PRAISE FOR *ALL HELL BREAKING LOOSE*

"[Klare] illuminates the prescient warnings the Pentagon has issued to the United States national and homeland security apparatus . . . A highly readable synthesis of the Pentagon's thinking on climate change that will quickly be considered seminal reading on the subject."

—Nathan P. Jones, *Small Wars Journal*

"A valuable look at strategic thought and planning . . . Though the White House may not believe that the climate is changing for the worse, the U.S. military does."

—*Kirkus Reviews*

"Michael Klare has done a masterful job of capturing key points in the U.S. military's pragmatic approach to climate change. As he shows, the military is building resilience in its own training, testing, and ability to respond, and is clear-eyed about warming's effects in catalyzing chaos and crises abroad that it may be called upon to respond to."

—General Ron Keys, U.S. Air Force (retired), chairman of the CNA Military Advisory Board

"Michael Klare does an exemplary job of recounting not only how military leaders view climate change differently than politicians on either end of the political spectrum, but why they do so. Seamlessly weaving together a narrative of Pentagon reports and compelling testimony, he shows that the military sees climate change as a threat to its capacity to defend the nation."

—John Conger, former Principal Deputy Under Secretary of Defense (Comptroller)

ALSO BY MICHAEL T. KLARE

*The Race for What's Left: The Global Scramble for the World's Last Resources*

*Rising Powers, Shrinking Planet: The New Geopolitics of Energy*

*Blood and Oil: The Dangers and Consequences of America's Growing Petroleum Dependency*

*Resource Wars: The New Landscape of Global Conflict*

*Light Weapons and Civil Conflict: Controlling the Tools of Violence*

*World Security: Challenges for a New Century*

*Rogue States and Nuclear Outlaws: America's Search for a New Foreign Policy*

*Low Intensity Warfare: Counterinsurgency, Proinsurgency, and Antiterrorism in the Eighties*

*American Arms Supermarket*

*Supplying Repression: U.S. Support for Authoritarian Regimes Abroad*

*War Without End: American Planning for the Next Vietnams*

Ellen Augarten

MICHAEL T. KLARE

## *All Hell Breaking Loose*

Michael T. Klare is the author of fifteen books, including *Resource Wars* and *The Race for What's Left*. A contributor to *Current History, Foreign Affairs, The Nation*, and *Scientific American*, he is the Five College Professor Emeritus of Peace and World Security Studies at Hampshire College and a senior visiting fellow at the Arms Control Association. He lives in Northampton, Massachusetts.

# ALL HELL BREAKING LOOSE

## THE PENTAGON'S PERSPECTIVE ON CLIMATE CHANGE

MICHAEL T. KLARE

PICADOR

METROPOLITAN BOOKS HENRY HOLT AND COMPANY NEW YORK

Picador
120 Broadway, New York 10271


Printed in the United States of America
Originally published in 2019 by Metropolitan Books
First Picador paperback edition, 2020

Maps by Glenn Ruga based on designs by Michael T. Klare

Library of Congress Control Number: 2019948301
Picador Paperback ISBN: 978-1-250-77294-7

Designed by Kelly S. Too

Our books may be purchased in bulk for promotional, educational, or business use. Please contact your local bookseller or the Macmillan Corporate and Premium Sales Department at 1-800-221-7945, extension 5442, or by email at MacmillanSpecialMarkets@macmillan.com.

Picador® is a U.S. registered trademark and is used by Macmillan Publishing Group, LLC, under license from Pan Books Limited.

For book club information, please visit facebook.com/picadorbookclub or email marketing@picadorusa.com.

picadorusa.com • instagram.com/picador
twitter.com/picadorusa • facebook.com/picadorusa

10 9 8 7 6 5 4 3 2 1

## CONTENTS

# ALL HELL BREAKING LOOSE

# INTRODUCTION

Shortly after assuming the presidency in 2017, Donald Trump rescinded Executive Order 13653, "Preparing the United States for the Impacts of Climate Change," a measure that had been signed by President Barack Obama in late 2013. The Obama order, steeped in the science of climate change, instructed all federal agencies to identify global warming's likely impacts on their future operations and to take such action as deemed necessary to "enhance climate preparedness and resilience." In rescinding that order, Trump asserted that economic competitiveness—involving, among other things, the unbridled exploitation of America's oil, coal, and natural gas reserves—outweighed environmental protection as a national priority. Accordingly, all federal agencies were instructed to abandon their efforts to enhance climate preparedness and to abolish any rules or regulations adopted in accordance with Executive Order 13653.[1] Most government agencies, now headed by Trump appointees, heeded the president's ruling. One major organization, however, carried on largely as before: the U.S. Department of Defense.

In accordance with the 2013 Obama directive, the Department of Defense (DoD) had taken significant steps to mitigate its contributions to global warming, such as installing solar panels on military installations and acquiring electric vehicles for its noncombat transport fleet. More important, the Pentagon leadership, in a January 2016 directive, had called on the military services to assess "the effects of climate change on the DoD mission" and act where necessary to overcome "any risks that develop as a result of climate change."[2] All those endeavors, presumably, were to be suspended following President Trump's 2017 decree. But while discussion of climate change has indeed largely disappeared from the Pentagon's public statements, its internal efforts to address the effects of global warming have not stopped.[3] Instead, a close look at Pentagon reports and initiatives reveals that many senior officers are convinced that climate change is real, is accelerating, and has direct and deleterious implications for American national security.[4]

In responding to this peril, the military leadership has not sought to position itself as a significant actor in the national debate over climate change. Well aware of the partisan nature of that debate and reluctant to become embroiled in domestic politics, senior officials have said relatively little about the causes of warming or other controversial issues. But for many officers, neither the dangers posed by global warming nor the imperative of addressing those threats have disappeared because a climate change skeptic had entered the White House. From their own experience, they know that many U.S. allies are experiencing severe drought and other harsh consequences of warming, exacerbating internal divisions and triggering violent conflict. They have watched as the military services have been called upon again and again to assist state and local authorities in coping with the aftereffects of exceptionally ferocious hurricanes, often mounting mammoth relief operations that lasted for many weeks or months. And they are keenly mindful of the fact that the military's own bases are coming under assault from rising seas, extreme storms, and raging wildfires.

Senior U.S. military officials have, therefore, continued to identify warming as a significant threat to American national security, despite the official guidance from the White House. "When I look at climate change, it's in the category of sources of conflict around the world and things we have to respond to," said General Joseph F. Dunford Jr., Chairman of the Joint Chiefs of Staff, in November 2018. "Shortages of water, and those kinds of things . . . are all sources of conflict. So, it is very much something that we take into account in our planning as we anticipate when, where and how we may be engaged in the future and what capabilities we should have."[5]

## INSTITUTIONAL ENDANGERMENT

To note that global warming poses a formidable threat to American national security is not to say that warming has necessarily been elevated above other perceived threats. In fact, the Department of Defense has made it clear that China and Russia constitute America's principal security threats and will remain so for some time to come.[6] Rather, top military officials perceive climate change as a secondary but insidious threat, capable of aggravating foreign conflicts, provoking regional instability, endangering American communities, and impairing the military's own response capabilities. Worse yet, warming's impacts are expected to grow increasingly severe, complicating the Pentagon's ability to address what it views as its more critical tasks. Ultimately, some officers fear, it could make fulfillment of those tasks nearly impossible.

To appreciate the military's perspective on the climate change threat, it's necessary to grasp something essential about the military leadership itself. Whatever else they may say, career officers will tell you that they've chosen a career in the military out of a deep belief in its overarching mission: to protect the homeland and defeat the nation's enemies. To succeed at this mission, they will explain, the military must be constantly vigilant and prepared, fully capable at every moment of undertaking any task or operation assigned by the president. Fighting and winning wars is, of course, their ultimate duty; but short of actual combat, their principal responsibility is to ensure that America's forces possess the *capacity* to win those wars. Accordingly, anything that detracts from that capacity represents, by definition, a threat to national security. And climate change, by undermining the military's ability to fulfill its primary strategic responsibilities, is widely feared to constitute exactly that sort of peril.

Senior commanders are well aware that there is an intense national debate over climate change and that some politicians—including President Trump and most of his cabinet—doubt the reality or imminence of planetary warming. But they have also seen evidence of warming for themselves (especially if they've served in drought-stricken areas of the Middle East and Asia, as a significant majority of them have done), and know that scientific evidence overwhelmingly confirms the climate change prognosis. Even more important, military officers are practical people and careful managers of *risk*. While they can never know for sure when and where the next security threat will arise, they must prepare themselves for any plausible contingency, and devastating climate change forecasts fall in this category. Even if the science of global warming still has a margin of uncertainty, they will say, it is close enough to being certain that the armed services must account for it in their future planning and take whatever steps they can to mitigate its harmful consequences.[7]

There is, therefore, a direct clash between current White House doctrine on climate change and the Pentagon's determination to overcome climate-related threats to military preparedness. A vivid illustration of this ongoing confrontation comes from the DoD's efforts to assess the danger that climate change poses to its domestic installations. Although many of America's combat-ready forces are deployed in or near potential hot spots abroad, the Pentagon relies on stateside bases to train and supply those forward-deployed units—so any threat to the operational utility of domestic facilities would endanger critical military operations. Military bases are launch platforms, and you "can't fight a war unless you've got a place to leave from," said General Gerald Galloway, formerly a senior officer at the Army Corps of Engineers.[8]

In 2015, after it became clear that rising seas would make many key coastal installations vulnerable to flooding and storm damage, Congress directed the Department of Defense to conduct a full-scale assessment of climate-related threats to all U.S. military bases. In response to that congressional directive, the DoD commenced a detailed survey of such risks to every one of its major facilities—a total of over thirty-five hundred installations. An interim report on that endeavor, "Climate-Related Risk to DoD Infrastructure: Initial Vulnerability Assessment Survey," was released in January 2018. It indicated that of the thousands of bases and installations queried, over half reported exposure to at least one climate-related impact, and many identified multiple effects. The greatest reported impact was from drought, with 782 facilities (22 percent of all U.S. bases) experiencing some drought conditions; in addition, 763 bases reported impacts from strong winds, 706 from severe flooding, and 210 from wildfires.[9] These remarkable numbers seemed to astonish even the DoD personnel who drafted the report. "If extreme weather makes our critical facilities unusable or necessitates costly or manpower-intensive work-arounds," they wrote, "that is an unacceptable impact."[10]

These findings attracted considerable press attention, both because of the magnitude of the dangers revealed and because of what seemed like a surprising willingness by the DoD to issue a report contrary to Trump administration views on global warming.[11] But it soon became apparent that the survey was only released after Pentagon officials—presumably acting under pressure from the White House—scrubbed the report of numerous references to climate change and the melting of the Arctic ice cap. Following its release, the *Washington Post* obtained an earlier draft of the report, dating from 2016, and revealed that the draft version had referred to climate change twenty-three times, while the text released to the public in 2018 mentioned it only once; instead, it had substituted terms like *extreme weather* or simply *change*. Discussions of rising sea levels and the melting of Arctic sea ice were also removed from the public version of the interim report, further diminishing the overall impression of warming's threat to U.S. military installations.[12]

The *Post*'s disclosure of this crude attempt to alter the tone of the assessment survey sparked widespread outrage in Washington. In July 2018, forty-four members of Congress—including ten Republicans—wrote to Secretary of Defense Jim Mattis and insisted that the final survey report provide an accurate account of warming's potential impacts, with "candid assessments" of base vulnerabilities.[13] If White House officials had hoped to erase climate change from the discourse on military preparedness, they failed utterly. Instead, their efforts at censorship and the subsequent congressional outrage only increased public awareness, generating fresh coverage of the topic.

Indeed, when Hurricane Michael swept through the Florida Panhandle a few months later and inflicted catastrophic damage on Tyndall Air Force Base, observers were quick to make the link between climate change and the vulnerability of U.S. bases. Tyndall, home to some thirty-six hundred Air Force personnel and a large share of the nation's super-sophisticated F-22 Raptor fighter planes—each costing some $339 million—sits on a narrow peninsula jutting out into the Gulf of Mexico, affording it little protection from high winds and surging seas.[14]

"We often don't associate climate change with threats to America's military, yet Hurricane Michael showed us how very real that threat is," wrote Lieutenant General Norman Seip, former commander of the 12th Air Force, in an op-ed. The hurricane "caused hundreds of millions of dollars' worth of damage to vital national security assets," he pointed out.[15] (The damage to Tyndall has since been estimated in the many billions of dollars, as discussed in chapter 7.) General Seip concluded his commentary with an observation that reflects the deep anxiety of many senior officers: "The damage to bases such as Tyndall may be catastrophic for the base itself, but it's only the beginning. Storms will continue to become more extreme and impact the ability of our armed forces to fight and win our nation's wars." The implications of this, he said, are inescapable: "Assessing and addressing the threat of climate change is critical for the future viability of our force."[16]

As a result of continuing congressional pressure and the impact of disasters like that experienced at Tyndall, the issue of military base vulnerability has refused to go away. At the behest of Congress, the DoD was required to produce yet another assessment of the problem in 2019. Although still displaying the muted tone of the department's 2018 report, the new version nevertheless revealed deep anxiety about the safety of key U.S. military installations. Regarding the risk to coastal bases, for example, it warned that "sea level changes magnify the impacts of storm surge, and may eventually result in permanent inundation of property." Drought, wildfires, and desertification were also identified as significantly threatening the future viability of critical facilities.[17]

## A UNIQUE AND ESSENTIAL VOICE

The uproar over the base vulnerability survey is revealing in many ways. To begin with, the 2018 assessment itself—even when scrubbed of most references to climate change—provides a grim picture of warming's mounting threats. Hundreds of key military installations, it shows, are imperiled by rising seas, high winds, and heavy flooding from extreme storm events, while hundreds more are at risk from drought and other climate effects. Even in its censored, toned-down version, the report still underscores the vulnerability of America's military infrastructure to the severe effects of a warming planet.

Just as significant, the episode demonstrates that despite the president's attempts to purge all climate change considerations from the federal government, senior military officials remain profoundly concerned about the impacts of global warming. As the 2018 report itself suggests, the immobilization of American bases by severe climate effects would be an "unacceptable impact." In accordance with this outlook, the military services are persevering with many of the initiatives undertaken in previous years to better prepare their forces and facilities for warming's harsh effects. These endeavors may now be described as responses to "extreme weather" or some other such euphemism, but there is no disguising the fact that they're intended to guard against the ravages of climate change.[18]

For the rest of us, however, the most important takeaway from this episode may be that the senior military leadership has fashioned an independent assessment of climate change, one that diverges in significant respects from how climate change often gets discussed elsewhere. While climate skeptics still claim that warming is not occurring at all or will have only minimal effects, the base survey report unequivocally demonstrates that senior military officials agree that climate change is under way and is having significant impacts *now.* Many U.S. bases, they contend, are already at risk of recurring inundation from rising seas and extreme storm events. At the same time, in contrast to climate activists' frequent focus on warming's threat to the natural environment and endangered species, Pentagon analysts instead highlight its deleterious effects on vulnerable populations, fragile states, and brittle institutions around the world. They see climate change as ratcheting up global chaos, which in turn means a greater likelihood of U.S. involvement in ugly foreign wars. "Stresses such as water shortages and crop failures," notes Rear Admiral David Titley, former chief oceanographer of the U.S. Navy, "can exacerbate or inflame existing tensions within or between states. These problems can lead to state failure, uncontrolled migration, and ungoverned spaces."[19]

Such comments by senior military leaders, both active-duty and retired, should be afforded close scrutiny by all of us. At stake is not just the "future viability" of America's armed forces—though that is obviously a matter of serious national concern. Rather, what these officers have to say about warming's effects on the military also tells us a lot about what we can expect for our own country, and for the world at large.

Consider, for example, the climate-related threats to military installations—the material infrastructure of bases, ports, radars, power plants, communications towers, and supply systems that enable American troops to assemble, train, deploy, and fight as needed. Those military systems are identical in many ways to the fundamental elements of civilian infrastructure needed by any modern industrial society—and, in many cases, are interspersed with their civilian equivalents in numerous communities across the country. It follows that if the armed services are worried about the safety and survival of *their* vital systems, we should be equally worried about the dangers to *ours*.

The Pentagon's ill-fated base survey released in January 2018 provides useful instruction in this regard. Attached to the report are several maps of the United States identifying the bases that have reported problems from heavy flooding, extreme temperatures, prolonged drought, and other climate impacts. These maps are covered with hundreds of dots—each representing an affected base—scattered from one end of the country to the other, with heavy concentrations along the Atlantic, Pacific, and Gulf coasts (reflecting, in part, the siting of numerous naval facilities there). Although the distribution of those endangered facilities does not coincide exactly with the largest concentrations of the nation's civilian population, it is close enough to indicate that a large percentage of Americans—including the residents of Los Angeles, San Francisco, San Diego, New York City, Boston, Philadelphia, Miami, and Washington, D.C.—live in close proximity to a military facility that can expect to suffer from the severe effects of climate change.[20] If the armed services worry about the future survival of those installations, should we not be worrying about the fate of all the cities, towns, and suburbs located in the same general area?

## Multiple Vulnerability Areas

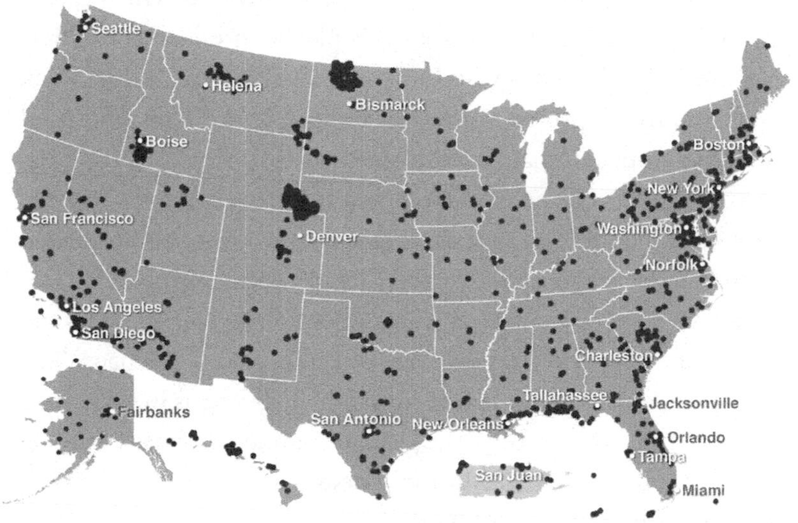


And while our concerns, understandably, are often focused on thc severe effects that climate change will have at home, we dare not ignore what the military has to say about warming's impacts on foreign nations that already suffer from resource scarcities and so are especially vulnerable to its harsh effects. As global temperatures rise, Pentagon analysts believe, those nations are likely to come under increasing pressure, with the weakest among them falling prey to civil unrest, ethnic strife, and state collapse. The most immediate consequence of such failures, those analysts contend, will be an increased call on U.S. forces to provide humanitarian aid and security services, often in the form of what are termed "stability operations." But other repercussions, as Admiral Titley suggests, could include widespread chaos, mass migrations, and increased terrorist activity—all of which would inevitably affect the United States itself.

Indeed, the picture that emerges from absorbing the military's analysis of climate change is of a future in which global warming wreaks havoc across the planet, producing multiple disasters simultaneously and jeopardizing the survival of weak and resource-deprived states everywhere. If the Pentagon itself dreads a troubled, chaotic world like this—even if solely out of its own institutional concern about military "overstretch"—all the rest of us should be at least as alarmed. A world of multiple failed states, vast "ungoverned spaces," and recurring mass migrations would pose mammoth challenges for the United States, no matter how hard we try to avert our eyes from the chaos. The collapse of economic and governmental institutions in numerous areas of the globe would disrupt vital trading networks and help foster deadly pandemics. In the worst-case scenarios, the major powers will fight over water and other vital resources, producing new global rifts and potentially involving the United States in full-scale wars with nuclear-armed belligerents.

Senior officials at the Department of Defense and the American intelligence community have peered into the future and seen this world. They have mapped out its basic parameters and calculated its likely effects. And their prognosis is grim: unless we act now to halt planetary warming and fortify our society against those climate effects that are already unavoidable, the American military will lose its capacity to defend the nation from multiple foreign perils, while the homeland itself will be ravaged by storms, floods, droughts, fires, and epidemics.

THIS BOOK WAS written in the belief that the American military and intelligence communities have something unique and valuable to contribute to the national conversation on climate change. Their viewpoint is not—and was never intended to be—a reinforcement of one or another of the existing partisan positions on the issue. Rather, their concerns bear on the very capacity of the military to defend this nation against all manner of assault. It is a perspective that deserves attention from us all.

*All Hell Breaking Loose* is constructed as a synthesis and interpretation of the military's thinking about climate change and its implications for the armed services and American national security. It is organized in a manner intended to replicate the spectrum of dangers that American military analysts see arising from a warming planet, roughly in order of their perceived magnitude. It also shows how the U.S. military has acted to minimize the threat posed by climate change, both by reducing its own contributions to the greenhouse effect and by working with the militaries of friendly nations to better adapt to a warming planet. In assembling this material, I have sought to faithfully reproduce the views and assessments of military commanders and analysts; but the overall structure of the book, and the hypothetical hierarchy of climate perils it rests on, is entirely my own.

A quick note on sources: in preparing to write this book, I examined hundreds of Pentagon and intelligence community reports, studies, directives, and statements, as well as the testimonies of senior military officers before assorted committees of Congress. In addition, I spoke with dozens of retired and active military officials, some cited in the pages that follow. My understanding of the military profession and military attitudes on climate change was further enhanced by extensive dialogue with serving officers while delivering talks at such institutions as the National War College, National Defense University, Army War College, Naval War College, Air University, Naval Postgraduate School, and the Naval Academy at Annapolis. I learned greatly from all the men and women I encountered at those institutions, and hope they will continue to highlight the dangers posed by climate change and undertake concrete measures to halt its advance. In this, I take heart from the words of U.S. Secretary of Defense Chuck Hagel. "We must be clear-eyed about the security threats presented by climate change, and we must be proactive in addressing them," he declared in 2014. "Defense leaders must be part of this global discussion."[21]

1

# A WORLD BESIEGED

## The Climate Threat to American National Security

On Tuesday, April 9, 2013, the Senate Armed Services Committee convened, as it always does in the early spring, to review the "posture," or strategic outlook, of the U.S. Pacific Command (Pacom). As Pacom's responsibility encompasses most of Asia, including China, North Korea, and the Indian subcontinent, its security review naturally attracts considerable attention from the Senate's defense-oriented members. Among those attending the hearing that day were Democrats Carl Levin of Michigan, Jack Reed of Rhode Island, and Tim Kaine of Virginia; on the Republican side were James Inhofe of Oklahoma, John McCain of Arizona, and Lindsey Graham of South Carolina. The sole witness before the committee was Admiral Samuel J. Locklear III, a forty-year Navy veteran and Pacom's senior commander.

In his prepared remarks for the hearing, Admiral Locklear began by providing the assembled senators with an overview of

Pacom's "security environment," or the aggregation of threats, trends, and political conditions under which American forces were obliged to operate. Topping the list of these challenges, he said, were China's rapidly modernizing military capabilities and North Korea's pursuit of nuclear weapons, followed by a number of territorial disputes, including those between China and its neighbors in the East and South China Seas. Not far behind those well-known perils, however, he listed a range of less familiar, unconventional threats—arising not from ongoing military rivalries but from resource scarcity, population growth, and climate change. "Increasingly severe weather patterns and rising sea levels threaten lives and property, and could even threaten the loss of entire low-lying nations," he declared.[1]

After his opening statement, Admiral Locklear came under intense questioning from members of the Armed Services Committee. Most of those present wanted to focus on the leading items in his threat assessment, notably the dangers posed by China and North Korea. Senator Levin, as the committee chair, began the process by raising a series of queries regarding U.S. and South Korean preparedness for a possible military provocation by North Korea. Locklear, no novice at this sort of thing, patiently explained the steps he and his fellow officers were taking to counter threats from the North, assuring the senators that U.S. and South Korean forces were fully prepared to deal with any conceivable North Korean provocation.[2] Senator McCain turned the discussion to China, asking if Pacom was closely monitoring military developments in that country. Once again, Locklear offered assurances that he and his staff were fully prepared for any eventuality.[3]

When it was his turn to ask questions, Senator Inhofe, however, introduced an entirely new line of inquiry. A former real estate developer and state official with strong ties to Oklahoma's oil and gas industry, Inhofe had long used his position in the Senate to dismiss climate science as, in his words, a "hoax." On this occasion, he set aside the threats posed by China and North Korea to challenge Locklear about his assertion that global warming had something to do with Asia's unfolding security situation. "Admiral, I'd like to get clarification on one statement that was, I think, misrepresented," he began, referring to some comments Locklear had made in an earlier press interview. "It was in the *Boston Globe*, reporting that you indicated—and I'm quoting now from the *Boston Globe*—'the biggest long-term security threat in the Pacific region is climate change.'" Was this really what he meant to say, Inhofe asked Locklear, or had his words been distorted by "environmental extremists" who believe "we're spending too much on defense?"[4]

Admiral Locklear, a ramrod-straight graduate of Annapolis who'd been commanding ships for decades, was not about to be intimidated. No, he responded, his remarks had not been misrepresented by reporters from the *Globe*. In that interview, Locklear explained, he'd begun, as he always did, by discussing the threat posed by China and North Korea. But after that, he said, "we started to talk about the long-term, the long-long-term," and at that point climate change had entered the discussion. As he'd told those reporters from the *Globe*—and now informed the attending senators—global warming would come to exert an ever-increasing influence on security conditions in the Asia-Pacific region. And then, as if to validate this assessment, Locklear offered Inhofe a mini-lecture on how climate change was transforming the security environment in Pacom's area of responsibility (AOR).

Of the several billion people in the region, Locklear said, "about 80 percent of them live within 200 miles of the coast, and that trend is increasing as people move towards the economic centers which are near the ports and facilities that support globalization." At the same time, those coastal areas are becoming increasingly vulnerable to the effects of climate change, especially rising seas and extreme storm events. Consequently, when severe events do occur, ever-larger populations are affected and the result is humanitarian disasters of mammoth proportions. According to the U.S. Agency for International Development, Locklear told Inhofe, an estimated 280,000 people in Pacom's AOR died from natural disasters between 2008 and 2012, and another 800,000 people were displaced.[5]

"Now, they weren't all climate change or weather-related, but a lot of them were due to that," Locklear said. Accordingly, "when I think about our planning and I think about what I have to do with allies and partners and I look long-term, it's important that the countries in this region build the capabilities into their infrastructure to be able to deal with the types of things that—"[6]

At this point, Senator Inhofe cut him off, not wanting to hear any more of this. Wasn't it true, he asked, that "many scientists disagree" with the proposition that "the climate is changing"? Locklear offered no such affirmation. Inhofe then tried to secure the admiral's endorsement for the full-scale exploitation of America's domestic energy supplies—including, presumably, all of its oil, coal, and natural gas—again without receiving much reaction from the admiral. Finally, Inhofe changed the subject entirely by asking Locklear about China's involvement in Africa, essentially ending the discussion of climate change.[7]

That extraordinary exchange between Senator Inhofe and Admiral Locklear can be interpreted in many ways. On one level, it exemplified the clash of cultures between the political elite, who can say just about anything as long as they keep winning elections, and the military leadership, who are totally loyal to the chain of command and rarely speak out of turn unless they're absolutely certain of the facts. It also highlighted the degree to which global warming had become a divisive political issue in the United States, with a prominent member of Congress using a once-a-year review of American strategy in Asia to instead score points on the climate front. Most of all, it exposed a fundamental difference of perception regarding the reality and consequences of climate change. For Senator Inhofe and his allies, warming is a dubious or debatable matter, requiring no immediate action in response; for Admiral Locklear and other senior officers, it is an observable reality, with significant and deeply worrisome implications for American national security.

Senior military officers do not, as a rule, clash with ranking members of Congress on a sensitive issue like climate change, generally preferring to limit their public comments to topics falling within their areas of expertise—strategy, weaponry, enemy capabilities, and so on—while leaving most political matters to the civilian leadership to resolve. For Admiral Locklear to have spoken out so forcefully at that April 2013 hearing could only mean one thing: he had come to view climate change as an issue that had become relevant to his *professional responsibility* as overall commander of all U.S. forces in a critical part of the world. Global warming may not have been the most urgent threat facing his forces, but it was already altering the security environment in his AOR, and appeared poised to have an even greater impact in the years to come.

## THE MILITARY'S EVOLVING ASSESSMENT OF CLIMATE CHANGE

The realization that climate change is a distinct threat to American national security did not occur overnight. Rather, it represents the culmination of more than a decade's worth of research, reflection, and analysis by senior members of the military establishment and their counterparts in the intelligence community—a systemic effort undertaken by those communities to educate themselves on climate change and its manifold consequences, especially as they bear on American national security.

The military's altered perspective can be traced back to the 2007 publication of *National Security and the Threat of Climate Change*, the first major study to view global warming as a security concern. Published by the CNA Corporation, a Pentagon-funded think tank originally known as the Center for Naval Analyses, the report was unequivocal in its conclusions. "Projected climate change poses a serious threat to America's national security," it began. "The predicted effects of climate change over the coming decades include extreme weather events, drought, flooding, sea level rise, retreating glaciers, habitat shifts, and the increased spread of life-threatening diseases. These conditions have the potential to disrupt our way of life and to force changes in the way we keep ourselves safe and secure."[8]

*National Security and the Threat of Climate Change* had an enormous influence on the military community, not only because of its analytical rigor but also because of the identity of its authors. In preparing the study, CNA general counsel Sherri Goodman, a former deputy undersecretary of defense for environmental security, assembled a military advisory board made up of high-ranking retired officers, including General Gordon R. Sullivan, former chief of staff of the Army, and Marine General Anthony C. Zinni, former commander of the Central Command. By their own admission, these officers were not particularly well informed on the science of global warming prior to their involvement in the project, but agreed to be briefed by some of the top experts in the field.[9] In the process, they became convinced that climate change was a real and growing danger—comparable, they indicated, to the major threats the country had encountered over the span of their careers, ranging "from containment and deterrence of the Soviet nuclear threat during the Cold War to terrorism and extremism in recent years."[10]

Global warming represented such a significant threat to U.S. security, the CNA study argued, because it increased the likelihood of internal unrest and state collapse in vulnerable states abroad, endangering key American allies and generating new and hazardous tasks for the U.S. military. In articulating this assessment, the report's authors introduced a new expression to the lexicon of climate change analysis: *threat multiplier.* "Many governments in Asia, Africa, and the Middle East are already on edge in terms of their ability to provide basic needs: food, water, shelter and stability," the study noted. "Projected climate change will exacerbate the problems in these regions and add to the problems of effective governance." In this manner, "climate change acts as a threat multiplier for instability in some of the most volatile regions of the world."[11]

Although the CNA report largely focused on the dangers arising from instability and state collapse in the developing world, it also warned of warming's threat to more developed countries, including the United States itself. "Projected climate change will add to tensions even in stable regions of the world," the study predicted, with the greatest dangers arising from climate-related pandemics and mass migrations. "The U.S. and Europe may experience mounting pressure to accept large numbers of immigrant and refugee populations as drought increases and food production declines in Latin America and Africa"—an accurate prophecy if ever there was one. On top of this, the study anticipated, "extreme weather events and natural disasters, as the U.S. experienced with Hurricane Katrina, may lead to increased missions for a number of U.S. agencies," including "our already stretched military."[12]

The U.S. military's understanding of climate change as a threat to national security received further amplification the following year with the release of a document produced by the National Intelligence Council, an arm of the Central Intelligence Agency responsible for long-range projections. The NIC report, titled *National Security Implications of Global Climate Change to 2030*, agreed that climate change could undermine the stability of key U.S. allies, especially those already suffering from resource scarcity and internal friction. "Climate change could threaten domestic stability in some states," the study concluded, "potentially contributing to intra- or, less likely, interstate conflict, particularly over access to increasingly scarce water resources."[13]

After the publication of those two studies, the perception of climate change as a threat to American national security spread widely among military professionals, and in 2010 it received its first official recognition in the Pentagon's *Quadrennial Defense Review* (QDR). As its name suggests, the QDR constitutes a periodic synthesis of Pentagon thinking on the global strategic environment and the military's preferred responses. The previous edition, released in 2006, had not even mentioned climate change, focusing instead almost entirely on the "long war" against terrorism. By contrast, the 2010 QDR incorporated many of the points raised in the 2007 CNA study and the 2008 NIC report. "Assessments by the intelligence community indicate that climate change could have significant geopolitical impacts around the world, contributing to poverty, environmental degradation, and the further weakening of fragile governments," the QDR stated. "Climate change will contribute to food and water scarcity, will increase the spread of disease, and may spur or exacerbate mass migration."[14] Global warming as a threat to American national security had now become a basic tenet of the country's official military doctrine.

In the years that followed, this amplified view of national security became increasingly evident in the speeches and statements of senior military officials. Especially noteworthy in this regard was Secretary of Defense Chuck Hagel (in office from 2013 to 2015), who explicitly identified global warming as a major security concern. Under his guidance, the concept of climate change as a threat to national security was inscribed in formal military directives and documents, including the 2014 edition of the QDR and in that year's *Department of Defense 2014 Climate Change Adaptation Roadmap*. "Climate change will affect the Department of Defense's ability to defend the Nation and poses immediate risks to U.S. national security," the 2014 road map avowed—strong language for an official Pentagon statement.[15] Equally robust language can be found in the 2015 *National Security Strategy* released by the Obama White House, which declared forthrightly that "climate change is an urgent and growing threat to our national security."[16]

Designating something as a "threat to national security" has enormous implications for the armed services. It means, at the very least, that the services must rigorously monitor the danger and be prepared to take whatever action may be required to overcome it. Looking further ahead, it means they must be trained and equipped to engage in a wide variety of military missions that could arise as a consequence of it, including diverse emergencies occurring simultaneously in several areas of the world. And since the armed forces themselves are at risk from the effects of climate change, the situation also requires adapting troops, bases, and military equipment to a hotter planet with more extreme weather conditions.

## THREATS ACROSS MULTIPLE REGIONS

As analysts at the Department of Defense were calculating the security implications of rising world temperatures, their counterparts at the military's overseas command centers were noting the climate impacts already visible within their areas of operation and reporting back to Washington on the resulting dangers. While Admiral Locklear was particularly forthcoming in such reportage during his 2013 testimony before the Senate Armed Services Committee, he is hardly alone among senior military officials in identifying these perils. Other high-ranking officers have also noted that climate change is altering the environment in which their forces and those of their allies may be compelled to fight, generating new risks and obstacles. Although always careful to insist that they remain focused on more familiar threats—Russian assertiveness, say, or the tenacity of terrorist groups like al-Qaeda and the Islamic State—those admirals and generals, like Locklear, have stated that warming is impeding their capacity to undertake critical operations.

The Department of Defense has divided the world into a mosaic of six massive regions and established a "geographic combatant command" for each one: the Pacific Command, Central Command, Africa Command, European Command, Northern Command, and Southern Command.* By law, all American military forces deployed within any one of those territories—whether drawn from the Army, Navy, Air Force, or Marine Corps—fall under the authority of the senior geographic combatant commander, such as Admiral Locklear when he headed

* In May 2018, the Pacific Command was renamed the Indo-Pacific Command, to reflect a greater emphasis on the Indian Ocean area.

**Unified Combatant Commands Areas of Responsibility**

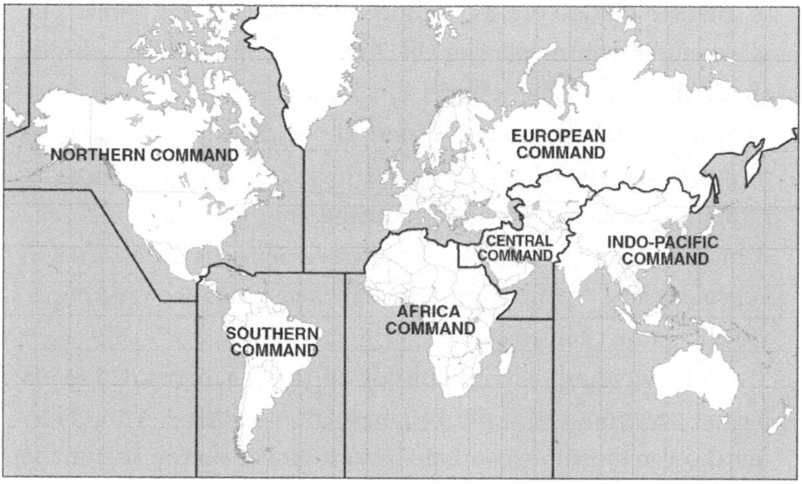

Pacom from 2012 to 2015. This officer is responsible for assessing the security environment in his or her AOR and taking steps to overcome any vulnerabilities identified thereby, whether from conventional military threats or unconventional perils, such as those posed by economic turbulence, severe drought, and population shifts.

Ordinarily, the most common settings in which the Pentagon's regional commanders have expressed their concerns over global warming and its regional effects have been the annual hearings convened by the House and Senate Armed Services Committees, like that in which Admiral Locklear testified in April 2013. Read through the transcripts of those proceedings, and you will find recurring references to warming's disruptive impact on U.S. and allied combat readiness in the region being discussed. While serving as head of the Southern Command, for example, General John F. Kelly—later chief of staff in the White House under President Trump—regularly spoke of the growing threat of extreme storms in the Caribbean and the resulting risk of "mass migration events."[17] More recently, General Thomas D. Waldhauser, commander of the Africa Command, has testified about the deleterious effects of climate change on the security equation in the Sahel region of North Africa. "Changing weather patterns, rising temperatures, and dramatic shifts in rainfall contribute to drought, famine, migration, and resource competition," he told the Senate Armed Services Committee in February 2019. "As each group seeks land for its own purposes, violent conflict can ensue."[18]

To better grasp the magnitude of these dangers, Congress has on occasion tasked the Department of Defense with collating those regional assessments into a global survey of climate change impacts. The most detailed of these, *National Security Implications of Climate-Related Risks and a Changing Climate*, was released in 2015. Based on reports submitted by officials of the six geographic combatant commands, it provides an overview of global warming's observed and anticipated impacts within each command's area of responsibility. The report from Pacom, for example, reiterated the findings on sea-level rise and extreme storm activity addressed by Admiral Locklear in his 2013 testimony. Similar perils were identified by the Southern Command, which includes the Caribbean islands and Central and South America. The Caribbean basin, Southcom reported, is already at risk from coastal flooding, and will become far more so as the oceans rise and storms become increasingly intense.[19]

Other geographic combatant commands described different dangers in their reports. The Central Command, which covers large parts of the Middle East, unsurprisingly warned of protracted drought and water scarcity. "Climate changes heighten competition [for water] at the national or subnational level in an already arid region," it declared. As regional temperatures rise, this competition "could be more dangerous as actors seek to protect limited resources."[20] The Africa Command focused on the growing risk of societal disintegration resulting from extreme drought and deadly pandemics. As warming advances, it suggested, "climate change will exacerbate existing economic, social, and environmental vulnerabilities," a process that "may tip states toward systemic breakdowns."[21] The threat of mass migrations arising from extreme drought, coastal flooding, food scarcity, and state collapse was a recurring theme in several of these reports, including those submitted by Africom, Centcom, and Southcom.

Yet another set of concerns was expressed over the rapid warming of the Arctic. Two of the combatant commands—the Northern Command (which has responsibility for North America) and the European Command—oversee AORs extending deep into the Arctic region. As polar ice disappears, this area is opening up to oil and natural gas extraction as well as to increased commercial shipping activity; this, in turn, is driving greater military involvement by neighboring powers, especially Russia. Climate change has, in fact, created a "new ocean" that must now be protected against oil spills, illegal commerce, and geopolitical contention. As a result, the Pentagon noted, both Northcom and Eucom "are concerned with security risks arising from increased shipping, military operations, and resource exploration in the Arctic as the icecap melts."[22]

Finally, the 2015 DoD report identified another key area that can expect to suffer from the severe effects of climate change: the United States itself. Just as the Indo-Pacific region and the Caribbean are being exposed to increased storm damage and heavy flooding, so, too, is this country. As in those other regions, moreover, populations are growing in low-lying areas along the U.S. coasts, magnifying the risk of mega-disasters. America's armed forces, as a result, will be called upon more frequently to provide emergency relief and assistance at home, much as they have abroad.[23]

In summarizing these findings, the Department of Defense affirmed that climate change is real, observable, and significantly affecting American national security. "We are already observing the impacts of climate change in shocks and stressors to vulnerable nations and communities, including in the United States, and in the Arctic, Middle East, Africa, Asia, and South America," the report concluded. At first, the poorest and most resource-deprived of countries will suffer the greatest harm from extreme climate effects, but in time every nation on Earth will be affected. "Even resilient, well-developed countries are subject to the effects of climate change in significant and consequential ways," it stated.[24]

In a more recent survey of these dangers, released in January 2019, the Department of Defense showed that regional commanders continue to observe and worry about the effects of warming in their areas of responsibility. Centcom, for example, noted that "current and historic climate conditions are factored into theater campaign plans, including water scarcity which is a recurring issue in the region." Similarly, at Africom, "climate impacts and drivers of instability and factional conflict are fully integrated into planning efforts."[25]

Whether serving in Africom, Centcom, Pacom, or any of the Pentagon's other geographic combatant commands, most senior U.S. officers have had at least some firsthand exposure to the extreme effects of climate change. Many of them have seen how warming is undermining the stability of nations whose support and steadfastness the United States relies on for the successful implementation of its global strategies. Looking into the future, they recognize that rising world temperatures are likely to increase the pressures on the more vulnerable of those states, and have begun to factor that into their long-range planning. They realize, too, that these pressures will only increase over time, producing ever more severe challenges to social cohesion and state survival.

## THE NEW "LADDER OF ESCALATION"

During the Cold War, military analysts used the term *ladder of escalation* to describe the increasingly intense and destructive stages of combat one might expect in a direct confrontation between the United States and the Soviet Union. Such a hypothetical sequence typically began with small-scale clashes employing conventional weapons, continued to massive army-on-army tank battles, then the first use of tactical nuclear weapons, and concluded with a strategic nuclear barrage and mutual annihilation. Although most serving officers would probably contest the analogy, it is evident that many envision something approximately similar in the climate sphere: a spectrum of increasingly severe disasters resulting in ever more complex and demanding missions for American military forces.

At the low end of this imaginary scale are disaster relief operations, where the armed services might be called upon to provide emergency support to a developing nation for a week or two before resuming its normal duties. Next along in complexity are extended operations in developing countries facing state collapse, where humanitarian aid would need to be combined with counterinsurgency missions. A third level involves military deployments spanning multiple countries, driven by warming-related shocks to energy systems or food supply chains that stretch across the globe. Further yet up the ladder would be American involvement in disputes among the world's major powers, which could come into direct conflict over vital supplies of water or other critical resources. Finally, ranking even higher than those—at least as far as impact on the homeland is concerned—would be catastrophic climate emergencies inside the United States itself, requiring a substantial commitment of the military's unique capabilities.

This sequence of ever more demanding and dangerous scenarios roughly coincides with the progression of increasingly severe climate effects we can expect from a warming planet. As the Intergovernmental Panel on Climate Change reported in its October 2018 synthesis of scientific research on global warming, by 2040 average world temperatures are projected to rise by 1.5 degrees Celsius (2.7 degrees Fahrenheit) over preindustrial levels; by the end of the century, if drastic action is not taken soon to curb global emissions of carbon dioxide and other greenhouse gases, they could climb much higher than that. Even with just a 1.5°C increase, the IPCC indicated, the planet will experience a wide array of harsh consequences, including deadly prolonged heat waves, more frequent and protracted droughts, increasingly ferocious storm activity, diminished crop yields, and, not least, rising sea levels. If and when temperatures climb beyond 1.5 degrees Celsius, those effects are certain to be intensified and augmented by other catastrophic events.[26]

The Pentagon's imaginary ladder of climate escalation does not match up exactly with this scientific projection of warming's future effects, since the likelihood of U.S. military involvement in foreign calamities and conflicts depends as much on the relative survival capacity of affected states—a largely social and political matter—as it does on the intensity of climate pressures. From this perspective, societies already suffering from scarcity and internal strife will reach the point of collapse first while more stable and affluent states will survive longer. Nevertheless, there is a clear understanding among military and intelligence officials that a growing number of states will reach the brink of collapse as warming advances, and so America's armed forces will be called upon ever more frequently to engage in relief and stability operations.

What would these climate-related scenarios look like in practice? Drawing on Pentagon reports and statements, complemented by interviews with current and former military officials, it is possible to visualize this new ladder of escalation, starting with relatively simple disaster relief operations and ending with great-power conflicts abroad and major calamities at home.

## Humanitarian Disaster Relief

On the lowest rung of this hypothetical ladder are what the Department of Defense calls humanitarian assistance and disaster relief (HA/DR) operations, typically involving the delivery of emergency food, water, and medical supplies to disaster-stricken countries following a major hurricane, typhoon, or other climate-related catastrophe. Ordinarily, such operations entail the deployment of American forces to the site of the disaster to help deliver relief supplies and provide medical care and other emergency services until those could be performed by local authorities—at which point, all American military personnel are expected to depart.

America's armed forces have long performed such operations, both as a "goodwill" effort, to demonstrate Washington's compassion for the victims of disaster, and as a display of American military prowess. Senior officers are worried, however, that the need for such missions will grow in the years ahead, as extreme weather events occur more often and rising seas place heavily populated coastal areas at ever greater risk.[27] This was, in fact, the concern expressed by Admiral Locklear in his 2013 testimony before the Senate Armed Services Committee. Officials also worry that such operations will prove increasingly complex and hazardous, as extreme events grow in severity and occur more frequently in heavily populated, ethnically torn areas. Any delays or perceived bias involving aid deliveries there could trigger riots and looting, putting at risk the lives of American military personnel sent to provide emergency food and shelter.

## Support for Beleaguered Foreign Governments

Next up the hypothetical ladder of escalation are limited military operations intended to assist a friendly foreign government facing internal unrest as a result of severe drought, widespread crop failure, or other consequences of climate change. Ever since American officers began to consider the impact of global warming on U.S. security, this has widely been assumed to be among the most common climate-related missions that American soldiers will be called on to perform on a regular basis. "Climate change can make already unstable situations worse, sometimes catastrophically so," Admiral Titley testified in July 2019. "Large-scale human suffering often accompanies these situations . . . U.S. military forces are frequently directed to these areas and our troops are placed at risk.[28]

Complicating all this is the challenge of what the national security literature terms *states of security concern* or *states important to U.S. national security interest.*[29] These (typically unidentified) nations, presumably, are ones that house American military bases, possess vast stores of oil or other vital resources, or are otherwise of critical importance to American security—and, like their poorer and less privileged neighbors, are considered highly vulnerable to the increasingly severe effects of climate change. Needless to say, any extended U.S. military involvement in countries of this significance would entail a commitment of forces and capabilities far grander than that associated with support missions in smaller states of less strategic importance. Presumably, it would entail the deployment of major ground combat units plus any needed air and naval support—essentially, the sort of commitment we have seen in Iraq and Afghanistan.

### Disruptions to Global Supply Chains

Ranking even higher on the scale of escalation is the prospect of large-scale "climate shocks" that trigger a succession of failed states and mass migrations. Lower-level contingencies, such as humanitarian disasters and sociopolitical instability, are largely projected to occur one at a time, with each event confined to a particular country; as warming progresses, however, there is a strong potential for the sudden disruption of international food chains or energy systems, resulting in widespread panic, flight, and instability. Unexpected events of this sort would have immense consequences for societies and polities around the world; some governments, already weakened by warming's effects, could find this an insurmountable challenge.

For the U.S. military, climate shocks of such magnitude would pose a range of demanding challenges. A succession of failed states is likely to trigger massive waves of human migration and help spread infectious diseases, producing disarray across the planet. Several states of strategic importance might also face collapse at the same time, prompting a large-scale commitment of American power. Any of these scenarios, alone or in combination, would place an enormous strain on American combat capabilities and force national leaders to make difficult choices about where and how to employ military force.

## Great-Power Discord

An even more consequential issue is the impact of climate change on the stability of the international system and the relationships among its most powerful actors. While the earliest victims of global warming are expected to be poor and divided countries of the developing world, every nation on Earth, even the strongest and wealthiest, will in time be battered by warming's severe effects. Initially, the more privileged states will largely experience those effects *indirectly*, as they are besieged by waves of desperate "climate refugees" seeking to escape from their increasingly uninhabitable homelands; as time goes on, however, they will also suffer from the *direct* impacts of climate change, whether in the form of extreme storms, prolonged heat waves, heavy flooding, or water scarcity.

From a U.S. security perspective, the major powers' growing vulnerability to global warming will have multiple acute consequences. At the very least, it will endanger the stability of the international political order and the global trading networks upon which American prosperity rests; equally at risk are the military alliances that augment U.S. power and influence abroad. As conditions deteriorate, the United States could face an even more perilous outcome: conflict among the great powers themselves. Although few believe that climate change will be the immediate trigger for a great-power war anytime soon, some analysts foresee a moment when global warming will bring existing rivalries to a head, perhaps over competition for oil or water. While seemingly unlikely now, such scenarios could become more plausible if global trading systems collapse and warming diminishes the availability of critical natural resources. The Arctic, where warming is opening up new areas for resource exploitation and where the interests of several major powers collide, is seen by many U.S. military analysts as one possible site for such conflict.

## Domestic Disasters

Alongside the projections of increasingly severe climate-related disasters abroad is the prospect of a similar pattern of escalating calamities at home. The United States, no less than the rest of the world, is expected to suffer from rising sea levels, more frequent and severe storms, protracted droughts, and catastrophic wildfires. As it has in the past, the Department of Defense will be called upon to assist local authorities in dealing with such events by providing emergency health services and by rescuing people trapped by fires or floods. Historically, such episodes have occurred infrequently, typically following an unusually powerful hurricane; with the advent of global warming, however, the frequency and severity of extreme climate events is growing, generating ever-increasing demands for the military's assistance. This became especially evident in the late summer of 2017, when Hurricanes Harvey, Irma, and Maria pummeled Texas, Florida, and Puerto Rico, prompting an unprecedented U.S. military response (as described in chapter 6).

As warming progresses in the decades ahead, the United States can expect to be ravaged by ever more severe climate effects, triggering more frequent and more complex civil disasters. Scientists largely agree, for example, that large stretches of

America's Atlantic Ocean and Gulf of Mexico shorelines are at risk of being submerged by rising seas in coming decades, imperiling the future habitability of many urban and suburban areas. Security experts also worry about the vulnerability of vital national infrastructure—such as highways, rail lines, airports, refineries, power stations, and electrical transmission lines—that occupy low-lying coastal areas and so are at particular risk from sea-level rise and storm flooding.[30] As these perils become more pronounced, the Pentagon told Congress in 2015, it anticipates a "substantial involvement of DoD units, personnel, and assets" in disaster relief and recovery operations at home.[31]

## ALL HELL BREAKING LOOSE

Even more worrisome than any of the disasters in this ladder of escalation is the significant likelihood that a number of them could occur at the same time or in close succession at various locations across the globe. Climate shocks that envelop large parts of the world simultaneously would cause widespread instability; the accompanying mayhem and erosion of governmental services would, in turn, facilitate the outbreak of deadly pandemics and create further panic and disorder. The major powers, previously relatively immune to warming's harshest effects, could face catastrophic threats themselves and battle one another over access to critical resources. Such a panoply of simultaneous disasters occurring at numerous sites around the world—including at home—would generate multiple, ultimately unmanageable demands on America's military capabilities.

Senior officials are normally reluctant to discuss scenarios this calamitous, but there's no doubt they've given them considerable thought. As early as 2003, the head of the DoD's Office of Net Assessment, the legendary Andrew Marshall (sometimes called "Yoda" by Pentagon admirers for his far-seeing intelligence), commissioned a study on warming's potential to produce planet-wide catastrophes.[32] The resulting document outlined a future in which climate change reaches a catastrophic tipping point, such as the collapse of the Atlantic Ocean's underlying current system. That could wreak havoc with global weather patterns, leading to wars over vital resources and the potential disintegration of major powers.[33] Similarly, a 2013 study by the National Research Council warned of the potential for increasingly menacing outcomes as severe climate events occur more frequently and start to overlap with one another. Given what we have learned from scientific modeling, the NRC asserted, "it is prudent for security analysts to expect climate surprises in the coming decade," and for such calamities "to become progressively more serious and frequent thereafter, most likely at an accelerating rate."[34]

These scenarios are further complicated by forecasts showing a substantial climate threat to domestic U.S. military bases from storm surges, severe droughts, rising seas, and recurring wildfires.[35] This threat to the Pentagon's installations at home, combined with an increased tempo of climate disasters abroad, conjures up the military's worst nightmare: a future in which the armed forces are called upon to overcome multiple emergencies around the globe while many of their bases are out of commission and large numbers of their troops are engaged in domestic relief operations, leaving them ill-equipped to address any major threats at all.

America's military officials are very clear about what they see as their primary professional obligation: to defend this nation against its most dangerous adversaries, notably Russia, China, Iran, and North Korea. A future in which the military services' ability to perform this role is compromised by climate-related contingencies at home and abroad is not, therefore, one that senior officers can contemplate with ease. Rather, they view warming as a serious threat to the successful fulfillment of their primary responsibilities, and so as something that must be resisted. Fighting against global warming is not, for most of them, a question of ideological preference or political engagement. Rather, it is matter of ensuring that the armed forces will be spared the most extreme climate contingencies imaginable, and so remain able to concentrate on Russia, China, and other perils at the core of their mission.

This perspective explains the military's strategy for confronting global warming. It does not aim to halt the advance of climate change but rather to slow its progress and, if possible, prevent escalation to the most severe climate scenarios described above. To this end, it calls for concerted action on two fronts: on one, reducing the services' own contributions to global warming, through reductions in their greenhouse gas emissions; on the other, assisting the militaries of foreign nations in improving their ability to cope with extreme disasters and provide emergency assistance as needed. This approach was first articulated in the 2010 edition of the QDR and has remained Pentagon policy ever since.

Military commanders are well aware that climate policy is largely a matter for civilian leaders to determine, and that the military alone cannot stop global warming. Nevertheless, senior officials believe it is their responsibility to mitigate the impacts of warming in the interest of national security. As Secretary Hagel put it, "Politics or ideology must not get in the way of sound planning." The armed forces, he declared, "must prepare for a future with a wide spectrum of possible threats, weighing risks and probabilities to ensure that we continue to keep our country secure."[36] It is from precisely this perspective that Admiral Locklear confronted Senator Inhofe in April 2013, and it is from this outlook that he and other officers have sought to tackle the very real challenges of climate change.

2

# HUMANITARIAN EMERGENCIES

## Climate Disasters, Civil Disorder, and U.S. Military Relief Operations

On November 2, 2013, the Joint Typhoon Warning Center in Honolulu, Hawaii, detected a tropical depression in the western Pacific Ocean, some 265 miles east-southeast of the Micronesian island of Pohnpei. By November 4, the developing storm, now moving in a westerly direction, was upgraded to a tropical storm and assigned the name Haiyan (a Chinese feminine given name). Drawing energy from the warm waters of the Pacific, the storm continued to gain strength and on November 6 was categorized as a super typhoon, with sustained winds exceeding 195 miles per hour and gusts reported up to 235 mph. Two days later, Haiyan smashed into the eastern Philippines as the most powerful storm ever recorded to strike land.

After traversing Samar Island, Super Typhoon Haiyan crossed Leyte Bay—site of a famous naval battle in World War II—and barreled across the central Philippines, devastating the islands of

Leyte, Bohol, Cebu, and Negros, among others. It then headed out into the South China Sea and eventually struck southern China, where it inflicted more damage before eventually dissipating. Wherever it crossed over land, Haiyan left scenes of vast wreckage and suffering. And while it is impossible to convey the full extent of Haiyan's destruction, official statistics from the Philippines give some sense of the catastrophic damage there: 6,293 people killed and 28,689 injured, 1.1 million homes damaged or destroyed, and 4 million individuals displaced.[1]

Haiyan's greatest impact was felt on Leyte Island, and particularly in and around Tacloban, the island's largest city. A thriving commercial hub with a population of about 220,000 at the time of the disaster, Tacloban occupies a low-lying stretch of land at the head of San Pablo Bay, which opens into Leyte Gulf and the western Pacific. Shaped like a narrow funnel, the bay proved a natural corridor for the stormwaters whipped up by Typhoon Haiyan. Compounding the city's vulnerability, many of Tacloban's residents were poor fishermen who resided in informal settlements—shantytowns, really—erected on swampland adjacent to the waterfront. When Haiyan struck the city on November 8, it brought not only ferocious winds and driving rain, but also a storm surge estimated at some fifteen to twenty feet: enough to submerge the shantytowns, the local airport, and much of the rest of the city.[2] At least 90 percent of Tacloban's buildings were destroyed, all essential services were disabled, and thousands of people were killed or injured.[3]

For those who survived the storm, the aftermath was a nightmare. The city center was completely leveled, with debris strewn everywhere and corpses littering the landscape. "We have bodies in the water, bodies on the bridges, bodies on the side of the road," said Richard Gordon, chairman of the Philippine Red Cross.[4] Stores were closed or demolished, food was in short supply, and clean water nearly impossible to find. "Survivors staggered up and down Tacloban's streets," said one observer, "many of them beg[ging] for supplies."[5] The city's main hospital had no electrical power and most of its equipment was destroyed; it was unable to provide adequate care for many of those injured in the storm, resulting in yet more deaths.[6]

Haiyan's pummeling of Tacloban produced what relief experts term a *complex emergency*—one that involves not just the loss of life and destruction of essential infrastructure but also powerful shocks to the underlying social fabric. With water mains broken and no food or medicine reaching the city, some survivors resorted to looting. "The looting is not criminality, it is self-preservation," said the city's administrator, Tecson John Lim; still, it produced clashes with store owners and police.[7] There were also reports that a Red Cross aid convoy was stampeded by hungry survivors seeking food and water, with police firing at and killing some members of the desperate crowd.[8] Many residents complained that the central government in Manila was slow to deliver relief aid and, when it finally did do so, showed favoritism in the allocation of supplies—providing more to well-connected families and less to disadvantaged communities.[9] Though slow to provide emergency relief, the central government was quick to respond to the looting, deploying army units equipped with armored personnel carriers to patrol the city's streets.[10]

The international media soon began broadcasting images of the wreckage and the growing social chaos in Tacloban. Arriving a few days after Haiyan ripped through the city, CNN's Anderson Cooper, who had famously reported in 2005 on the dismal governmental response to Hurricane Katrina in New Orleans, was equally critical of what he witnessed in Tacloban. "It looks like the end of the world, [and] for many here it is," he said. "It is not getting better day by day. . . . You would expect maybe a feeding center would have been set up five days after the storm. We haven't seen that, certainly not in this area."[11] Such dispatches, no doubt amplified by intelligence reports collected by the American Embassy in Manila and other U.S. government sources, evidently made a big impression on President Obama. "I think all of us have been shaken by the images of the devastation wrought by Typhoon Haiyan," he declared.[12] On November 9, Obama ordered a full-scale response to the crisis. In addition to promising a substantial donation of humanitarian aid, he ordered the Department of Defense to employ all available resources in assisting civilian agencies in the delivery of emergency relief.

Soon after receiving Obama's order, Secretary of Defense Chuck Hagel directed the U.S. Pacific Command, then headed by Admiral Locklear, to mobilize its formidable assets for the government-wide emergency effort. Two days later, Hagel ordered the USS *George Washington*, a nuclear-powered aircraft carrier with more than eighty aircraft, to proceed from Hong Kong (where it had been on a port visit) to the storm-affected area in the Philippines, along with its support group of two cruisers, two destroyers, and assorted supply vessels.[13] The Pentagon dubbed the burgeoning relief effort Operation Damayan, meaning "help in time of need" in Filipino.

Oversight of Operation Damayan was delegated to the Pacom command staff in Hawaii. Moving swiftly, Locklear established Joint Task Force (JTF) 505 to encompass all U.S. military assets—Army, Navy, Marines, Air Force, and Special Forces—committed to the emergency effort. A forward operating base for JTF-505 was established at Camp Aguinaldo, near Manila, and military units from throughout the Pacific were given orders to deploy to the storm-ravaged area.[14] At the height of this effort, JTF-505 encompassed approximately fourteen thousand U.S. military personnel plus sixty-six aircraft, the *George Washington* carrier group, and a dozen other surface vessels—an extraordinary commitment of military resources for an activity other than war.[15]

Between November 9, when Secretary Hagel gave the order to commence relief operations, and December 1, when JTF-505 was stood down, a very large share of Pacom's deployable assets was devoted to Operation Damayan. These assets—including both equipment (helicopters, cargo planes, amphibious vehicles, portable generators) and personnel (medics, engineers, supply and communications technicians, and others)—were used to clear roads and airstrips, deliver food and water supplies to hard-hit areas, restore water and power lines, provide emergency medical assistance, and evacuate those in extreme danger. In many stricken areas, the U.S. military was far more visible than the Philippines armed forces, which were widely criticized for their meager emergency-response capability.[16] By the conclusion of Operation Damayan, American forces had conducted more than thirteen hundred flights in support of relief operations, delivered over twenty-five hundred tons of relief supplies to devastated areas, and evacuated more than twenty-one thousand people.[17]

## CLIMATE CHANGE AND THE PENTAGON'S DISASTER-RELIEF MISSION

Humanitarian aid missions like Operation Damayan represent the lowest rung on the Pentagon's hypothetical "ladder of escalation" when it comes to climate change. As exemplified by that episode, such endeavors typically involve the commitment of assorted U.S. military units in emergency relief operations for a limited duration, followed by their rapid withdrawal once local civilian agencies have assumed responsibility for essential services. The U.S. military has long been performing humanitarian assistance and disaster relief (HA/DR) missions of this sort, both to boost America's image abroad and to demonstrate—to allies and adversaries alike—its ability to quickly mobilize massive resources. "We sent some 14,500 soldiers, sailors, airmen, and Marines in response to that catastrophic event," said Marine General Stephen Cheney of Typhoon Haiyan. "We were the only country that's capable of doing that, of deploying that amount of forces that amount of distance."[18] But however gratifying these operations can be for the troops involved, many senior officers worry that such calls on U.S. forces will become problematically more frequent as global warming advances.

That concern arises both from the officers' own personal observations and from scientific research on the topic, which conclusively demonstrates that rising world temperatures are generating storms of ever-increasing scale and ferocity. This is especially evident in the case of tropical cyclones (known as typhoons when arising in the Pacific, hurricanes when arising in the Atlantic), which have grown measurably stronger in recent years.[19] Although scientists readily admit that it can be difficult to attribute any individual storm to climate change, Super Typhoon Haiyan was widely perceived by many of them as a direct manifestation of global warming. "Typhoons, hurricanes and all tropical storms draw their vast energy from the warmth of the sea," explained Will Steffen, director of the Australian National University's climate change institute, shortly after Haiyan struck the Philippines. "We know sea-surface temperatures are warming pretty much around the planet, so that's a pretty direct influence of climate change on the nature of the storm."[20]

In fact, recent studies have shown that the world's oceans

are warming at an even faster rate than previously suspected. In 2014, the Intergovernmental Panel on Climate Change reported that the oceans' upper levels warmed by approximately half a degree Celsius (0.9 degrees Fahrenheit) between 1971 and 2010. In 2018, however, scientists using more precise measurements determined that the warming was at least 40 percent greater.[21] A faster rate of ocean warming implies, among other things, a greater risk of intense storm activity. "What we can certainly say is that a warmer world will have riper conditions for more extreme hurricanes," said Zeke Hausfather of the University of California, Berkeley, a coauthor of one of those studies. "The warmer the ocean waters, the more potential for energy for these storms."[22]

The increase in severe storms and accompanying storm surges is especially hazardous for island states like Indonesia and the Philippines, and for countries with extended coastlines such as China, Bangladesh, and Vietnam, where major population centers are often located in low-lying coastal areas. Many of these countries have transitioned in recent years from reliance on agriculture to extensive engagement in manufacturing and export trade, with a corresponding growth in population and urbanization. This growth has very often been concentrated in coastal zones, near major ports, airports, and sea-lanes. According to the IPCC, low-elevation coastal zones (LECZs) occupy only 2 percent of the world's land surface but contain 10 percent of its population.[23] That percentage, moreover, is expected to climb in the coming decades, as opportunities for income generation in rural areas decline—a consequence, in part, of droughts induced by global warming—and growing numbers of people migrate to cities in the LECZs.[24]

Sea-level rise, another consequence of global warming, will only add to the risk in those areas, as it will increase the vulnerability of low-lying coastal zones to seawater intrusion during extreme storms. As global temperatures climb, the world's oceans will absorb even more heat and gradually expand, steadily encroaching on the LECZs. Just how great this increase will prove to be is a matter of some speculation, as it will depend to a considerable extent on the degree to which nations succeed or fail in curbing their greenhouse gas emissions. Depending on what assumptions are made regarding those emissions, the IPCC reported in 2014, the global mean increase in sea level will range from 0.3 to 1.0 meters by 2100, or approximately 1 to 3 feet.[25] But some scientists have calculated that the rapid melting of the Greenland and Antarctica ice sheets could lead the oceans to rise by 6 feet or more during that time.[26] Even without that scenario, an increase in the global sea level of just one to three feet would be enough to endanger numerous cities located in low-lying coastal areas during extreme high tides and storm surges.

Officers from the Pacific Command, which oversaw Operation Damayan and a host of other major HA/DR operations, are particularly aware of the extent to which powerful storms, flooding, and other climate-related factors are altering the security environment in their area of responsibility. Admiral Locklear, who clashed with Senator Inhofe at the Senate Armed Services Committee hearing in 2013, sounded a similar warning the following year at a meeting of the Atlantic Council. "I've got 52 percent, 53 percent roughly of the world [population] in my AOR," he noted. "And a lot of it's at sea level. A lot of it's nearly below sea level. . . . And guess what? They're all moving closer to the littorals so they can access the jobs and access the global economy." As a consequence, "the implications for any climate change or any changes in weather patterns or sea level changes are much more dramatic for this mass amount of population."[27]

A similar assessment was provided in 2019 by one of Locklear's successors at what had been rechristened the Indo-Pacific Command. Asked by Senator Elizabeth Warren of the Senate Armed Services Committee to discuss the impact of climate change on operational readiness in his area of responsibility, Admiral Philip S. Davidson replied: "The immediate manifestation, ma'am, is the number of ecological disaster events that are happening." In just the past few months, he indicated, the Indo-Pacific Command had been called on to assist with emergency relief operations in the U.S.-administered Northern Mariana Islands after they were struck by Super Typhoon Yutu. "Our assistance in terms of humanitarian assistance and disaster relief, our ability to command and control, to marshal troops, to deliver logistics, is important training for the region."[28]

For Admiral Locklear and his successors, the consequences of all this are unmistakable: the U.S. military will be called upon again and again to conduct major disaster relief operations like Damayan. "If there's one thing I tell everybody that comes to work for me," Locklear said in 2014, it is this: "'While you're here you may not have a conflict with another military, but you will have a natural disaster that you have to either assist in or be prepared to manage the consequences on the other side.' And that has been true every year."[29]

## EXTREME STORMS IN AFRICA AND THE CARIBBEAN

Given the Asia-Pacific region's vulnerability to severe typhoons and sea-level rise, it is hardly surprising that Admiral Locklear devoted so much attention to those perils in his assessment of Pacom's leading security concerns. But that region is by no means the only one to be at risk from extreme storms and elevated seas in the years ahead. In fact, almost every corner of the planet will be hammered by the punishing effects of climate change. The precise nature of this assault may vary from place to place—inland areas will suffer more from heat waves, droughts, and mega-fires; coastal areas more from hurricanes, typhoons, and sea surges—but the severity of extreme climate events is projected to grow everywhere.[30] As a result, regional combatant commands in other parts of the world are also assessing the climate perils in their areas of responsibility and contemplating the likely increase in their HA/DR operations.

In some regions, American forces will encounter conditions not unlike those expected in the Asia-Pacific region. This is especially true of the Caribbean and coastal areas of Central America and Africa, which face the same sort of threat from cyclones and sea-level rise as do the islands of the Pacific and Indian Oceans. In all those regions, as elsewhere in the developing world, large numbers of people have been migrating to urban areas along the coasts in search of economic opportunity, thereby increasing the potential scale of human tragedy and asset losses from future storm events. The concentration of so many people in these exposed areas is also contributing to an increased risk of infectious disease in the aftermath of natural disasters, which often result in the breakdown of public services and the contamination of water supplies.[31]

The Caribbean islands and coastal areas of Central America are thought to be at particular risk from the severe effects of climate change. Not only are the surrounding seas rising, endangering vital economic assets and infrastructure, but the region is highly exposed to Atlantic hurricanes, which have grown stronger as the oceans have warmed.[32] With government adaptive capacity limited in most countries, rising unemployment and mass migrations are predictable outcomes. "Warming seas and their link to storm energy are especially worrisome for Central

America and small Caribbean island nations that do not have the social infrastructure to deal with natural disasters," the CNA Corporation warned in its landmark report on climate change and American security.[33]

Just how severe the impacts of climate change can prove to be was well demonstrated in 2017, when a series of hurricanes lashed the Caribbean islands before barreling on to Puerto Rico and the U.S. mainland. With surface temperatures in the Atlantic unusually warm—an indisputable consequence of climate change, in the view of many analysts—these storms absorbed immense energy from the ocean and delivered it with shocking force.[34] Hurricane Irma, which struck the tiny island of Barbuda on September 6 and destroyed everything in its path, produced the strongest recorded winds of any hurricane to emerge in the open Atlantic, with some gusts reaching over 183 miles per hour. After pulverizing Barbuda and forcing its entire population of fifteen hundred people to flee, Irma inflicted immense damage on the British overseas island territory of Anguilla and the Franco-Dutch island of Saint Martin/Sint Maarten, destroying its entire infrastructure.[35] Those and other islands were then pummeled by Hurricane Jose, impeding relief and repair operations, and then devastated again by Hurricane Maria several weeks later.

Coming in such close succession, those hurricanes (and the massively destructive Hurricane Harvey, which struck the Houston area just a few weeks before Irma's appearance) were widely viewed as incontrovertible evidence of global warming's mounting threat to island states and low-lying coastal regions. "The small islands have been saying for so many years in the climate change discussions that this is possible," said Walton Alfonso Webson, the ambassador of Antigua and Barbuda to the United Nations, at an emergency General Assembly meeting called to address the disasters. "It's no longer possible. It's happened."[36]

As in the Asia-Pacific region, this climate-related increase in humanitarian disasters is expected to generate a growing "call" on the U.S. military to conduct disaster relief missions. After Hurricanes Irma, Jose, and Maria struck the Caribbean, for instance, the Southern Command activated Joint Task Force-Leeward Islands (JTF-LI) and deployed it to the affected area with orders to assist local authorities in relief operations.[37] At its peak strength, the task force included more than three hundred military personnel, as well as ten Army and Marine helicopters, four Air Force C-130 Hercules aircraft, and the Navy's amphibious ship USS *Wasp*.[38]

Such missions are likely to prove increasingly necessary in the years ahead, as temperatures climb and extreme storms occur more frequently. Given the Caribbean basin's proximity to the United States—and the ever-present anxiety over mass migration from affected areas to U.S. territory—the American military is sure to place a high priority on HA/DR missions in this part of the world. But Africa is also expected to generate a growing demand for emergency relief operations. Sea-level rise, the CNA noted, could "result in the displacement of large numbers of people on the African continent, as more than 25 percent of the African population lives within 100 kilometers (sixty-two miles) of the coast." Such displacement, it added, is likely to result in widespread chaos, hunger, and disease, endangering state stability and spurring massive waves of migration. Overwhelmed local authorities are sure to plead for international assistance, with the U.S. military expected to play a leading role.[39]

Responsibility for American military participation in international relief operations in the Caribbean, Central America, and Africa lies with the geographic combatant commands with jurisdiction over U.S. forces in those areas: Southcom in the case of Central America and the Caribbean, Africom in the case of Africa. Just as Admiral Locklear and his staff oversaw Damayan in the Philippines, the senior officers in those commands are responsible for planning and managing any HA/DR missions conducted by U.S. military contingents within their respective AORs. As directed by the Department of Defense, these officers are required to "incorporate the risks posed by current and projected climate variations into their planning, resource requirements, and operational considerations."[40]

In complying with this directive, each combatant command has developed contingency plans in accordance with its assessment of its AOR's distinctive challenges and response requirements. Southcom, the DoD told Congress in 2015, "identifies coastal flooding to be a particular concern for parts of the Caribbean basin due to climate change–related sea level rise." Africom, for its part, "assesses humanitarian crisis as the most likely climate-related risk within its AOR, foremost due to the impact that devastating events like drought and disease could have on vulnerable populations and on state stability in places already struggling with fragility and conflict."[41]

The commanding officers of Africom and Southcom have generally not been as articulate as Admiral Locklear when it comes to global warming. General John F. Kelly of the Marine Corps, who commanded Southcom from 2012 to 2016 (and was named secretary of Homeland Security in January 2017 before transitioning to the White House staff later that year), used his annual testimony before Congress to emphasize the threat posed by transnational criminal organizations. Similarly, Marine General Thomas D. Waldhauser, who assumed command of Africom in July 2016, has largely emphasized the threat from terrorist groups such as al-Shabaab and Boko Haram. Nevertheless, both officers stated that climate effects and natural disasters were significant features of the security environment in their respective AORs and noted that planning for and undertaking HA/DR operations constituted a major component of their day-to-day activities, much of this undertaken in conjunction with the military forces of partner nations.

Despite his reluctance to specifically invoke climate change in his 2015 congressional testimony—possibly motivated by a fear of provoking a clash like that between Senator Inhofe and Admiral Locklear—General Kelly seems to have been fully aware of potential security risks linked to global warming. Recall that in the DoD's report to Congress that same year, Southcom identified "climate change–related sea level rise" as a particular concern in the Caribbean basin. With this in mind, Kelly's testimony regarding the region is especially revealing. "Contingency planning," he told Congress, "prepares our organization to respond to various scenarios," including "Caribbean mass migration." He also indicated that Southcom had requested $28 million to develop infrastructure at the U.S. naval base at Guantánamo—site of the controversial detention center for foreign terrorism suspects—to house refugees "in the event of a maritime mass migration."[42] While it is possible to imagine a number of scenarios that might trigger mass migration, coastal flooding and resulting economic damage from "climate change–related sea level rise" have to be prominent among them.

General Waldhauser has been more explicit in identifying climate change as a source of instability in his AOR. In the southern Sahel, he noted, persistent drought and resulting desertification have "created strong competition between the region's farmers and herders who migrate across borders searching for usable land"—a pattern with a strong potential for inciting armed conflict. These trends, moreover, threaten to overwhelm the capacity of weak or ineffective governments, "who are unable to respond and cope with their already serious, on-going political, economic, and social challenges." To help these governments, Waldhauser indicated, Africom was working with their armed forces to slow the pace of environmental degradation and better prepare them for humanitarian disasters.[43]

Like their counterparts at Pacom and Southcom, officials at Africom worry about the impacts of rising oceans and extreme storm events, particularly as some of Africa's major cities are located at sea level. More than elsewhere, moreover, they fear the outbreak of infectious diseases that could spread rapidly in crowded, unsanitary urban environments and produce widespread mayhem. Africom played a critical role in the 2014 U.S. response to the Ebola epidemic in Liberia, and warming temperatures are expected to spur the outbreak of more such pandemics in the years to come.[44] Given Africa's large and growing population, Waldhauser testified in 2018, any future outbreaks of Ebola or other infectious diseases would produce a crisis whose "scale and scope would be significant." Accordingly, preparation for pandemic-related relief missions constitutes a top HA/DR priority for Africom.[45]

Africom's rapid-response capability was put to the test in March 2019, when Mozambique, Malawi, and Zimbabwe were battered by Cyclone Idai, one of the strongest storms to assault Africa in recent decades. Bringing winds with speeds exceeding 120 miles per hour and torrential rainfall, Idai flooded much of central Mozambique and destroyed 90 percent of the buildings and infrastructure in Beira, Mozambique's fourth most populous city. Millions of people were rendered homeless and large numbers exposed to the risk of cholera and other infectious diseases.[46] To help that country cope with the storm's severe effects, Africom mobilized Combined Joint Task Force-Horn of

Africa (CJTF-HOA), deploying senior officers and supply planes to assist in the delivery of emergency relief supplies to Beira.[47]

Pacom, Southcom, and Africom are the three commands most likely to be engaged in climate-related HA/DR missions in the years ahead, a reflection of the high vulnerability of their AORs to severe storms, droughts, and sea-level rise. The Pentagon's other combatant commands, however, are also bound to be involved in activities of this sort. The Central Command, for example, could face massive humanitarian disasters arising from prolonged drought and water scarcity. Although most of Centcom's attention is focused on the conflicts in Iraq, Syria, and Afghanistan, it also "monitors resource scarcity (e.g., water, food, energy) in its arid AOR" and "accounts for this factor in its planning," the DoD told Congress in 2015.[48]

## IT CAN ONLY GET MESSIER

As the tempo of international relief operations picks up, U.S. military officials will consistently wish for one thing: for American forces to be swiftly dispatched, effectively used to address the emergency, and just as swiftly withdrawn once local authorities are able to take over the task of recovery. This is the most desirable process, they believe, in order to prevent valuable U.S. combat assets from being diverted to nonmilitary activities for an extended period of time.[49] During Operation Damayan in the Philippines, for example, Pacom's leadership was noticeably eager to redeploy the *George Washington* to other missions in the Pacific, and did so within days of its arrival at Leyte.[50] Quick in, quick out—that's the military's preferred scenario for HA/DR.

But while American commanders are determined to keep things short and simple, it may not always be possible for them to do so. In fact, as global temperatures rise and socioeconomic stresses increase, HA/DR missions are likely to prove ever more demanding and hazardous as time goes on. Increasingly powerful storms, combined with a greater concentration of people and economic activities in large coastal cities, will produce disasters of unprecedented scale and complexity, requiring larger and more protracted commitments of U.S. forces in future missions.

These forces will have to deal not only with the widespread collapse of infrastructure but also with social and political antagonisms, typically arising from historical grievances and from perceptions that government assistance is being allocated in an inequitable or incompetent manner. People moving from rural to urban areas usually arrive with few resources or political connections and so are compelled to settle in squatter settlements on the urban fringe, which are particularly vulnerable to flooding and storm surges. Lacking ties to local elites, the new arrivals are often the last to receive emergency aid when disaster strikes, generating fierce animosity toward the powers that be.[51] American troops deployed to a disaster zone could thus be forced to protect aid workers against mob violence, or become embroiled in intergroup disputes over the allocation of aid supplies.[52] Under these circumstances, U.S. military personnel could be targeted if perceived as playing favorites in the distribution of aid, or as failing to intervene when one group monopolizes relief supplies at the expense of others.

Another risk for American forces deployed in overseas disaster zones is that they may be inserted into a country that's divided into warring camps along ethnic, religious, or ideological lines, with one side or another perceiving the United States as an implacable adversary. This was a concern in planning for Operation Damayan in the Philippines, as members of the New People's Army—the armed wing of the Communist Party of the Philippines—had been active in some storm-affected areas and could have posed an impediment to American relief operations. As it turned out, the NPA declared a cease-fire following the storm's aftermath, eliminating any potential for a clash with U.S. forces.[53] In the future, however, it may not always be possible to secure such a benign outcome, and American soldiers may find themselves in a situation where the delivery of emergency aid entails the risk of combat with hostile forces.

This is especially likely to be the case in Africa and the Middle East, where many disaster-prone areas are already the site of conflict among various factions and where resource scarcity—especially involving water—often constitutes a major factor in the disputes. Any U.S. relief operation in water-stressed regions will, as a result, risk becoming entangled in these ongoing conflicts. That prospect is a particular concern for the U.S. Central Command, which operates in a region of persistent conflict and recurring drought. Global warming is bound to heighten the competition for water, Centcom reported in 2015, and this competition "could be more dangerous as actors seek to protect limited resources."[54]

Yet another complication could arise from the need to rescue American citizens (and perhaps those of other friendly nations) from areas stricken by severe climate events and a resulting breakdown in social order. When Hurricane Maria destroyed most of the infrastructure in Saint Martin/Sint Maarten in 2017, for example, depriving residents of water and electricity and constricting food supplies, it was not long before looting broke out; in some cases, it was accompanied by armed violence. Most of this was aimed at shopkeepers, but some foreign tourists also reported being robbed at gunpoint in their hotel rooms. Eventually, Dutch Marines were sent to help restore order on the island and the U.S. military evacuated over two thousand American citizens, flying them on C-130 transport aircraft to Puerto

Rico.[55] As far as it is known, this effort proceeded without any shots being fired, but it is easy to imagine that future missions of this sort—in more remote and contested areas—will not prove bloodless.

All of this, needless to say, is a source of considerable anxiety to U.S. military officials as they contemplate future engagement in climate-related relief operations. This concern was first voiced by the authors of the CNA Corporation's pathbreaking 2007 study of climate change and American national security. "In light of the potential magnitude of the human crisis that could result from major weather-related natural disasters and the magnitude of the response and recovery efforts that would be required," it stated, "stability operations" carried out by U.S. and partner militaries in the course of such efforts "will likely occur more frequently."[56] The term *stability operations* typically means the application of force in maintaining order: everything from the protection of aid workers to riot control and peacekeeping operations. Recognizing this, former White House chief of staff John Podesta recommended that any U.S. military forces committed to HA/DR missions be trained and equipped to undertake such supplemental activities. "Army and Marine Corps troops may need to receive training in how to provide disaster relief in potentially hostile environments," he wrote.[57]

## THE SPECTER OF DISASTER "CLUSTERING"

Historically, the U.S. military has taken great pride in its unique capacity to provide emergency assistance in response to foreign catastrophes. "Our country is a compassionate, generous and caring nation with a long history of aiding those around the world who are impacted by disasters," said Admiral Kurt Tidd at the start of Southcom's relief operation in the Caribbean following Hurricane Maria.[58] Presumably, American military officials in future years will be no less inclined to undertake such relief operations. But if anything can be deduced from the scientific literature on global warming, it is that the number and severity of extreme climate events is bound to increase in the decades ahead. In consequence, the U.S. military will be called upon ever more frequently to assume leadership in the world's response to these disasters. "Although some of the emergencies created or worsened by climate change may ultimately be managed by the UN, nations will look to the United States as a first responder in the immediate aftermath of a major natural disaster or humanitarian emergency," John Podesta noted. "The larger and more logistically difficult the operation, the more urgent the appeal will be."[59] But this naturally raises a critical question: How many of these appeals can the United States say "yes" to without undermining its own security?

This dilemma will become ever more acute in the years ahead. When spaced out, major humanitarian aid operations can be accommodated by America's military with relative ease. If such operations were to occur in rapid succession, however, they would begin to place a heavy strain on U.S. forces, undermining their ability to perform other vital missions. The situation could prove especially problematic if several major disasters erupted simultaneously or in quick succession. A major shift in atmospheric jet streams, for example, could result in large-scale weather changes and trigger multiple disasters simultaneously.[60] As noted in a 2013 National Research Council report, "clusters of extreme events may occur as a result of a random co-occurrence of extreme events in different places that have different causes," or they may "result from large-scale climate processes that serve as common causes of events in disparate places." As global temperatures rise, the incidence of such clusters will become "progressively more serious and more frequent," the NRC indicated, and will occur "at an accelerating rate."[61]

Such a "clustering" of extreme events and accompanying calls on U.S. military assistance might mean that all the available forces in a combatant command would be already tied up in response to one emergency when another broke out in the same region. Yet this is exactly the sort of scenario, the NRC noted, that is becoming more likely as a result of climate change. America's future capacity to conduct HA/DR and other key operations could be compromised, it added, "because U.S. government resources . . . deployed to deal with a security or humanitarian concern related to the first event in a cluster might be unavailable or less available to deal with a second or subsequent extreme event."[62]

A foretaste of what this might look like was offered by Hurricanes Harvey, Irma, and Maria, which struck Houston, the Florida Keys, and several Caribbean islands within the span of several weeks. Although each hurricane had its distinctive trajectory and characteristics, all were propelled by the same climate-related factor: abnormally high ocean temperatures in the eastern Atlantic, where the storms originated. In response to these storms, the Department of Defense mobilized a vast array of forces to provide emergency assistance, a task that involved both Southcom and Northcom (which bears responsibility for homeland defense). As we will see in chapters 6 and 7, those operations proved an immense challenge for the DoD, forcing it to quickly shift assets from one locale to another even as some of its own installations were inundated by the storms.

As the number of emergencies increases, will the American military continue to relish its role as "first responder," especially as the scale, complexity, and riskiness of the missions grow?

Given senior officers' concerns about long-term diversions of valuable combat assets to nonstrategic missions—which automatically, in their view, diminishes their ability to address more acute threats to American security—many will surely view this prospect with growing anxiety. Indeed, the National Intelligence Council warned of just such an outcome in its 2008 National Intelligence Assessment on climate change and U.S. national security. "As climate changes spur more humanitarian emergencies," it declared, "the international community's capacity to respond will be increasingly strained [and] the United States, in particular, will be called upon to respond. The demands of these potential humanitarian responses may significantly tax U.S. military transportation and support force structures, resulting in a strained readiness posture and decreased strategic depth for combat operations."[63]

This gets to the heart of American officers' anxiety over climate change and its impact on U.S. national security. While they do not see global warming as a *direct* threat to American security, at least not in the short term, they do view it as a source of recurring crises and disasters abroad—events that could trigger an unending series of U.S. emergency response operations, gradually degrading the military's ability to fight and defeat America's adversaries. In this sense, climate change poses a clear threat to national security, albeit through an indirect path of causation. If critical U.S. combat assets like the USS *George Washington* are perpetually tied down in emergency response operations because of global warming, America will be unprepared for battle—and thus, in a very real way, laid low by climate change.

3

# STATES ON THE BRINK

## Resource Scarcity, Ethnic Strife, and Government Collapse

In January 2012, following the far-flung political upheaval we know as the Arab Spring, a rebellion led by Tuareg militants erupted in northern Mali, a former French colony in northwestern Africa. Fiercely independent, the largely nomadic Tuaregs had long resisted domination by others, including the French colonialists and, after their departure in 1960, the postcolonial government in Bamako, the country's capital, located in Mali's agricultural south. An earlier uprising by the Tuaregs, lasting from 2007 to 2009, had ended in a cease-fire and promises of assistance by the government; but now, with government authorities reneging on their promises of development aid and vast stores of modern arms suddenly available from the looted arsenals of war-racked Libya, the Tuaregs chose to renew their struggle. In short order, the rebels conquered all government strongholds in the northern part of the country and occupied many key towns, including the fabled city of Timbuktu. Soon thereafter, leaders of the rebellion declared an independent state, Azawad, in the areas under their control—electrifying the Islamic world and generating anxiety throughout Europe and Africa.[1]

For radical Islamists, the establishment of Azawad represented an extraordinary opportunity: a chance to institutionalize a fundamentalist version of their faith across a large tract of territory. Before long, the Tuaregs were joined in Timbuktu by Islamic zealots from a variety of extremist factions, including Ansar Dine ("Defenders of the Faith") and al-Qaeda in the Islamic Maghreb (AQIM), the North African branch of the Pakistan-based terrorist organization. Once arrived in Mali, the militants of Ansar Dine and AQIM imposed Sharia law in rebel-controlled areas and destroyed centuries-old monuments and libraries deemed to be idolatrous.[2] Although the original Tuareg rebels and AQIM did not see eye-to-eye in all matters—the newcomers espoused a far more rigid form of Islam than most of the Tuaregs—their combined forces succeeded in conquering additional territory and reaching the outskirts of Bamako.[3]

As the rebel forces gained momentum on the battlefield, Mali experienced a second shock: a group of young army officers overthrew the government in Bamako, claiming they had been abandoned by their superiors and left to fight the well-armed insurgents with insufficient arms and ammunition. Mali's long-reigning president, Amadou Toumani Touré, fled the city as the military junta took control.[4] Intense pressure by other African leaders persuaded the junta to transfer power to Malian civilian authorities a few weeks later, but stability was never fully restored. Conflict between the military and a succession of civilian leaders ensued while efforts by neighboring states to help the Malian army regroup and oust the rebels faltered. After several months of turmoil, the French government—fearful of a

## The Sahel Region of North Africa

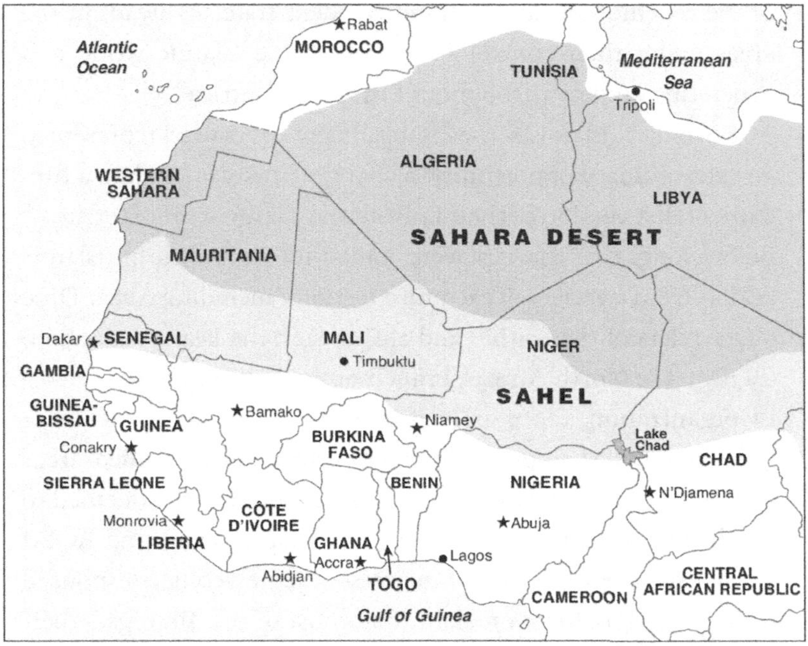

rebel takeover in Bamako and the spread of Islamic extremism to neighboring countries—chose to intervene, deploying several thousand combat troops in the country in January 2013. Those forces, aided by troops from other African countries and backed by American logistical and surveillance support, eventually succeeded in driving out the rebels from their strongholds in the south and restoring government control over large areas of the north.[5]

Driven out of Mali's main population centers and hounded by French and international forces, most of the surviving Tuareg forces signed a peace agreement with the Malian government in 2015.[6] However, some factions of the rebel movement refused to sign the agreement, and have continued to stage attacks on French troops and UN peacekeepers ever since, occasionally inflicting significant casualties.[7] The United States, fearful of growing terrorist activity in the area, continues to support French operations in northern Mali and has been expanding its own military presence in the region.[8] In October 2017, four members of a U.S. military patrol died when pursuing a terrorist suspect along a remote stretch of the Mali-Niger border.[9]

Although the United States played only a secondary role in dealing with the original Tuareg rebellion—mainly just ferrying French troops to the battlefield and providing them with intelligence data—the Malian conflict made a significant impression on American security officials. For one thing, it represented al-Qaeda's first sustained penetration into sub-Saharan Africa, opening a new front in the "Long War" against terrorism. Until that point, extremist violence of the al-Qaeda variety had largely been confined to North Africa and the Persian Gulf area; AQIM's incursion into Mali gave it a significant foothold in sub-Saharan Africa.[10] American officials also worried about potential spillover effects from the Malian upheaval, fearing the outbreak of parallel rebellions in neighboring countries with similar ethnic and economic divisions. But most of all, the Malian conflict attracted U.S. attention because it was viewed by many analysts as the first of an expected series of civil conflicts provoked, at least to some degree, by climate change.

To be absolutely clear, American analysts never claimed that the conflict in Mali was *directly caused* by climate change. Rather, in consonance with the "threat multiplier" model described in chapter 1, it has been suggested that global warming significantly exacerbated the underlying social, political, and economic conditions behind the Tuareg revolt. The Tuaregs live in a region known as the Sahel—literally, in Arabic, the "shore" of the Sahara Desert, with the desert to the north and savanna grasslands to the south. "The northern Sahel zone is particularly hard hit by the consequences of climate change," noted Dona J. Stewart in an assessment of the Malian conflict written for the U.S. Army War College. "Drought and desertification have increased the population's vulnerability and raised levels of food insecurity." Average rainfall in Mali had dropped by 30 percent over the fifteen years preceding the revolt, and droughts had become more frequent and prolonged—effects that were proving especially harmful for the Tuaregs, who inhabited the most arid and drought-prone areas of the country. With ever rising temperatures, moreover, the southern edge of the Sahara Desert was expanding into the Sahel by approximately thirty miles per year, overtaking once-extensive grasslands. This forced the nomads to either move farther south—encroaching on lands occupied by sedentary agriculturalists, who often fought back—or to abandon their herds and move to the cities. As a result, Stewart indicated, climate change was putting "even greater strains on the population and society," thereby increasing "the potential for instability."[11]

A very similar assessment was later provided by General Waldhauser, commander of Africom, in his 2018 testimony before the House Armed Services Committee. When asked about the impact of climate change on security conditions in his area of responsibility, Waldhauser pointed to the situation in Mali. "The Sahel has been receding," he indicated. "This has had a significant impact on groups like the Tuaregs, whose history is of pastoralists, of herders; they move to where the water and the grasslands are for their livestock and cattle." Rising temperatures and desertification have endangered their nomadic existence by drying up traditional grazing areas and provoking clashes with other groups over access to water. "This causes disagreements in terms of who owns or who can use these water rights for the livestock," said Waldhauser, in many cases leading to violence.[12]

Climate change was not, of course, the only significant factor in sparking the Tuareg rebellion. Extreme poverty is a fact of life for many of Mali's citizens, and persistent governmental incompetence and corruption have added to their distress. What's more, the bulk of Mali's population is concentrated in the agricultural south, and most government officials historically come from there; unsurprisingly, what little funding the government can spare for social and economic development has been channeled to farming communities in that region, often to the particular benefit of well-connected local elites. The Tuaregs had always found themselves last in line when it came to the allocation of government assistance, and the unmet promises of aid from the 2009 cease-fire further increased their frustration.[13]

Given this multiplicity of factors, it is impossible to determine to what degree global warming was a decisive factor in precipitating the Malian conflict. What matters, in the view of American security analysts, is that the warming *did* play an important role, and one that is likely to be replicated elsewhere.[14] A 2014 study by the CNA Corporation (a successor to its highly influential 2007 report on climate and national security) pointed out that the same conditions considered responsible for the Tuareg rebellion—desertification, resource scarcity, ethnic distrust, and governmental venality—could be found in many other developing nations, raising the specter of additional Mali-like upheavals and the collapse of friendly governments. "The recent Malian conflict fits a pattern of other such conflicts in Africa's Sahel region, including Darfur, South Sudan, Niger, and Nigeria," the CNA Corporation observed. In all those nations, it noted, global warming had resulted in diminished food and water supplies, adding to the desperation of local populations and stoking interethnic hostilities. With national governments unable or unwilling to manage the situation, extremists were moving in and exploiting people's grievances, "transforming resource competition into ethno-political conflict."[15]

## THE FAILED STATE SYNDROME

Ever since American security officials first began considering the impacts of climate change on American national security, the potential for Mali-like insurgencies has been among their greatest concerns. Although the countries affected by such discord may not be viewed in Washington as possessing great strategic significance in their own right, the disintegration of their state institutions can result, it is widely believed, in widespread chaos and starvation, producing a massive humanitarian catastrophe. That, in turn, could trigger waves of outward migration, generating fresh havoc in neighboring countries, some of which might possess greater geopolitical importance. The absence of state authority could also allow for the emergence of vast "uncontrolled spaces"—remote areas in which terrorists and other extremists could flourish. Any of these factors, alone or in combination, could prompt an American president to order U.S. forces to the affected area.

As one might imagine, military endeavors of this sort would look rather different from the humanitarian aid missions described in the previous chapter. When engaging in HA/DR operations, American forces are serving largely as emergency aid workers, providing relief supplies and medical care as needed to disaster sites unreachable by other organizations; they may employ armed force on occasion, to stop looting or protect aid convoys besieged by desperate survivors, but are otherwise operating in a noncombatant role. Intervening in a crisis situation where assorted armed groups are fighting over access to vital commodities poses an entirely different set of challenges. On such a mission, American forces might have to combat ethnic militias or insurgent bands while protecting the delivery of emergency assistance and provide essential government services for an extended period of time—a far more complex and hazardous undertaking. What is encompassed here, then, is the second rung on the hypothetical "ladder of escalation" of climate change scenarios.

The critical difference between these more complex operations and standard-fare HA/DR missions is the status of government authorities in the country involved. In ordinary humanitarian aid activities, it is assumed that American forces will play a significant role in delivering supplies and providing emergency services only for a short period of time, while local authorities regroup and begin the task of recovery. In those sorts of operations, explains Bert B. Tussing of the U.S. Army War College, the American military has no interest "in retaining control over the country they have committed to assist." Rather, "we would prefer to restore to power appropriate civil authorities. They are the ones who, over the long term, will remain behind to provide for the governance and well-being of their own people."[16] In the case of Mali-like crises, however, local authorities may fade away in the face of armed insurgents, or become just another faction in a multiethnic conflict. Under such circumstances, any U.S. forces sent to deal with the situation would not necessarily be able to rely on support from local authorities, nor could they plan for a quick withdrawal on the assumption that effective governance will soon be restored.

From very early on, therefore, concern over the prospect of "failed" and "fragile" states has been a prominent theme in the military's discussion of global warming. Many countries of the developing world, in this analysis, are already on the edge of dissolution because of resource scarcity, ethnic discord, and leadership venality; climate change, by further diminishing the supply of critical resources and generating severe natural disasters, can push them over the edge to collapse. As a country's critical supplies of food, water, and shelter decline, various groups within the population will fight for access to whatever remains. If, under these circumstances, the government fails to act in an equitable manner, ensuring that every group obtains at least minimal survival needs, violence will erupt between those favored by the government and those neglected by it—precisely the scenario that unfolded in Mali.

This stark prospect was first sketched out by the CNA Corporation in its original 2007 report on climate change and national security. "Economic and environmental conditions in already fragile areas will further erode as food production declines, diseases increase, clean water becomes increasingly scarce, and large populations move in search of resources," it warned. "When the conditions for failed states increase—as they most likely will over the coming decades—the chaos that results can be an incubator of civil strife, genocide, and the growth of terrorism."[17]

In the absence of a functioning state, the CNA report noted, essential services and the economy would disintegrate, forcing helpless citizens to arm themselves or join ethnic militias in a desperate bid for survival. This would inevitably accrue to the benefit of extremist organizations, which typically promise aid and protection in return for loyalty. For U.S. military officers, such a scenario is bound to be among the most fearsome outcomes of climate-related state collapse. "You may also have a population that is traumatized by an event or a change in conditions triggered by climate change," said General Anthony Zinni, former commander of Centcom, in the 2007 report. "If the government there is not able to cope with the effects, and if other institutions are unable to cope, then you can be faced with a collapsing state. And these end up as breeding grounds for instability, for insurgencies, for warlords."[18] All of this, of course, increases the likelihood of U.S. military intervention in such situations.

Ever since the publication of the CNA report, the notion that climate change would lead to failed states and significant security threats to the United States has permeated the military discourse. Those concerns were accorded considerable attention, for example, in a strategic assessment released in 2010 by the U.S. Joint Forces Command, the organization then responsible for mobilizing U.S.-based forces for deployment to overseas combat areas.* Given that responsibility, the Joint Forces Command sought to identify the global trends shaping potential battle zones, or what it called the "operating environment," publishing its findings in a document called the *Joint Operating Environment* report (*JOE*). The 2010 edition of the *JOE* is particularly notable because the Joint Forces commander at that time was General James Mattis, later President Trump's choice to be secretary of defense.

In a foreword to the *JOE*, General Mattis stressed the necessity of examining current trends, including climate change, to ensure U.S. success on future battlefields.[19] The *JOE* itself identified water scarcity, global warming, and mass migrations as being among the most prominent developments in this regard, and devoted particular attention to the threat posed by state collapse in areas where U.S. troops may be deployed. "Weak and

---

* In 2011, the Joint Forces Command was disassembled in what was described as a cost-saving measure and its various constituent parts were shifted to other organizations, including the Northern Command.

failing states will continue to present strategic and operational planners serious challenges, with human suffering on a scale so large that it almost invariably spreads throughout the region," it declared. Under these circumstances, "the Joint Force may be called upon to provide order and security in areas where simmering political, racial, ethnic, religious, and tribal differences create the potential for large-scale atrocities."[20]

In time, this outlook became assimilated into official DoD doctrine and the pronouncements of senior officials. This is evident, for example, in General Waldhauser's 2019 testimony before the Senate Armed Services Committee. "Environmental degradation and the overuse of natural resources exacerbate weak or ineffective governments who are unable to respond and cope with their already serious, on-going political, economic, and social challenges," he declared. Because of this, he said, Africom was working with partner militaries in Africa "to build the capability and capacity of governance, infrastructure, and defense institutions" and so, hopefully, reduce the risk of state collapse and its attendant maladies.[21]

For American military planners, the conclusion is inescapable. As global temperatures rise and more states confront the perils of instability and dissolution, the United States will be called upon ever more frequently to help preserve order.

## WATER, FOOD, AND INSTABILITY

The widely held perception among American security officials that climate change is a potential source of political instability and state disintegration largely rests on their belief that global warming is endangering the supply of vital resources—notably food, water, and arable land—in areas already suffering from scarcity and intergroup hostility. To some degree, this premise derives from the personal observations of American military personnel, especially those who have served in overseas combatant commands like Africom and Centcom. Mostly, however, it relies on scientific research in the field and extensive study by U.S. military and intelligence agencies. From 2008 to the present, the U.S. Intelligence Community (IC) and the Department of Defense have been issuing periodic reports summarizing the work of civilian and military experts on the connections among climate, resources, and conflict. These reports, in turn, have served as the foundation for the military's broader strategy documents and policy planning on climate change and national security.

This work began with the 2008 publication by the National Intelligence Council of its National Intelligence Assessment (NIA) titled *National Security Implications of Global Climate Change to 2030*. Drawing heavily on research conducted by major scientific organizations, including the National Oceanic and Atmospheric Administration and the Intergovernmental Panel on Climate Change, the NIC report sought to evaluate the effects that climate change would have on state stability and intergroup conflict over the ensuing twenty years. "We assess that climate change alone is unlikely to trigger state failure in any state out to 2030," it concluded, "but the impacts will worsen existing problems [and] could threaten domestic stability in some states."[22]

An especially pivotal factor in this equation, according to the 2008 assessment, is climate-related water scarcity. Drawing on extensive scientific research, the NIA projected that many areas of the world, especially in Africa, Asia, and the Middle East, could expect significant declines in rainfall as warming advanced, producing a corresponding contraction in food production. "Scientific studies indicate that climate change is likely to cause agricultural losses, possibly severe in the Sahel, West Africa, and southern Africa," it stated. With food and water supplies in steady decline and many local governments incapable of addressing the resulting hardship and bitterness, both intergroup and antigovernment violence were a predictable outcome.[23]

The intelligence community's perceived linkages between global warming, resource shortages, and conflict found a ready audience within the military establishment, many of whose members had served in Iraq and Afghanistan and seen firsthand the impact of water scarcity on hard-pressed populations. Continuing concern over this topic induced the National Intelligence Council to conduct a new study of the climate resource conflict connection, focusing specifically on water. This resulted, in 2012, in the publication of *Global Water Security,* the first official IC document on the subject. Described as an "Intelligence Community Assessment" (ICA)—and thus reflective of the views of all IC members, including the CIA, NIC, NSA, and so on—the report was intended to gauge how water scarcity and related problems would impact U.S. national security over the ensuing thirty years.[24]

Based on its review of the available scientific data, the NIC staff drew a bleak picture of the future water situation. Not only was global warming resulting in diminished rainfall in many areas, but it was also eradicating mountain glaciers whose meltwater feeds crucial river systems, such as the Ganges, Indus, Mekong, and Yangtze. As a result, an ever-greater share of the world's population was destined to live in areas of severe water stress, with insufficient supplies to meet minimum daily requirements.[25] This increase in water stress, the ICA suggested, was bound to increase social and political tensions, especially in countries where large segments of the population depend on agriculture for their livelihood and where some groups enjoyed better access to water than others—a frequent source of friction throughout human history.* At this point, the government response becomes crucial. If local authorities succeed in resolving emerging water disputes in a fair and pragmatic fashion, the outbreak of violent conflict can be averted; if they prove incapable of doing so or are seen to be favoring one group over another in the allocation of scarce water supplies, the danger will be multiplied. "Water shortages, and government failures to manage them, are likely to lead to social disruptions, pressure on national and local leaders, and potentially political instability," the intelligence assessment warned.[26]

Always lurking behind these investigations of climate change and water scarcity is the critical issue of *food* availability. Without adequate supplies of water, crop production and animal husbandry are virtually impossible, a devastating state of affairs for those whose livelihood is tied to the land. Moreover, as food supplies contract, prices always rise, causing misery for people who live in poverty and devote a large share of their income to food purchases.[27] In places where government authorities are widely considered corrupt or overly beholden to privileged elites, sudden jumps in food prices can provide the spark that sets off antigovernment protests and so-called food riots. That's precisely what happened in many countries following a worldwide spate of such price spikes in 2008.[28]

---

* For the most part, the risk of instability and conflict due to water scarcity was assumed in this report to arise *within* states, stemming from local disputes over access to water holes and streams. But the 2012 assessment also envisioned the possible outbreak of water-related conflict *between* states, notably over the allocation of water from shared river systems such as the Nile, Jordan, Indus, and Brahmaputra. This possible outcome of climate change will be examined in chapter 5.

In recognition of this water-food-instability nexus, the U.S. Intelligence Community followed up its study of water risks with one devoted to food. That report, *Global Food Security*, was released in 2015, again in the form of a National Intelligence Assessment. Like the earlier report on water, the assessment on food was decidedly pessimistic. Global demand, it said, was growing much faster than the anticipated increase in supply; existing agricultural systems, as currently configured, are simply not capable of feeding an ever-growing world population. And if meeting the world's future food requirements was difficult to begin with, climate change will make the task infinitely more challenging. As weather patterns change, the assessment noted, rainfall will decline and prolonged heat waves will occur more regularly in many areas, substantially reducing the production of certain key food crops. The output of corn and wheat—basic staples for many people around the world—was said to be at particular risk, as both crops require large amounts of water and are typically grown in areas expected to experience periodic droughts and increasingly high temperatures.[29]

As in the case of water scarcity, the 2015 report noted that future shortages of food crops—and accompanying high prices—represent potential causes of unrest and conflict, especially when combined with other sources of instability. Such disorder could take a variety of forms. In one such scenario, reminiscent of the events in Mali, "clashes between farmers and pastoralists" could erupt "as government policies, natural resource constraints, and pressure due to climate change push these two groups into closer proximity." In another scenario, government efforts to boost agricultural output by transferring poorly documented tribal lands to large agribusiness companies—a practice derisively called "land grabs"—could provoke armed resistance from those whose traditional homelands were being appropriated in this fashion.[30]

The IC's reports on water and food security were careful to note that, as with other climate change issues, resource scarcities *alone* are unlikely to spark widespread conflict. When scarcities arise, societies with competent governance and a high degree of social stability tend to cope in a practical and effective manner, avoiding the outbreak of conflict; indeed, a capable response to crisis can be a source of invigorated solidarity. The problem arises when food and water shortages amplify other key factors that lead to instability, particularly preexisting intergroup hostilities and corrupt, ineffectual governance. When a society is deeply divided and some sectors of the population enjoy greater access to vital resources than others, a climate-related crisis—especially one in which the government shows favoritism in the distribution of development aid and relief supplies—can rapidly escalate from civil unrest to armed violence.

By the mid twenty-teens, this understanding of the complex relationships among climate change, resource scarcity, ethnic antagonisms, and governmental ineffectiveness had been thoroughly integrated into the strategic outlook of senior American officers—especially among those who served in geographic combatant commands such as Africom, Centcom, and Pacom. "GCCs generally view climate change as a security risk because it impacts human security and, more indirectly, the ability of governments to meet the basic needs of their populations," the DoD told Congress in 2015. "Communities and states that are already fragile and have limited resources are significantly more vulnerable to disruption and far less likely to respond effectively." Climate changes "can generate new vulnerabilities (e.g., water scarcity) and thus contribute to instability and conflict even in situations not previously considered at risk."[31]

## COUNTRIES OF STRATEGIC IMPORTANCE

When discussing states at risk from the disruptive forces of climate change and resource scarcity, the authors of the various reports and statements cited above largely speak in general terms of certain regions or subregions, such as the Sahel, that they believe are particularly sensitive to the effects of climate change. They rarely mention any specific countries by name, and when individual nations are mentioned, they are usually weak and marginal states like Mali, whose fragility is well established. The documents do, however, make periodic references to "countries of strategic importance to the United States," also identified as "states important to U.S. national security interests." These countries, one assumes, are considered vital because of their size, location, natural resource endowments, contributions to U.S.-led military operations, or some combination of all of those factors. They are also, presumably, included on a watch-list of countries that are thought to be at risk of civil strife and state collapse, though they cannot be directly identified as such in public documents for fear of alienating their leaders.

Although the Intelligence Community is understandably vague about the identity of such states, the very fact that they've received so much attention in the IC reports has enormous significance for the U.S. military establishment. It suggests, above all, that intelligence analysts have serious concerns about the ability of some key allies to survive the severe impacts of climate change, along with worries that their collapse could endanger U.S. national security and thereby trigger American military intervention. Needless to say, any U.S. military engagement in countries falling into this category is likely to entail a much larger commitment of troops and equipment than would be the case in responding to a similar crisis in a less-significant, less-populated country such as Mali. In all likelihood, it would also involve far greater danger.

It is tempting, of course, to speculate about the identity of the countries listed on the IC's hypothetical watchlist of climate-endangered nations of strategic importance. Some hints can be garnered from the various reports and statements cited above and from other Pentagon documents. Among the possible candidates, three countries stand out in particular: Pakistan, Nigeria, and Saudi Arabia.

## Pakistan

There is no doubt that Pakistan is considered a "country of strategic importance to the United States." Not only is it a vital (if not always wholehearted) partner in the war on terror, but it also possesses a substantial arsenal of nuclear weapons whose security is a matter of enormous concern to Washington. Should those munitions wind up with rogue elements of the Pakistani military (some of whose members are believed to maintain clandestine links to radical Islamic organizations), or even worse, should Pakistan descend into civil war and the weapons fall into untrustworthy or hostile hands, the safety of India and other U.S. allies—as well as of American forces deployed in the region—would be at grave risk.[32] Ensuring Pakistan's stability has, therefore, long been a major U.S. security objective, prompting regular deliveries of American arms and other military aid.[33] Yet despite billions of dollars in U.S. aid, Pakistan remains vulnerable to social and ethnic internal strife. Increasingly, it is also at risk from the effects of climate change. In the words of the National Research Council, "Pakistan presents a clear example of a country where social dynamics and susceptibility to harm from climate events combine to create a potentially unstable situation."[34]

Farming is the principal economic activity in Pakistan, and so ensuring access to water is an overarching government concern. This means, above all, harnessing the flow of the Indus River—the country's main source of water for irrigated agriculture, as well as for much of its electrical generating capacity. Pakistan's rising population (projected to climb from 189 million people in 2015 to 310 million in 2050) and its growing cities and industrial enterprises are placing an immense strain on the Indus, leading to competition among farmers, industrialists, and urban consumers. With water and power shortages becoming an increasingly frequent aspect of daily life, public protests—sometimes turning violent—have erupted across the country. In one particularly intense bout of rioting, following a prolonged power outage in June 2012, protesters burned trains, blocked roads, looted shops, and damaged banks and gas stations.[35]

But however bad things might be in Pakistan today, climate change is likely to make conditions far worse in the years ahead. Prolonged droughts are expected to occur with increasing regularity, posing a severe threat to the nation's agricultural sector and further reducing the supply of hydroelectric power. Of particular concern is the likelihood that warming will affect the glaciers in the high Himalayas that provide much of the water for the Indus—especially during the dry season, when no monsoon rains fall. Scientists believe that these glaciers are slowly losing mass as a result of rising temperatures and eventually will disappear, posing a severe threat to the Indus and other key Asian rivers.[36] Warming may also increase the intensity of some monsoon downpours, resulting in massive flooding (as occurred in 2010) and the loss of valuable topsoil, further adding to Pakistan's woes. With the competition for available land and water resources bound to increase, and Pakistan already divided along ethnic and religious lines, widespread civil strife becomes more and more likely, possibly jeopardizing the survival of the state.[37]

Compounding Pakistan's mounting challenges is the persistent absence of a functioning civilian government with the authority and capacity to address the country's long-term problems. Corruption is endemic at every level of government, and the military—Pakistan's most cohesive institution—controls many key levers of power. In 2018, the military leadership engineered the judicial ouster of Nawaz Sharif, a prime minister they considered insufficiently pliable, and helped orchestrate the election of Imran Khan, a former playboy and cricket star. Khan has promised to overcome Pakistan's structural handicaps, including water and energy shortages, but few believe he is capable of achieving much. The stage is being set, therefore, for future outbreaks of social and economic unrest.[38]

It is impossible to predict exactly how the United States might respond to a systemic breakdown of state governance in Pakistan. One thing is clear, though: at the earliest sign that the country's nuclear weapons are at risk of falling into the hands of hostile parties, the American military would respond with decisive force. In fact, research conducted by the nonpartisan Nuclear Threat Initiative has revealed that the Joint Special Operations Command (JSOC) and specialized Army units have been training for such contingencies for some time and have deployed all the necessary gear to the region. In the event of a coup or crisis, the NTI revealed, "U.S. forces would rush into the country, crossing borders, rappelling down from helicopters, and parachuting out of airplanes, so they can secure known or suspected nuclear-storage sites." Recognizing that any such actions by American forces could trigger widespread resistance by the Pakistani army and/or various jihadist groups, the

U.S. Central Command, which has authority over all American forces in the region, has developed plans for backing up JSOC personnel with full-scale military support.[39]

## Nigeria

Like Pakistan, Nigeria receives recurring attention in the literature dealing with states deemed at risk of internal strife and collapse. One of America's key partners in Africa, it, too, faces severe risk from the effects of climate change, and, like Pakistan, suffers from endemic corruption, resource scarcity, and ethnoreligious strife.

Nigeria is the most populous nation in Africa, with some 180 million people, and is one of the world's major producers of oil and natural gas. According to oil giant BP, it possesses Africa's second-largest reserves of oil (after Libya) and its largest reserves of natural gas; in 2018, its petroleum output of two million barrels per day made it the top producer in the region.[40] But although fortunate in its hydrocarbon wealth, Nigeria has long suffered from internal divisions along ethnic, religious, and regional lines, and its governing elites have regularly been accused of unfettered avarice and corruption. In recent years it has also come under attack from violent extremist organizations, notably the Islamic terrorist group Boko Haram. In recognition of Nigeria's strategic importance and the threat it faces from violent extremism, the United States has provided its government with considerable military and economic assistance.[41]

While the most immediate threats to Nigeria's stability come from extremist groups like Boko Haram in the north and separatist movements in the Niger Delta region in the south, the country is also facing a growing challenge from climate change. This danger is particularly acute in Nigeria's north and north-

## Lake Chad Region of Africa

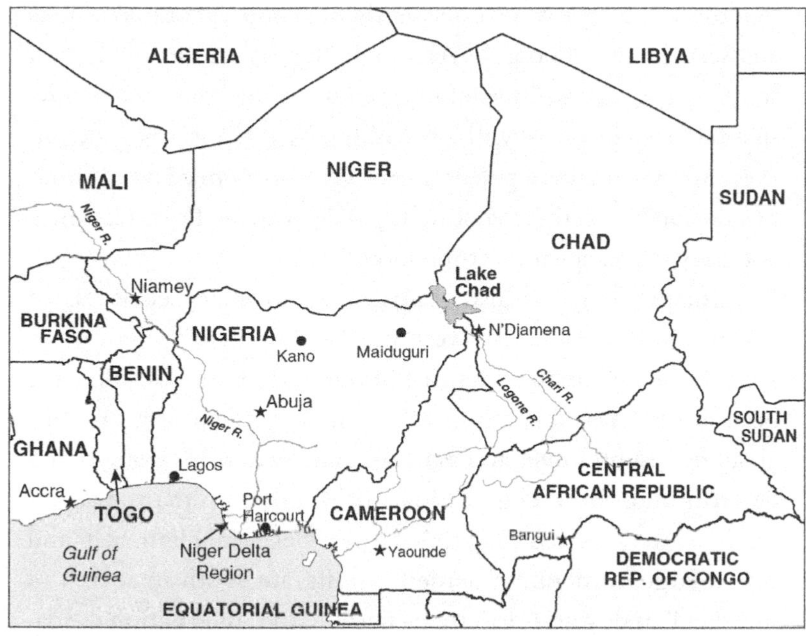


east, which abut the Sahel region and have been suffering from low rainfall and relentless drought. These effects have been particularly evident in the Lake Chad region of the northeast, the epicenter of the Boko Haram insurgency. Once a thriving locale for fishing and irrigated agriculture, Lake Chad has shrunk to less than one-fifth of its original size due to global warming and water mismanagement.[42] As fishing and agriculture decline, local people have struggled to feed themselves and earn a livelihood; and, with the government doing little to address the problem (or, worse, responding in a harmful and divisive fashion), Boko Haram has been able to attract significant local support. "Economic conditions in the region have become increasingly dire, creating resentment, grievances, and tensions within and among populations," the CNA Corporation noted in a 2017 report on global water stress. "Boko Haram exploits this situation to recruit followers, offering them economic opportunities and secured livelihoods."[43] Although Nigeria's military has had some recent success in subduing Boko Haram, the group (now split into two factions, with one calling itself the Islamic State in West Africa) remains a potent threat. With economic and environmental conditions there continuing to deteriorate, Boko Haram is not likely to disappear any time soon.[44]

Climate change is also contributing to increased levels of violence in Nigeria's northwest and "Middle Belt," where thousands have died and some three hundred thousand people have been displaced as a result of ethnic strife—much of it brought about by disputes over access to land and water.[45] "Drought and desertification have degraded pastures, dried up many natural water sources across Nigeria's far-northern Sahelian belt and forced large numbers of herders to migrate south in search of grassland and water for their herds," the International Crisis Group (ICG) reported in 2017.[46] Herders migrating into the savanna of the central states have heightened the pressure on farmland, increasing the frequency of disputes over crop damage. As in Mali and other states along the Sahel, there is an ethnic and religious component to the strife: the nomadic groups in Nigeria's north include the predominantly Islamic Fulani, who have clashed with majority Christian communities living farther south. With the government doing little to remedy the situation, "these disagreements increasingly turn violent," the ICG observed.[47]

As in Pakistan, Nigeria's response to these challenges has been hampered by a lack of effective governance. Although the current president, Muhammadu Buhari, is personally considered untainted by graft, he is widely accused of protecting political allies from criminal investigation. Nigeria's military leadership has also been accused of pocketing funds intended for frontline troops, hampering the fight against Boko Haram.[48] Buhari was reelected in a hard-fought contest in February 2019, promising to reinvigorate the battle against corruption and Boko Haram, but few observers expect much progress on either front.[49]

Although not directly involved in the internal strife in Nigeria, the United States has provided considerable aid to the Nigerian military in its campaign to eradicate Boko Haram and other militant groups. Most of this has been provided through regional security programs, such as the Trans-Sahara Counterterrorism Partnership (run by the State Department) and the Global Security Contingency Fund (run jointly by State and the DoD), which is aimed at bolstering counterinsurgency and border-defense capabilities in the Lake Chad region.[50] Some of the aid, though, has been supplied directly, in the form of military training and financing for arms transfers. American Special Forces and Army Infantry specialists have been deployed to the Nigerian Army Infantry School, for instance, to help train soldiers committed to the fight against Boko Haram.[51] While still relatively modest, these endeavors provide a preview of larger-scale U.S. intervention in Nigeria should such action be deemed necessary.

### Saudi Arabia

Also high on the list of key U.S. allies with considerable vulnerability to climate change is the Kingdom of Saudi Arabia. Saudi Arabia is, of course, the world's leading supplier of petroleum; its output, estimated in 2019 at 12 million barrels per day, is essential to the smooth functioning of the global economy, and it has proven reserves of some 298 billion barrels.[52] The Kingdom, ruled since 1932 by the Al Saud family, also plays a critical role in U.S.-led efforts to contain Iran and to combat terror organizations in the Persian Gulf region.[53] For years, Saudi Arabia has been the leading customer for American weaponry, signing orders for $62 billion's worth of advanced armaments between 2008 and 2015.[54] President Trump has been particularly outspoken in his support of the Al Saud regime, visiting Riyadh on his first trip abroad in 2017 and regularly playing host to Crown Prince Mohammed bin Salman, the Kingdom's de facto ruler.[55]

A relatively prosperous nation (due to its colossal oil income) with a population of nearly thirty million people, Saudi Arabia occupies a mostly arid peninsula inserted between North Africa and Southwest Asia. Possessing little surface water, the Kingdom relies on underground aquifers—many at risk of depletion—and the desalination of seawater for the bulk of its drinking water.[56] But desalination is not practical for large-scale irrigation purposes. With scant rainfall to rely on, Saudi Arabia can produce only a small share of its total food intake, and instead depends on imports for the bulk of its requirements. To ensure an uninterrupted stream of grain and vegetable imports, the Saudi government has financed the acquisition of large agricultural estates in other countries, particularly Ethiopia and Sudan, to grow crops for Saudi consumption—a practice often condemned as land grabbing.[57]

Even without global warming, Saudi Arabia is likely to face a confluence of perils. As its water supply diminishes, the quality of life deteriorates. Meanwhile, its population has been expanding, but employment opportunities have not kept up. The Kingdom's massive oil wealth provides some bulwark against these pressures, but if the world's reliance on petroleum begins to decline—a probable outcome of global efforts to curb emissions of carbon dioxide—it may prove inadequate to satisfy a restive populace.[58] Rising world temperatures are bound to exacerbate many of the Saudis' problems and make day-to-day life much more stressful, thereby amplifying these disruptive forces. "Saudi Arabia sits in the middle of the world's climate furnace," James A. Russell of the Naval Postgraduate School wrote in 2016. "There are few hotter, drier places on the planet, and it's only going to get worse as the world continues to dump carbon into the atmosphere."[59]

Temperatures are predicted to rise in the Middle East at twice the global average rate, and to reach increasingly oppressive levels in the years ahead.[60] A 2015 study published in *Nature Climate Change* concluded that by midcentury, many parts of the Arabian Peninsula could regularly experience summer daytime highs exceeding 122 degrees Fahrenheit, more than most people can endure for any length of time.[61] "Our results expose a specific regional hotspot where climate change, in the absence of significant [reduction in carbon emissions], is likely to severely impact human habitability in the future," said the study's authors.[62] Among the areas likely to be afflicted with such life-threatening temperatures are Jeddah and Mecca, site of the sacred Muslim ritual of the hajj, which involves substantial outdoor worship.[63] With water supplies dwindling and lethal heat waves regularly scorching the region, Saudi Arabia, much like other states in the region, could face internal unrest and antigovernment upheavals.

At present, the House of Saud appears to be in full control of the country. Despite occasional outbreaks of unrest, the government has largely succeeded in suppressing outright dissent while providing its younger citizens with sufficient economic incentives to discourage any Arab Spring–like revolt. But events in 2017–18 suggested greater disarray beneath the surface. In November 2017, Crown Prince Mohammed bin Salman rounded up hundreds of Saudi princes and entrepreneurs and incarcerated them for months in a Riyadh luxury hotel. This was done, it was claimed, to force them to surrender billions of dollars in ill-gotten financial assets—but also, in the view of many, to squelch internal opposition to his continued rule.[64] Then, in October 2018, Prince Mohammed was linked to the execution, at the Saudi consulate in Istanbul, of Jamal Khashoggi, a columnist for the *Washington Post* who was a fierce critic of the Saudi regime; again, observers hinted at deeper strains within the Kingdom.[65] Although Mohammed remains in control, and continues to enjoy strong support from the White House, these events cast doubt on the regime's ability to manage any severe crises that might erupt in the years ahead.

American leaders have always expressed fidelity to the Saudi royal family and, on occasion, have pledged military force to ensure the uninterrupted production of the country's oil. In 1981, when supporters of the Islamic Revolution in Iran began fomenting for a similar outcome in Saudi Arabia, President Ronald Reagan insisted that any such drive would be crushed by American forces. "There's no way," he told reporters at the time, "that we would stand by and see [the Kingdom] taken over by anyone that would shut off that oil."[66] Nearly ten years later, when Iraqi forces occupied Kuwait and appeared to threaten major oil fields in neighboring areas of the Kingdom, President George H. W. Bush authorized the deployment of U.S. troops to defend those areas under what was called Operation Desert Shield—the prelude, as it turned out, to the invasion of Iraq in Operation Desert Storm.[67] How American leaders would respond to a climate-related future threat to the Saudi regime's survival cannot be known in advance, but there can be no doubt that U.S. war planners have devised a variety of plans for possible intervention if circumstances warrant such action.

## CONTINGENCY PLANNING

There are, undoubtedly, also other countries on the undisclosed list of "states of security concern"—nations that are seen as being at risk due to the extreme effects of climate change and are deemed potential sites of U.S. military intervention if conditions were to deteriorate. Egypt comes to mind, as do Indonesia, Kenya, and the Philippines. The continued stability of each of these countries is unquestionably considered important by American strategists, and all of them are vulnerable to some combination of sea-level rise, prolonged drought, food scarcity, and protracted heat waves. At present, all of them possess reasonably capable governments, but when faced with extreme disasters—such as Typhoon Haiyan in the Philippines—they have not always performed with grace and proficiency. All of these countries, and other states one might place in the same category, are likely to face a series of increasingly severe climate assaults in the years to come, and it's anyone's guess as to whether they will survive with their governmental institutions intact.

As part of their regular duties, each of the Pentagon's geographic combatant commands is required to maintain reasonably up-to-date contingency plans at the regional ("theater") and national level within its area of responsibility. If U.S. forces are ordered to respond to some crisis in an assortment of conceivable scenarios, these highly classified plans dictate which combat units will conduct what sorts of maneuvers in what sequence. All of these plans existed long before climate change became a concern for war planners, but, since its emergence, global warming has been specifically factored into these blueprints. The combatant commands "use their Theater Campaign Plans, Operation Plans, Contingency Plans, and Theater Security Cooperation

Plans as a means to identify or take into account climate risks," the Pentagon informed Congress in 2015.[68]

Exactly how these assorted plans are being modified by concerns over climate change cannot be determined with any sort of precision without access to classified material. From various DoD statements and documents, though, it is clear that senior leaders envision a future in which American forces will be obliged to conduct hybrid missions that combine humanitarian assistance, combat operations, some degree of civil administration and law enforcement, and possibly the restoration of water and power supplies. Several of these aspects have figured in recent U.S. military deployments abroad, including the emergency response to Typhoon Haiyan and the interventions in Iraq and Afghanistan. Future engagements will, no doubt, prove equally complex and challenging.

The American military may not be preparing for "climate wars" as such, but it certainly anticipates that global warming will undermine the stability of many countries whose survival is deemed important to U.S. security, and accordingly knows that it may be called upon to intervene in such cases to avert chaos and calamity. This might entail limited support activities, as in Mali; but as warming engulfs more strategically significant states, it could result in far more extensive operations. Just how severe this challenge will prove to be will depend not only on the pace of warming but also on the ability of friendly governments to overcome an onslaught of increasingly severe climate shocks.

# 4

# GLOBAL SHOCK WAVES

## Food Shortages, Energy Crises, Pandemics, and Mass Migrations

Russia had never experienced anything like it before. Temperatures began rising to oppressive levels in May 2010 and by the end of June were breaking all previous records. July proved even hotter, with temperatures in Moscow averaging some twenty-five degrees Fahrenheit above normal, occasionally exceeding 100 degrees Fahrenheit. Thousands of wildfires broke out across the country, including some close to the capital; the smoke was so thick that flights were grounded at Moscow's airports and people were warned to stay indoors unless absolutely necessary. Even military installations were threatened by the flames, prompting Russian authorities to relocate artillery shells from a base near Moscow for fear they would ignite and set off a massive explosion.[1] President Dmitry Medvedev declared a state of emergency across much of the country, and Prime Minister Vladimir Putin (then planning another run for the presidency) was filmed in shirtsleeves overseeing relief operations in burned-out areas.[2]

As the heat wave gained momentum and fires raged across the country, Russia's vast agricultural sector was severely affected. Hundreds of thousands of hectares of farmland were burned, and approximately one-fifth of Russia's annual wheat harvest went up in smoke.[3] Patriarch Kirill, the head of the Russian Orthodox Church, made a nationwide appeal for the faithful "to unite in one prayer to God that He send rains to our scorched soil."[4] On August 5, with little rain expected for weeks to come and fears brewing of a domestic food crisis, Prime Minister Putin imposed an embargo on all exports of wheat and other grain products.[5] In response to his order, rail cars loaded with fresh grain were intercepted across Russia and rerouted from export ports to granaries in the interior.[6]

The summer heat wave inflicted a grim toll on Russia. An estimated five thousand people died from smoke-related health complications in Moscow alone, while another hundred thousand were rendered homeless and had to be evacuated from fire-scorched areas. The cost of the wildfires, including both lost crops and damaged homes and infrastructure, was estimated at many billions of dollars.[7] But Russia was not alone in suffering the consequences of its abnormally high temperatures. As Putin's decision to ban grain exports reverberated in the global food markets, food shortages and price spikes hit other countries, producing widespread havoc and misery. What started out as an exceptional Russian weather phenomenon thus combined with other destabilizing factors elsewhere—income inequality, high youth unemployment, and governmental corruption, among others—to generate a worldwide shock wave.

Scientists are normally reluctant to attribute any single weather event to global warming, but the Russian heat wave of

2010 was so far off the charts that it defied any other explanation. Not only did the summer inferno break all local temperature records by a wide margin, but it lasted longer than any previous heat wave and afflicted a much larger swath of territory, encompassing nearly all of western Russia along with large parts of Ukraine and Kazakhstan. After examining Russian weather patterns stretching back many years, scientists from NASA's Goddard Institute for Space Studies and Columbia University's Earth Institute concluded that "the extreme summer climate anomalies" of 2010 almost certainly had to be "a consequence of global warming" as the probability of their occurring "in the absence of global warming was exceedingly small."[8]

At the same time, global warming amplified the worldwide spike in food prices by decimating grain harvests in other regions of the world as well. Unusually heavy spring rains that year had washed away seeds and topsoil in key producing areas of Canada, reducing the summer wheat crop there by an estimated 35 percent.[9] Abnormal summer monsoonal rains and resulting floods in Pakistan inundated one-fifth of that country, destroying much of its prime cropland and adding to the pressure on global grain supplies.[10] Wheat exports from Australia, a major producer, were sharply curtailed by a prolonged drought, while in China drought conditions began to emerge in the northeast, the country's principal grain-producing area. Global food prices, already elevated by August, soared after Russia imposed its ban on wheat exports, and continued rising after China's leaders—fearing the consequences of drought—began making huge grain purchases on the international market. The relentless rise in prices may not have been especially burdensome for China, with its mammoth financial reserves, but proved devastating for poor countries in Africa and the Middle East, which rely on grain imports for a large share of their food intake and were now being forced to pay much more for desperately needed provisions.[11]

The disruptive consequences of all this were first made manifest in Mozambique, beginning just a few weeks after Putin's August 5 decision to ban grain exports. A relatively poor country on Africa's southeastern flank, Mozambique—like other countries in the region—is highly reliant on imported cereals, and the sudden rise in wheat prices caused an immediate food crisis. At the end of August, the government eliminated subsidies on food, causing the price of bread to jump by 30 percent and stirring widespread dissent. Within days, violent protests broke out in the capital city of Maputo, bringing the city to a virtual halt and prompting a harsh government crackdown. At first, officials refused to reinstate the subsidies, prompting even more protests and further violence, leaving twelve people dead and more than four hundred injured. Only after the government backed down and acceded to the protesters' demand for renewed food subsidies was order restored.[12]

But this was only the beginning. Like Mozambique, the nations of the Middle East and North Africa (MENA) were also particularly sensitive to spiking grain prices, being heavily reliant on food imports to satisfy their basic requirements. According to a 2009 report by the World Bank, the Arab states of MENA import at least half of all the food calories they consume, more than any other group of nations. "As the largest net importers of cereal," the study noted, "Arab countries are more exposed than other countries to severe swings in agricultural commodity prices, and their vulnerability will probably be exacerbated in coming years by strong population growth, low agricultural productivity, and their dependence on global commodities markets."[13] The highly prophetic report singled out Egypt and Tunisia as especially vulnerable to disruptions in international grain markets, since bread constitutes a large share of their caloric intake and many of their citizens devote a significant proportion of their income—often 50 percent or more—to food purchases.[14]

By December 2010, the food-price shock wave that had been detonated by Vladimir Putin and afforded added momentum by panic buying in China had reached the MENA region with a vengeance. At this point, global wheat prices were roughly 90 percent higher than they had been at the start of the year, and other cereals were also trading significantly above their previous levels. As in Mozambique, the price of bread and other food staples underwent a precipitous rise, provoking civic unrest throughout the region. Many people in the MENA countries—especially the poor, the unemployed, and those otherwise excluded from the privileged elite—already harbored numerous grievances toward the authoritarian regimes in power, and the sudden spike in food prices generated an added sense of outrage.[15]

On December 17, a poor Tunisian street vendor named Tarek el-Tayeb Mohamed Bouazizi set himself aflame after government officials overturned his vegetable cart and confiscated his scale, depriving him of a way to earn a living. Almost immediately, protests broke out against the dictatorial regime of President Zine El Abidine Ben Ali, demanding both political reform and relief from high food prices. The protests in Tunisia inspired similar uprisings in neighboring countries, where mammoth crowds turned out to denounce their own corrupt and repressive governments. In Egypt, millions of protesters flooded Tahrir Square in central Cairo, defying armed police and paramilitary forces; large demonstrations were also held in the capitals of Libya, Jordan, and other Arab nations. Along with signs calling for the reform of sclerotic political institutions, many of the protesters brandished loaves of bread, signifying their resentment of the rising food prices.[16]

In what came to be known as the Arab Spring, a wave of revolutionary fervor swept through the region, permanently altering the political landscape and creating a host of new security challenges for the United States. In Egypt, the mass protests ultimately succeeded in precipitating the ouster of President Hosni Mubarak, a longtime ally of the United States; his immediate successor, Mohammed Morsi of the Muslim Brotherhood, was less beholden to Washington. (Morsi himself was soon overthrown in a military coup and replaced by General Abdel Fattah el-Sisi.) In Libya, an armed rebellion succeeded in toppling the dictatorship of Mu'ammar Gadhafi; in the aftermath of his ouster, however, the various rebel militias began fighting with one another for control of the country, leading to widespread chaos and the arrival of militants from al-Qaeda and the Islamic State. In Syria, peaceful demonstrations against the Bashar al-Assad regime were met with a vicious government crackdown, triggering a civil war that persists to this day. All of these, and related events in neighboring countries, opened fresh opportunities for the expansion of terrorist organizations and produced vast waves of human migration.[17]

## COMPOUNDING SYSTEM SHOCKS

The Arab Spring exemplified a new type of security threat from global warming: one arising not from a single natural disaster, limited in time and space, but from a *compound* series of events, spreading quickly across the planet. Such events—call them climate shock waves—are far more threatening than the dangers discussed earlier in this book, as they have the capacity to destabilize numerous states simultaneously rather than just one at a time. Moreover, they can also imperil the world-spanning trade and logistical systems upon which the international economic order—and American prosperity—rests. These systems, such as the grain markets so affected by the Russian heat wave of 2010, are essential for the well-being of almost every country on Earth, yet are highly vulnerable to global climate shocks. Other critical networks, such as the worldwide flow of energy and the global public health system, are equally at risk to shocks of this sort. When such systems fail, vital commodities become scarce and chaos may ensue—posing a severe risk to fragile states and a potential threat to U.S. national security. Accordingly, climate shock waves represent an even higher level of danger than the other warming-related perils we have examined up to this point.

The risks to national and international stability from climate shock waves have been a concern of America's military and intelligence communities for some time. In its initial 2008 National Intelligence Assessment on the security threats posed by climate change, the National Intelligence Council underscored America's reliance on reliable global networks. The United States, it pointed out, "depends on a smooth-functioning international system ensuring the flow of trade and market access to critical raw materials such as oil and gas, and security for its allies and partners." Climate change could imperil all of that, it noted, resulting in the downfall of friendly states, a loss of access to vital materials, and disruptions to "the global economy more broadly."[18]

Following the Arab Spring, the U.S. Intelligence Community sought to acquire a more sophisticated understanding of the role that climate change might play in triggering such far-reaching calamities. To this end, the IC commissioned the National Research Council of the American Academy of Sciences to conduct a study of warming's socioeconomic consequences, which was published in 2013 as *Climate and Social Stress: Implications for Security Analysis*. The NRC study examined a number of scenarios already discussed in earlier chapters of this book, including humanitarian disasters, resource scarcities, and state collapse. But it also included a section on "global system shocks," continent-spanning crises triggered by some combination of climate change and "globally integrated systems other than the climate itself." As world temperatures rise and global supply networks become more interdependent, the report noted, "there are numerous ways in which climate events could create shocks to integrated global social, economic, health, or technological systems and thus have effects far removed geographically from where the events occur."[19]

Because we have become so dependent on these global supply networks, the NRC's analysts concluded, a major climate event that disrupts or damages a significant component of them can inflict immediate and substantial pain. Many nations rely on those systems for deliveries of food, energy, and other vital commodities; when shortages of such goods arise, their prices soar and all those with limited means begin to suffer. If governments fail to address these challenges in a timely and equitable manner, unrest and conflict can erupt in multiple countries at once. Such upheavals can also produce follow-on effects, including mass migrations and pandemics, that undermine yet other countries. States that are already vulnerable to dissolution can fail one after another.[20]

The authors of the NRC report were particularly struck by the degree to which climate change is combining with globalization to increase the risk of upheaval. Not only are extreme climate events occurring more frequently, they noted, but warming's effects are being amplified by our reliance on international trading networks for essential goods and services—in particular, the globe-spanning matrix of pipelines, rail lines, and shipping lanes used to transport food and energy supplies. These networks are relatively robust under ordinary conditions, but can be severely disrupted by extreme climate-related events, as with hurricane damage to refineries, pipelines, and oil terminals.[21] To make matters worse, severe climate events are occurring more frequently in "clusters," magnifying the shock to the system—much as when the 2010 heat wave in Russia coincided with severe flooding in Pakistan and drought in China.[22]

Global supply chains' vulnerability to severe climate effects is especially evident in the case of food. The crops that account for a large share of the world's caloric intake—wheat, maize (corn), rice, soy beans, and a few others—require copious amounts of water to achieve maximum yield, along with temperatures that remain within a certain range. Always unpredictable in the best of times, these benign growing conditions will prove increasingly uncommon as severe heat waves, prolonged droughts, and catastrophic floods become the norm. Under these circumstances, shortages of one staple or another are likely to occur on a recurring basis.[23] On top of this, the number of grain-producing nations capable of generating a surplus for export is rather small, while the number of countries dependent on those few exporters for their essential food requirements is large. A clustering of extreme weather events that reduces or eliminates exports from just two or three of the major exporters would thus have a powerful effect on the global market, squeezing supplies for all importers and sending prices skyward.[24]

The disruptiveness of such price increases is amplified by the social and economic difficulties in a number of the countries dependent on food imports. In water-stressed areas of the developing world, many poor farmers—no longer able to secure an adequate livelihood from their increasingly barren fields as temperatures rise and rainfall diminishes—are migrating to the cities in search of alternative options, and must scramble to acquire food there. This trend, the NRC pointed out, can only increase these countries' vulnerability to global food-supply problems, creating larger urban populations that are particularly sensitive to food prices. With more displaced agriculturalists moving to the cities, it stated, "the dependence of low-income populations on imported food supplies provided by global markets may increase their vulnerability to climatic or economic events in other parts of the world that sharply increase the prices of the foods they have come to depend upon."[25]

This combination of circumstances, IC analysts believe, can only lead to more Arab Spring–like upheavals in the future—a risk given close scrutiny in the National Intelligence Council's 2015 report, *Global Food Security*. Although humans are theoretically capable of producing enough foodstuffs to meet the basic caloric requirements of everyone on the planet, that report indicated, large segments of the global population are vulnerable to food shortages and sudden price spikes of the sort witnessed in 2010–11 because of unreliable distribution systems, flawed government policies, and relentless poverty.[26] "We judge that the overall risk of food insecurity in many countries of strategic importance to the United States will increase," the NIC report concluded. "In some countries, declining food security will almost certainly contribute to social disruptions or large-scale political instability or conflict."[27]

This concern—that growing world food insecurity and climate-driven price spikes will generate widespread instability and conflict—continues to permeate U.S. strategic calculations. It is evident, for example, in the "worldwide threat assessment" delivered each year to Congress by the director of national intelligence on behalf of the IC as a whole. In his February 2018 presentation, the current director, Daniel R. Coats, stated that "extreme weather events in a warmer world have the potential for greater impacts and can compound with other drivers to raise the risk of humanitarian disasters [and] conflict," with "food shortages" and "price shocks" playing major contributing roles.[28]

## ENERGY SHOCK WAVES

Warming's threat to global food distribution networks has, in general, constituted the primary focus of U.S. military and intelligence analysts concerned about climate shock waves. However, they have also sounded the alarm about the potential for other highly disruptive events: breakdowns in global energy systems, outbreaks of global pandemics, and new, destabilizing mass migrations. As with a collapse of global food-supply chains, these climate shocks would involve extreme climate events that arise in one or more parts of the world and provoke havoc in many others, ultimately endangering American national security and prompting U.S. military action of some sort.

After global food supplies, American security analysts have worried most about warming's capacity to disrupt the world's vital energy systems. As with food supplies, today's world is highly reliant on global commerce for many essential fuels, especially oil and natural gas. While a handful of countries are largely self-sufficient in one or both of those fuels, most industrial powers—including Japan, the United States, and the EU countries—depend on imports for at least some of their energy needs. In 2018, for example, Japan relied on imports for nearly 100 percent of its petroleum requirements, the EU countries for 89 percent, and the United States for 25 percent. These import dependencies are expected to persist well into the future, with the developing nations of Asia assuming an ever-increasing share of global energy demand. China now relies on imported petroleum for 65 percent of its requirements and India for 82 percent; by 2040, their import dependence is projected to climb to 80 and 91 percent, respectively.[29]

It is true, of course, that some countries are working very hard to reduce their reliance on fossil fuels, including oil and natural gas, so as to diminish their contributions to global warming. Japan, for example, has reduced its oil consumption from a peak of 4.7 million barrels per day in 2012 to 3.9 million battels in 2018. Most European countries have also experienced a decline, with consumption by the European Union as a whole dropping from 14.8 million barrels per day in 2008 to 13.3 million barrels in 2018.[30] Some analysts believe, therefore, that the global demand for petroleum will gradually subside. But in many parts of the world, especially Asia, Africa, and the Middle East, oil consumption is projected to continue growing, especially as more people enter the middle class and purchase cars, trucks, and motorcycles; these surges in demand are expected to outweigh declines elsewhere, ensuring continuing increases in global oil consumption. The worldwide demand for natural gas is also expected to climb, as countries around the world work to phase out older coal-powered electrical plants. As a result of all this, the trade in oil and gas is likely to remain a critical feature of international commerce for decades to come.

To transport oil, coal, natural gas, and electricity from one end of the world to another, energy-exporting and -consuming nations have constructed a vast matrix of railroads, pipelines, transmission lines, and maritime shipping routes. On any given day, a large share of the world's energy supply is being transported via one of these vital conduits. According to BP, on an average day in 2018, some seventy-one million barrels of crude petroleum and refined fuels—approximately 75 percent of daily world output—were being shipped from one country to another; for natural gas, the share of world output in transit was about 24 percent.[31] In many cases, the pipelines and tankers used in carrying these supplies pass through or near areas of recurring conflict, such as the Middle East and North Africa; most of the time, moreover, they travel across areas vulnerable to storms, wildfires, flooding, and other climate-related disasters.

American security analysts have long been concerned about disruptions in the global flow of energy arising from war and political interference. Those concerns were given particular urgency in the 1970s following two crippling "oil shocks" generated by political turbulence in the Middle East—the first, occurring in 1973–74, when Arab members of the Organization of the Petroleum Exporting Countries (OPEC) imposed an embargo on exports to the United States in retaliation for its support of Israel in the October War of 1973; the second in 1979–80, following the Islamic Revolution in Iran. In response to those two oil shocks, the United States charged its military with taking ever greater responsibility for ensuring the safety of oil deliveries from the Persian Gulf.[32] Following the 1979 Soviet invasion of Afghanistan, President Jimmy Carter proclaimed that any hostile effort to impede those deliveries "will be regarded as an assault on the vital interests of the United States of America," and, as such, "will be repelled by any means necessary, including military force."[33]

To enforce that edict—quickly dubbed the "Carter Doctrine"—the Department of Defense established the Rapid Deployment Joint Task Force and assigned it responsibility for protecting Persian Gulf oil exports; that force later served as the nucleus of the U.S. Central Command. When Iraq invaded Kuwait in 1990 and appeared to be poised for an attack on Saudi Arabia, President George H. W. Bush invoked the Carter Doctrine to justify the deployment of American forces to the Gulf and the onset of what became Operation Desert Storm.[34] Although the United States no longer relies on Persian Gulf oil for a large share of its energy needs—as a result of advances in extraction technology, this country now obtains an ever-greater proportion of its energy needs from domestic shale formations—U.S. leaders continue to worry about the safety of the global oil flow, given its critical importance to the world economy. In particular, they worry about threats being made by Iranian leaders to block oil traffic through the Gulf in case of a U.S. attack on Iranian nuclear facilities; to counter any such move, Centcom has long deployed a powerful array of ships and planes in the region.[35]

But while American strategists continue to think about the threats to oil flow posed by terrorism and hostile powers, they are becoming increasingly concerned about dangers to the global web of energy systems arising from the effects of climate change. A great deal of the world's energy is transported via extended pipelines, shipping lanes, and transmission lines that are naturally at risk from such climate-related perils as severe flooding, turbulent seas, and major wildfires. This danger is compounded by the fact that, in search of ready access to maritime shipping channels, a very substantial proportion of the world's oil and natural gas infrastructure is situated in coastal areas, which in many cases are highly vulnerable to hurricanes and storm surges. As global warming advances, therefore, international energy trade will become increasingly susceptible to severe climate shocks.[36]

With the world increasingly dependent on these extended, highly vulnerable energy-supply networks, the NRC concluded in its 2013 report, future climate shocks could produce instant shortages and price hikes around the world, much as with the food-price shock waves it had studied.[37] In support of this assessment, the report pointed to a series of powerful hurricanes that struck America's Gulf Coast in the early years of the twenty-first century: Katrina and Rita in 2005, followed by Gustav and Ike in 2008. These storms damaged or destroyed many offshore rigs and disrupted operations at refineries and distribution facilities, sharply reducing U.S. oil and gas output and causing a spike in global prices.[38] Sea-level rise, the NRC noted, will amplify the disruptive consequences of future storms and hurricanes, as many power plants—both nuclear and coal-fired—are located in low-lying coastal areas; when storms occur, these plants are at risk of flooding, causing systemic damage and power outages. This occurred, for example, in the New York metropolitan region following Superstorm Sandy in 2012: several of the region's power plants, including all of its nuclear stations, were either damaged or experienced temporary shutdowns due to high winds and flooding.[39]

The NRC further noted that climate change may disrupt the global energy supply system in other ways. Prolonged droughts and heat waves can reduce the amount of water available to hydropower facilities and water-cooled thermoelectric power plants, cutting into the electricity delivered to international grids.[40] A disruption of just this sort occurred during a European heat wave in 2003 that was blamed for the deaths of over thirty-four thousand people. As river levels dropped in France—Europe's leading exporter of electricity—the government was forced to shut down several nuclear reactors for lack of adequate cooling water. This, in turn, resulted in a 50 percent decline in France's power exports, producing electricity shortages throughout the region.[41]

Major disruptions to the global energy system have occurred before, and no doubt will occur again in the future for a variety of reasons, including those cited above. Given the multiplicity of international networks available for energy delivery, the world economy can probably absorb several such disruptions happening sequentially, as they have in the past. What worried the authors of the NRC report, however, is the possibility that advancing climate change will result in several major disruptions occurring *simultaneously*, severely testing the ability of global supply networks to cope. Such a scenario, they warned, could produce significant energy shortages around the world and a rapid spike in prices. This, in turn, could result in an economic recession and political unrest. As happened with the 2010–11 spike in food prices, "an oil-price shock could increase instability, particularly in a situation that is already politically sensitive."[42]

Initially, such an outcome would prove most disruptive in developing countries that are highly dependent on energy imports and can ill afford a sudden spike in prices. But climate-related supply interruptions could also generate havoc in advanced nations that rely heavily on imports, as well as in energy-exporting states that depend on foreign sales to finance government operations. Any significant disruption in Persian Gulf oil exports, for example, will punish oil-producing countries as well as their overseas clients. As warming advances and global supply chains prove more unreliable, major energy-consuming nations may adopt a more nationalistic and militaristic stance toward energy, thereby generating yet additional international tensions. This could also lead to conflict among the major powers—a topic to be addressed in the next chapter.

## GLOBAL PANDEMICS

In addition to their concern about global food-price and energy-price shocks, American strategists worry about another potential climate-instigated shock wave: the rapid spread of lethal infectious diseases across the globe, causing widespread illness in multiple locations and, in so doing, adding to the pressures on already overstressed societies. Deadly pandemics have, of course, long bedeviled human society, going back to the outbreaks of plague that periodically decimated European populations. Modern medicine has helped reduce the risk of such calamities, but now climate change is threatening to overwhelm those gains. Rising world temperatures, increased precipitation, and higher levels of humidity all facilitate the spread of diseases transmitted by mosquitoes and other insects. Mosquitoes need pools of water to breed, and the hotter and wetter it is, the faster they can reproduce. As global warming widens the geographic extent of hot, moist breeding areas, the range of many virus-bearing mosquitoes will grow as well.[43]

Malaria, one of the deadliest diseases transmitted by mosquitoes, is already thought to be spreading from the tropics to temperate zones as a consequence of climate change.[44] Other "vector-borne" diseases, such as the Zika virus and dengue fever, are also expected to spread into new areas as global warming advances.[45] "Increased temperatures and more frequent and intense precipitation events can create conditions that favor the movement of vector-borne diseases into new geographic regions," the U.S. Global Change Research Program noted in its *Fourth National Climate Assessment*.[46] Adding to the danger of future pandemics is the looming breakdown of public health systems in many poor and conflict-ravaged countries. Epidemics that can effectively be controlled by medical authorities in well-functioning societies are likely to gain momentum when health systems collapse—an outcome that will prove increasingly likely as more and more states are impacted by climate shock waves.[47]

Globalization is also contributing to the risk of global pandemics, by facilitating air and sea travel from one corner of the world to another. "Outbreaks occurring in other countries can impact U.S. populations and military personnel living abroad and can sometimes affect the United States," the *Fourth Assessment* warned.[48] Unless a quarantine is imposed when a potential epidemic is first detected, visitors to a country with mosquito-borne diseases may become infected and return to their home country before any symptoms have appeared, potentially creating new centers of infection. In this manner, the effects of climate change could combine with international transportation networks to ignite a global health shock wave, akin to the food and energy shock waves described above.

As suggested by analysts at the National Research Council, climate effects and globalization are combining to increase the risk of global health shocks. "Weather and climate changes," they noted, "have the potential of interaction with other factors to alter both the geographic range and the intensity of transmission of a number of infectious diseases, thereby creating the potential for pandemics."[49] If these pandemics arise in or spread to developing nations with inadequate public health systems, they can lead to widespread panic and civic unrest, prompting terrified citizens to seek refuge in other countries—possibly carrying the pathogens with them and so igniting fresh outbreaks of contagion. Once this occurs, it is but a short step to a global humanitarian crisis, which could easily result in the involvement of the American military due to its unique ability to deploy on short notice to virtually any location on the planet and provide emergency services.[50]

All this was given dramatic immediacy by the West African Ebola epidemic of 2014–16, which ravaged Guinea, Liberia, and Sierra Leone and affected several other countries, claiming an estimated 11,300 lives. An often fatal viral disease, Ebola is thought to be transmitted to humans from bats and other wild animals, usually in situations where humans live in close proximity to such creatures and rely on them as a supplemental source of food, as is true in some poor, rural areas of Africa.[51] The 2014–16 Ebola outbreak, the most severe of its kind, first arose in Guinea and then quickly spread to neighboring Liberia and Sierra Leone when panicked citizens—some carrying the infection—moved from one country to another across poorly marked borders in search of safety from the outbreak. Local public health systems, poorly staffed and poorly equipped to begin with, quickly became overwhelmed as medical workers themselves came down with the disease. By some estimates, one in ten of Ebola fatalities during the early stages of the epidemic were among nurses, doctors, medical students, and other clinical staff.[52]

The Ebola epidemic also threatened to spread to other parts of the world as foreign health workers returned to their home countries after volunteering in one of the affected West African states and as panicked citizens of those countries traveled elsewhere in the hope of avoiding infection. Indeed, several Ebola cases were identified in Europe and the United States under exactly such circumstances, prompting fears of a global pandemic and accompanying social disorder. As an indication of what might occur, fighting broke out in Monrovia, the capital of Liberia, when police tried to cordon off the heavily infected neighborhood of West Point and panicked residents fought back.[53] For American security officials, it had all the earmarks of a potential international crisis.

In a remarkable expression of these fears, President Obama

explicitly warned of Ebola's threat to global security, announcing a major U.S. effort to combat the disease:

> In West Africa, Ebola is now an epidemic of the likes that we have not seen before. It's spiraling out of control. It is getting worse. It's spreading faster and exponentially. Today, thousands of people in West Africa are infected. That number could rapidly grow to tens of thousands. And if the outbreak is not stopped now, we could be looking at hundreds of thousands of people infected, with profound political and economic and security implications for all of us. So this is an epidemic that is not just a threat to regional security—it's a potential threat to global security if these countries break down, if their economies break down, if people panic. That has profound effects on all of us, even if we are not directly contracting the disease.

With stakes this high, combating the Ebola outbreak was declared a "national security priority," and every relevant arm of government would be mobilized to prevent its spread.[54]

To manage this effort and conduct its most urgent missions, Obama turned to the U.S. Africa Command. Africom, he announced in September 2014, would establish a "military command center in Liberia to support civilian efforts across the region," with General Darryl Williams, commander of Africom's U.S. Army contingent, overseeing the operation. This was an unusual arrangement, as the Department of Defense had never before conducted what it termed "a disease-driven foreign humanitarian assistance mission."[55] However, given the magnitude of the peril and the lack of any other institution capable of taking on such a Herculean task, Obama placed this responsibility on the U.S. military. "Our Department of Defense is better at that, our Armed Services are better at that, than any organization on Earth," he declared.[56]

At Obama's behest, Africom undertook a massive logistical effort in West Africa, establishing emergency hospitals and clinics in each of the three most heavily affected countries and providing support services for a bevy of doctors and other health workers flown in from the United States and other countries. At least three thousand U.S. military personnel participated in this extraordinary effort, dubbed Operation United Assistance. Although not directly involved in the medical treatment of patients—that task was performed solely by civilian personnel—these troops played a vital role in fighting Ebola by providing essential logistical support to the doctors and nurses on the front lines of treatment.[57]

For many observers, the Ebola epidemic of 2014–16 represents a preview of what can be expected in the future as global warming advances, certain infectious diseases extend their range, and vulnerable states prove unable to cope with the multiple challenges of extreme weather, resource scarcity, and inadequate public institutions. This peril was highlighted again in early 2019, as a fresh outbreak of Ebola occurred in parts of the Democratic Republic of the Congo, where inadequate government institutions and ethnic strife impeded efforts by the international community to provide emergency care. And, as the NRC points out, the danger will only increase as temperatures continue their rise and extreme events cluster together more frequently, undermining the ability of the international community to provide emergency relief and assistance. Should a pandemic occur at a time when international supply systems for medications are already impaired by climate change, the consequences would be dire.[58]

## MASS MIGRATION EVENTS

Whenever U.S. security analysts have considered the risks of climate change, a perpetual concern has been that extreme events and prolonged droughts could trigger a massive flight of desperate people seeking refuge in other locales, provoking chaos and hostility wherever they travel. This anxiety was evident in some of the analysts' earliest public statements on the national security implications of warming, and it has remained a major theme to the present day. In its initial 2007 report on climate change, for example, the CNA Corporation warned that severe climate effects "can fuel migrations in less developed countries, and these migrations can lead to international political conflict."[59] Defense Secretary Hagel sounded a similar note in his 2014 address to the Conference of the Defense Ministers of the Americas. "Drought and crop failures can leave millions of people without any lifeline, and trigger waves of mass migration," he declared.[60]

In talking about the risk of mass migrations, U.S. security analysts are typically discussing *long-term* pressures—such as prolonged drought and coastal erosion—that deprive people of their livelihoods and force them to move elsewhere in search of jobs and income. "When water or food supplies shift or when conditions otherwise deteriorate (as from sea level rise, for example), people will likely move to find more favorable conditions," the CNA explained.[61] The ongoing relocation of impoverished farmers from scorched inland areas to urban centers, for instance, fits this pattern. But American analysts also worry about *sudden-onset* climate events that would spark rapid, large-scale movements of people from one country to another, setting off a political firestorm. Such destabilizing events, which could become more frequent as global warming advances, are akin to the other types of climate shock waves discussed in this chapter.

A migratory shock wave of this type could be ignited by various kinds of climate events, such as a cluster of severe hurricanes or crop failures. If, under these circumstances, local governments prove unable to provide adequate emergency assistance or collapse entirely, vast numbers of people may simultaneously choose to move to adjacent (or even distant) countries in search of refuge and a new start in life. Some environmentalists are predicting that the numbers of such "climate refugees," as they have sometimes been termed, could reach into the hundreds of millions as global warming advances; others have cautioned against such predictions, saying the evidence for them is still inconclusive. Whatever the exact numbers, the arrival of large groups of outsiders—many, if not most, in need of substantial assistance—is bound to generate unease and, in all likelihood, hostility in the destination countries. The fact that the newcomers often differ in their race and religion from the natives only adds to the risk of antagonism.[62]

A foretaste of what this might look like was provided by the migratory surges from North Africa and the Middle East into southern Europe following the Arab Spring of 2011, as desperate residents of battleground countries such as Libya and Syria sought to escape the fighting and accompanying decline in economic conditions. The situation in Libya was particularly fraught for migrant workers from the Sahel region and sub-Saharan Africa, who made up as much as 10 percent of Libya's population prior to the revolt against Gadhafi. Those workers (mostly young men) had already fled their own countries because of drought, desertification, and joblessness, seeking low-level positions in various state-backed enterprises in Libya under the old regime. After Gadhafi's removal, they lost their jobs and faced intense hostility from native Libyans, who viewed them as interlopers and Gadhafi loyalists. Reluctant to return to their own impoverished countries, huge numbers of these migrant workers sought to move farther north, fleeing in rickety ships across the Mediterranean to Europe—where, if they survived the journey, they usually encountered fresh animosity.[63]

An even greater number of people sought to flee the fighting and abysmal living conditions in Syria. Beginning in 2012, and reaching a flood tide in 2015, vast multitudes of desperate Syrians sought to reach the relative security of Europe, mostly by traveling by raft from southwestern Turkey to Lesbos and other Greek islands in the Aegean Sea; from there they sought passage to wealthier European countries farther north, especially Germany, Austria, and Norway. Although welcomed at first by sympathetic Europeans (most notably German chancellor Angela Merkel), the Syrian refugees started arriving in such massive numbers that many residents of the receiving nations turned hostile, embracing measures such as fencing off their borders and using armed police to repel the migrants—steps taken by Hungary in 2015 as hundreds of thousands of refugees moved north from Greece.[64] With anti-refugee sentiment growing throughout the region, European officials were forced to adopt ever more stringent means to stem the flow, including mobilizing NATO's naval fleets to patrol waters of the Aegean Sea and assist the Greek coast guard in blocking migrant vessels from Turkey.[65]

When examining the causes of the massive migrant flood that overwhelmed Europe in 2015, most analysts have concluded that the principal driving forces were the ongoing violence in Syria and the lack of meaningful economic opportunities both there and in transit countries such as Jordan, Lebanon, and Turkey. Nevertheless, some analysts believe that climate change had a contributing role in sparking the migratory shock wave, largely by causing a severe drought in 2007–10 that decimated Syrian agriculture and drove impoverished farmers into overcrowded urban centers, where they helped launch the anti-Assad rebellion.[66] "Syria's drought has destroyed crops, killed livestock and displaced as many as 1.5 million Syrian farmers," observed John Wendle in *Scientific American*. "In the process, it touched off the social turmoil that burst into civil war," impelling millions of people to flee.[67] Other analysts discount the role of climate change in provoking the Syrian civil war and resulting migratory impulse, insisting on the primarily political nature of the conflict.[68] But even if warming's role was relatively modest in this case, the events of 2012–15 provide an indication of what we might expect from future migratory shock waves as temperatures rise, farming becomes untenable in vast areas of the planet, and masses of people move about in search of new ways to survive.

While Europe—given its proximity to climate-sensitive areas of Africa and the Middle East—is expected to prove the principal objective of many of these migratory surges, North America is also considered a likely destination for future mass migrations. The CNA Corporation, for example, has suggested that the greatest climate-related threat to American security—other than its direct impacts on the U.S. homeland itself—would arise from the migratory implications of climate disasters occurring in nearby countries, especially in Central America and the Caribbean. As warming advances, it noted, severe climate events will afflict many of these areas, destroying entire habitats and impelling millions of people to head north in search of refuge and employment opportunities.[69]

General John F. Kelly, while serving as commander of the U.S. Southern Command, spoke of such occurrences as "mass migration events," and emphasized the importance of taking steps to prevent future climate refugees from entering the United States. With that goal in mind, he told the Senate Armed Services Committee in 2014, "We regularly exercise our rapid response capabilities in a variety of scenarios, including responding to a natural disaster [and a] mass migration event."[70] In one such exercise, Southcom revealed, Kelly's staff established a Joint Task Force-Migrant Operations (JTF-MIGOPS) at Naval Station Guantánamo Bay to oversee a mock crisis-response mission. According to Rear Admiral Jon G. Matheson, deputy Joint Task Force commander of JTF-MIGOPS in 2013, this allowed Southcom to "flesh-out some of the processes and resources we would need if a mass migration were to occur."[71]

Southcom conducted another iteration of these exercises two years later, with Fort Sam Houston, Texas, serving as the host of a reconstituted JTF-MIGOPS. The 2015 exercise, a Pentagon reporter noted, "anticipated the mass migration of people from multiple Caribbean islands after a series of hurricanes devastate the area." With this in mind, "the goal of the exercise scenario was to effectively interdict and repatriate the migrants at sea who were attempting to enter the United States." In other words, the military services are practicing to do whatever might be needed to prevent large numbers of disaster-driven refugees from gaining access to U.S. territory.[72] As participants in the exercise explained, this means stopping migrant-laden ships at sea and transporting the migrants to the U.S. Navy base at Guantánamo, where they would be detained in giant tent camps until they can be ferried back to their home country.[73]

Whether originating in Africa, the Middle East, Latin America, or the Caribbean, mass migration events are destined to become more common in the years ahead as global warming takes an ever greater toll on the livelihoods and living conditions of people in highly exposed areas. As the European migrant crisis of 2015 demonstrates, moreover, such events are likely to prove highly disruptive and to trigger military-type responses. The construction of fortified border walls and fences is one expression of this, as are the preparations being undertaken by Southcom to house vast numbers of detained migrants at Guantánamo Bay. Wherever and whenever such events occur, the outcome is almost certain to prove wrenching and violent.

## WHEN SYSTEMS COLLAPSE

For American military and intelligence analysts, the implications of all this are hard to escape: as global warming advances, one climate shock after another will ricochet across the planet, leaving chaos and misery in their wake. Try to picture a food-price crisis occurring at more or less the same time as a major pandemic and a mass migration event: the resulting chaos, distress, and contention are almost unimaginable. The most likely consequence of such a multi-shock calamity would be the failure of fragile states and resulting anarchy—with the failures occurring not one at a time, as in some less fearsome scenarios, but one right after another, as during the Arab Spring. But it will not be just fragile states in the developing world that will suffer from the impacts of these shocks, but all nations, as the global networks on which we all rely for essential goods and services begin to break down.

The potential for systemic collapse of this sort was given close attention by the *Fourth National Climate Assessment*, released in November 2018. Like the NRC study before it, the *Fourth Assessment* highlights the world's growing reliance on global networks and the ways these systems have become inextricably linked—and so have become vulnerable to unexpected shocks. "A long history of research on complex systems," it noted, "has shown that systems that depend on one another are subject to new and often complex behaviors. . . . These behaviors, in turn, raise the prospect of unanticipated, and potentially catastrophic risks. For example, failures can cascade from one system to another." Climate change, it observed, is likely to provide exactly the sort of external jolt that could trigger such a cascade of failures, sowing havoc across the planet.[74]

For the United States, the breakdown of global systems would have many consequences, not least in the national security realm. Many U.S. allies, including those deemed of strategic importance, could be exposed to the disruptive effects of pandemics, mass migrations, and resource shortfalls, diminishing or eliminating their capacity to assist in U.S.-led security operations. Also, because the American economy is so closely linked to those of its major trading partners, any major economic disruption abroad will inevitably hurt businesses at home. "The impacts of climate change, variability, and extremes that occur outside the United States can directly affect the U.S. economy and trade through impacts on U.S.-owned, provided, or consumed services, infrastructure, and resources in other countries," the *Fourth Assessment* noted. American national security would be further affected by the increasing likelihood of foreign wars and humanitarian disasters—any of which could result in U.S. military action of one sort or another.[75]

As such crises unfold, the military's initial concern will be the much-noted risk of state collapse in developing countries, and the emergence of "ungoverned spaces" containing well-armed insurgents and terrorist organizations. Developments of that sort pose immediately identifiable threats to U.S. national security, and so, as discussed in earlier chapters, are likely to lead to the deployment of American forces in one capacity or another. Eventually, however, the global climate shock waves described in this chapter will begin to threaten not only weak states in the developing world, but also major powers in the club of wealthy, industrialized nations. The next chapter offers a closer look at how global warming is affecting the world's major powers—along with the global order upon which these countries (including the United States) rely for their continuing prosperity and security.

5

# GREAT-POWER CLASHES

## The Melting Arctic and Other Conflict Zones

In March 2016, some three thousand American military personnel joined twelve thousand soldiers from other NATO countries in Exercise Cold Response, the largest multinational maneuvers conducted in Europe's Far North since the end of the Cold War. The exercise, sponsored by the Norwegian military, was intended to enhance the fighting skills of combat units in Norway's near-Arctic environment. Conducted over several weeks in snow-covered mountain ranges near the port city of Trondheim, Cold Response 2016 featured large-scale armored engagements between allied defenders and an unidentified "aggressor" force.[1] The underlying strategic scenario for the exercise was not made public by U.S. officials at the scene, but it is not hard to reconstruct the gist of the plan from comments made by participating officers—and to conclude that the mock aggressor force was unmistakably Russian.

In the exercise scenario, the invading force entered Norway from positions above the Arctic Circle (Norway and Russia share a 122-mile land border at the extreme northern tip of Scandinavia) and made their way down toward populated areas in the south. Norway's small army managed to slow the invaders' advance, providing time for allied forces to stream in from bases elsewhere in Europe and in the United States. At that point in the scenario, hundreds of U.S. Marines conducted amphibious landings along Norway's coastal fjords while others flew to airstrips inland, picking up heavy weapons already prepositioned in large caves there before moving toward the battle zone. The arriving Americans then joined with Norwegian forces and other allied troops to overpower the invaders.[2]

While similar in many ways to other multinational exercises conducted throughout the year by the United States and NATO, Exercise Cold Response 2016 was unique in several significant ways. To begin with, of course, there was the sub-Arctic terrain in which it took place. The Norwegian training site was specifically chosen to acquaint American and allied soldiers—most of whose combat experience had been in the deserts of Iraq and Afghanistan—with the distinctive challenges of fighting in snow-covered, subzero conditions. "This exercise in particular was meant to get us out of our own home plate or back yard and operating in an area where we're not very familiar," said Marine Colonel Will Bentley. "We've been doing a lot of desert operations and operations in other areas. We have not operated in this extreme cold nor in Norway . . . in a [*sic*] quite a while."[3]

The exercise also highlighted a largely unknown feature of U.S. planning for possible combat with Russian forces in the Far North: the fact that the U.S. Department of Defense is storing vast quantities of military matériel in climate-controlled caves in Norway's mountainous interior for potential use by American forces. This program, initiated during the Cold War, was substantially expanded in 2014, when the Norwegian government gave the DoD the right to store advanced M1A1 Abrams main battle tanks in the caves, along with other heavy combat systems. The cave complex now contains enough tanks, artillery pieces, and other equipment to sustain a Marine Corps Air-Ground Task Force of some fifteen thousand combatants for thirty days of intense combat. Norwegian personnel maintain the equipment with the understanding that, if Norway were to be invaded, American troops would be flown into the area and use those weapons to help defend the country.[4]

Beyond practicing the retrieval of that heavy equipment and familiarizing American soldiers with the harsh conditions of Norway's Far North, Exercise Cold Response 2016 fulfilled another major goal: to signal to Russia and other major powers that the United States regards the Arctic as an important site of geopolitical contestation. The Arctic had, of course, been accorded considerable strategic significance during the Cold War era, when U.S. and Russian bombers and missiles were expected to fly over the North Pole while on nuclear attack missions—prompting both sides to establish radar sites and air bases there—but it had received little attention from military planners since then. More recently, however, the region has again attracted close attention, as allied strategists began contemplating the potential for clashes with Russia all along its western periphery. Believing that a time might come when fighting will erupt in or near the Arctic, American and NATO officials started taking steps to prepare their forces for combat in that unforgiving environment.

The few details provided regarding the scenario for Exercise Cold Response 2016 say little about the geopolitical backdrop for the simulated confrontation. But from the nature of U.S.

training operations and other indications, it is very clear that American military officials are seriously contemplating the possibility of great-power combat occurring in the Arctic region—arising not just as an extension of a clash erupting elsewhere in Europe but *independently*, as a consequence of developments in the Arctic itself. Because of the rapidly melting Arctic ice cap, this once inaccessible area has become open to oil drilling and other economic activities—an opening that has sparked the interest of many Arctic-facing nations, Russia most of all. As it has moved ever deeper into the Arctic in search of energy reserves to develop, Russia has also undertaken a major military buildup in the region, producing considerable anxiety for Norway and other U.S. allies.[5]

Significantly, the 2016 exercise assumed that the invading force entered Norway from its northern border with Russia, an area adjacent to the Kola Peninsula and a major concentration of Russian forces. Russia's Northern Fleet, a mainstay of its naval power, is based at Murmansk, only about seventy-five miles from that border. Murmansk was a bastion of Soviet strength during the Cold War era, housing ballistic missile submarines and other critical assets; it fell into decay following the USSR's collapse, but has been revived in recent years under President Vladimir Putin's patronage. Declaring the Arctic to be of vital importance to Russia's future economic strength, Putin created a new strategic command for the Arctic in 2014 and ordered the construction of new and expanded bases in the Kola Peninsula.[6]

In the view of U.S. strategists, the escalation of NATO-Russia tensions in Central Europe remains the most likely source of a great-power confrontation in Scandinavia. However, as the Arctic's hydrocarbon reserves become ever more accessible, states may clash directly over access to those resources, setting the stage for battle. In 2016, the DoD told Congress that while this scenario is unlikely in the short term, it will become more likely when the Arctic ice cap begins to disappear. "In the mid- to far-term, as ice recedes and resource extraction technology improves, competition for economic advantage and a desire to exert influence over an area of increasing geostrategic importance could lead to increased tension," the DoD stated. "These economic and security concerns may increase the risk of disputes between Arctic and non-Arctic nations over access to Arctic shipping lanes and natural resources."[7]

As we shall see, the Arctic could prove to be the first region of the world in which climate change plays a direct role in provoking conflict among the major powers. Although it may seem distant from the main centers of great-power confrontation, the polar region is encircled by Russia, the United States, and four other NATO members—Canada, Denmark (responsible for Greenland's defense), Iceland, and Norway. All of those countries have demonstrated an interest in exploiting the Arctic's hydrocarbon resources, and all except Iceland have commenced or announced plans to bolster their military capabilities there. China, though not an Arctic nation, has also expressed an interest in exploiting the region's resources, and is building icebreakers to facilitate such activities.[8] As this competition intensifies, the risk of conflict is bound to grow. And while the Arctic may prove to be the first site of climate-related great-power clashes, it is unlikely to be the last: other areas of the world harboring critical resources, especially water, will also be subject to warming's powerful impacts, and they, too, could experience wars among the major powers.

For the U.S. military, any great-power war arising from the impacts of global warming—whether involving the United States as a belligerent or not—would represent a significant leap up the ladder of escalation. Once such a conflict erupted, the pace and outcome of events would of course be largely decided by conventional military factors, such as the balance of forces on each side. Meanwhile, having triggered the conflict, climate change could also play a significant role in how it unfolds. In the Arctic, for example, an increasingly ice-free sea expanse would permit naval maneuvers not previously conceivable; for conflicts erupting elsewhere, higher temperatures could impede the performance of both machines and personnel.

No matter how the fighting progresses, any such war—like any conflict among the great powers—is certain to produce widespread death and destruction, with an unpredictable outcome. Always hovering in the background, moreover, is the prospect of nuclear weapons use and resulting catastrophe. Most of the major powers with a possible stake in future resource disputes, including China, Russia, India, Pakistan, and the United States, are armed with nuclear weapons, and all of them are modernizing and expanding their nuclear arsenals. Given all this, the potential for war in the Arctic and other potential climate-affected great-power battle zones requires close attention.

## "A WHOLE NEW OCEAN"

Of all the impacts of global warming, none is as conspicuous—or, some argue, as significant—as the melting of the Arctic ice cap. Temperatures are rising faster in the Arctic region than anywhere else on the planet—Anchorage, Alaska, for example, posted a statewide record high of 90° Fahrenheit in July 2019—and the ice cap is shrinking at a corresponding rate. The extent of winter sea ice floating on the Arctic Ocean was an astonishing 43 percent less in 2017 than it was in 1979, and its summer reach had shrunk by an equivalent amount; the ice cap is expected to shrink even more in the future, and could disappear entirely in summers soon to come.[9] As a consequence, oil and gas drilling operations can be undertaken for longer periods of time each year and can extend farther poleward. The melting ice cap also allows increased commercial transit through the Arctic—and, more worrisome from a strategic perspective, increased operations by naval vessels. "Think about the Arctic," former deputy undersecretary of defense Sherri Goodman told me in a May 2017 interview. "It's changing more rapidly than the rest of the planet, and recognizing that, we have to now be able to operate in the Arctic because we have a *whole new ocean*."[10]

The notion of the Arctic as a "whole new ocean" has been on the minds of U.S. military officials ever since they began to consider the issue of climate change and national security. "Open seas at the Arctic means you have another side of this continent exposed," observed Admiral Donald Pilling, former vice chief of naval operations, in a commentary attached to the landmark 2007 CNA study, *National Security and the Threat of Climate Change*.[11] As the military service most likely to be charged with protecting American interests in the Arctic, the Navy has often joined with the Coast Guard in calling attention to warming's impacts on the region. To provide the necessary analysis for these efforts, in 2009 Chief of Naval Operations Admiral Gary Roughead established Task Force Climate Change, charging it with producing a series of "road maps" for the Navy's adaptation to a changing Arctic.[12]

Up until this point, the armed forces had very little strategic guidance to rely on when developing plans for Arctic operations. The only formal statement on the issue, a National Security Presidential Directive released in January 2009 by the outgoing George W. Bush administration, spoke in vague terms about security issues in the Arctic. It indicated that the United States "is an Arctic nation, with varied and compelling interests in that region," of which resource extraction was identified as the most important. Given Bush's background in the oil industry, it is hardly surprising that he chose to emphasize expanded oil and natural gas drilling as the nation's principal Arctic objective. But the directive also acknowledged that any increase in economic activity in the Arctic could generate new security concerns, and so called for increased military attention to the region.[13]

The Navy's first Arctic road map took Bush's directive as its starting point. Even more than in the White House document, however, it stressed the impact of climate change on the Arctic's emerging geopolitical importance. "The Arctic is warming twice as fast as the rest of the globe," it noted. "While significant uncertainty exists in projections for Arctic ice extent, the current scientific consensus indicates the Arctic may experience nearly ice-free summers sometime in the 2030s." The retreating ice cap, it continued, would spur new economic and military activities in the region, including resource extraction, tourism, and intercontinental trade. "These developments offer opportunities for growth," the road map said, "but also are potential sources of competition and conflict for access and natural resources." Acknowledging that the Navy was unprepared, at that time, to deal with all such contingencies, it outlined a range of actions it needed to take to be better prepared for future Arctic operations, such as an increased tempo of training exercises and the installation of advanced surveillance and communications gear.[14]

In addition to undertaking a variety of steps to enhance its own capacity for operating in the region, the Navy has also sought to persuade leaders of the other armed services and the military establishment at large to focus greater attention on the challenges of a warming Arctic. These endeavors achieved their first significant success with Secretary of Defense Chuck Hagel, who took a personal interest in the topic. "Climate change is shifting the landscape in the Arctic more rapidly than anywhere else in the world," he declared in a November 2013 address at the NATO-sponsored Halifax International Security Forum in Nova Scotia. "As the Arctic changes, it creates new opportunities—and new challenges."[15]

Hagel used the occasion of his appearance at the Halifax Forum to release the DoD's *Arctic Strategy*, a Pentagon-wide policy brief modeled on the Navy's Arctic road map. "The Arctic is at a strategic inflection point," the DoD's brief proclaimed, a consequence of diminished sea ice and a resulting increase in energy extraction and other commercial activities. Inevitably, these changes would result in new and expanded responsibilities for the U.S. military, whether in responding to environmental disasters, ensuring the safe passage of American ships and aircraft, or protecting the homeland from attack. While expressing optimism that any future disputes arising in the Arctic would be resolved by peaceful means, the Pentagon brief enjoined the armed services to "prepare for a wide range of challenges and contingencies," including the use of force "to maintain stability in the region."[16]

In a more recent statement on Arctic policy, the 2016 *Report to Congress on Strategy to Protect United States National Security Interests in the Arctic Region*, the DoD again emphasized the growing geopolitical importance of the region and the need for increased American military involvement there. Two tasks in particular were identified as top Pentagon priorities. The first involved defending the nation's northern borders against attacks originating in the Arctic, an undertaking that was said to entail upgrading the detection and combat capabilities of the North American Aerospace Defense Command (NORAD), the joint U.S.-Canadian organization responsible for aerospace and maritime warning for North America. The second focused on enhancing U.S.

and allied capabilities to overcome hostile forces in the Arctic itself, which translated into forging closer ties with America's Arctic-oriented allies and an expanded program of joint military maneuvers along the lines of Exercise Cold Response.[17]

The authors of the 2016 DoD Arctic strategy were clear that the most acute future threat to U.S. security in the Arctic is likely to come from Russia, which is both the most ardent pursuer of economic activities in the region and also the country with the greatest concentration of military capabilities there. "Recent Russian strategy documents emphasize the importance of the Arctic region to Russia and its national economy," the Pentagon analysts indicated. Driving this outlook, in their view, is Moscow's intention "to use Russia's Arctic region as a national strategic resource base to support the country's socio-economic development."[18]

This perception of the Arctic as a major site of geopolitical contestation has grown even more entrenched under the Trump administration. "America's got to up its game in the Arctic," then secretary of defense Jim Mattis declared during a visit to Alaska in 2018. Not only was Russia projecting more power into the region, he said, but international energy firms were looking for further drilling opportunities there. "The reality is that we're going to have to deal with the developing Arctic," he noted.[19] With this in mind, the DoD has increased its operations in the Arctic, conducting periodic exercises like Cold Response 2016 and deploying additional U.S. troops in the region. In 2016, for example, the Marine Corps announced that it would station 330 soldiers near those caves in the Trondheim area of Norway—the first foreign troops to be based in Norway since World War II.[20]

Although Russia remains the preeminent concern of American strategists when addressing the Arctic, the DoD and the White House are also paying closer attention to China's emerging interest in the region. In January 2018, the Chinese government released its first Arctic Policy, stating that China was a "near-Arctic state" and that it intended to establish a "Polar Silk Road" for transportation and commerce across the region.[21] China's state-owned oil firms have established ties with key Arctic players, including Norway and Greenland, and announced plans to begin drilling in Arctic waters.[22] All this has alarmed American officials, who worry about growing Chinese involvement. "The U.S. is far from alone in seeing the region's value," observed Air Force secretary Heather Wilson and chief of staff General David Goldfein in a 2019 opinion piece. "China considers the Arctic as part of its Belt and Road Initiative and is establishing a presence through economic leverage with other Arctic nations."[23]

Concern over the growing presence of both Russia and China in the Arctic was a major theme of Secretary of State Mike Pompeo's May 2019 address to a meeting of the Arctic Council, an association of regional governments, in Rovaniemi, Finland. The Arctic "has become an arena for power and competition," he stated, "complete with new threats to . . . all of our interests in that region." Russia, he claimed, was militarizing the Arctic and impeding international commerce along the Northern Sea Route, which connects the North Pacific to the Barents Sea; China, for its part, was using economic investment in the region "to establish a permanent security presence." In response, the Trump administration was "fortifying America's security and diplomatic presence in the area"—which meant, among other things, "hosting military exercises, strengthening our force presence, [and] rebuilding our icebreaker fleet."[24]

## RESOURCE WARS AND OTHER ARCTIC CONTINGENCIES

By and large, the literature on Arctic geopolitics emphasizes the stated desire of the region's major powers to settle any disagreements that might arise among them in a peaceful manner. "Present geopolitical trends in the Arctic region lead intelligence assessments to predict it is unlikely the region will be the site of state-on-state armed conflict" anytime soon, the U.S. Navy suggested in its second *Arctic Roadmap*, released in 2014. Looking farther into the future, however, the Navy's strategists saw more reason to worry. As the ice cap melts and relations among the Arctic powers deteriorate, they said, "tensions could increase due to misperceptions and [inflammatory] rhetoric, as well as the unforeseen dynamics of economic interests in the region." Disagreements over contested resource zones might further exacerbate tensions, increasing the risk of armed conflict and creating new challenges for the Navy.[25]

What might cause the relative calm now prevailing in the Arctic to give way to armed conflict? Official U.S. sources are noticeably reluctant to detail such scenarios in unclassified public documents, but a persistent theme emerges in many of them: if conflict occurs, it will most likely arise out of disputes over the ownership of offshore resource zones or the flow of maritime traffic entering and exiting the Arctic Ocean. "Excessive extended continental shelf claims made by Arctic nations . . . may cause tension and create political uncertainty," the 2014 road map warned. "Given the resource wealth that could be at stake, a resulting standoff could indeed lead to disputes and military posturing by rival nations."[26]

When discussing the "resource wealth that could be at stake" in the Arctic, most analysts begin with its hydrocarbon deposits, believed to be among the world's largest remaining undeveloped reserves. According to the U.S. Geological Survey, the area north of the Arctic Circle possesses approximately 13 percent of the world's undiscovered oil resources along with 30 percent of its remaining natural gas.[27] Many of these reserves are located in areas under the undisputed control of one or another of the Arctic powers, but others are located in contested areas or in the polar region itself, whose jurisdiction has yet to be determined.[28] The region is also thought to harbor vast deposits of vital minerals, including iron, copper, uranium, and rare earths; Greenland is believed to contain especially significant deposits of such minerals, and prominent foreign mining firms—including some from China—have begun operations there.[29] Many valuable fish species reside in or migrate through the region, representing an increasingly valuable source of animal protein. As the ice cap shrivels, moreover, the Arctic could provide a cost-effective shortcut for maritime trade between the Atlantic and Pacific.

As these interests proliferate, American strategists believe, the risk of competition and conflict over the Arctic's resource wealth is bound to grow. "Relatively low economic stakes in the past and fairly well established [offshore development] zones among the Arctic states have facilitated cooperation in pursuit of shared interests in the region, even as polar ice has receded," Director of National Intelligence Dan Coats testified in May 2017. "However, as the Arctic becomes more open to shipping and commercial exploitation, we assess that risk of competition over access to sea routes and resources, including fish, will include countries traditionally active in the Arctic as well as other countries that do not border on the region [read: China] but increasingly look to advance their economic interests there."[30]

The risk of increased competition and conflict over valuable resources and trade routes was also highlighted by Secretary Pompeo in his May 2019 address to the Arctic Council. "Far from the barren backcountry that many thought it to be [in past decades]," he noted, "the Arctic is at the forefront of opportunity and abundance. It houses 13 percent of the world's undiscovered oil, 30 percent of its undiscovered gas, and an abundance of uranium, rare earth minerals, gold, diamonds, and millions of square miles of untapped resources." At the same time, "steady reductions in sea ice"—this said without identifying global warming as the cause—"are opening new passageways and new opportunities for trade." These developments, Pompeo added, have made the Arctic "the subject of renewed competition," which could get ugly if other actors, notably China and Russia, fail to play by accepted rules of international commerce.[31]

Russian officials also suggest that resource competition is likely to be the catalyst for future conflict in the Arctic.[32] "By 2050 about 30 percent of all hydrocarbons will be produced in the Arctic area," Vladimir Putin declared in 2017. "From an economic point of view, this is critically important." As global warming proceeds, moreover, "the navigation period in the Arctic zone will get longer," enhancing the value of Russia's Northern Sea Route, which traverses Russia's Arctic waters from one end of the country to the other. Given these high stakes, "we need to ensure the use of these routes, develop our economic activity in these areas, and ensure our sovereignty over these territories." Putin, like many of his top advisers, believes that this will inevitably lead to clashes with other major powers, who may seek to challenge Russia's claims to vital Arctic resources and trade routes. "Let us not forget about the purely military aspect of the matter," Putin avowed. "This is an extremely important region from the point of view of ensuring our country's defense capability."[33]

In accordance with the UN Convention on the Law of the Sea (UNCLOS), Russia has claimed an exclusive economic zone (EEZ) stretching 200 nautical miles out from its extended Arctic coastline, allowing it the undisputed right to exploit marine and mineral resources there. But for Russian authorities, as for those of neighboring countries, a major source of concern is control over development rights to waters of the Arctic extending *beyond* each country's EEZ. Under Article 76 of the Law of the Sea, coastal states can claim the exclusive development rights to their extended continental shelf up to 350 nautical miles offshore if they can convince the Commission on the Limits of the Continental Shelf, a UN-affiliated body, that their continental margin stretches that far out. Such claims to extended undersea rights can be highly contentious. Canada, Denmark (acting for Greenland), Norway, and Russia have all submitted or are in the process of submitting claims encompassing large swaths of the Arctic, presumably ones rich in oil and gas reserves; the United States, although not yet a signatory to UNCLOS, is collecting the data required to do so.[34] As these claims have yet to be thoroughly documented and submitted to the commission, it is not known whether any of them officially overlap. However, senior officials of Canada, Denmark, and Russia have all said that the Lomonosov Ridge—an underwater feature that straddles the North Pole, from Canada and Greenland on one side to northeastern Siberia on the other—constitutes a natural extension of their own nation's continental shelf, and so is theirs alone to develop. The danger, then, is that these countries will assert claims to the same stretches of undersea territory, conceivably triggering a future clash over valuable hydrocarbon assets.[35]

Such a confrontation may appear unlikely at this point in time, given the present difficulty of operating in the Arctic and the relative adequacy of resource reservoirs located below the Arctic Circle. As time goes on, however, the Arctic will become increasingly accessible due to climate change while energy supplies elsewhere may dwindle, altering the perceived geoeconomic equation. Under these circumstances, the various claimants to offshore Arctic territories could prove more unyielding in their assertions of sovereignty. "The Arctic is ours, and

# The Arctic Region

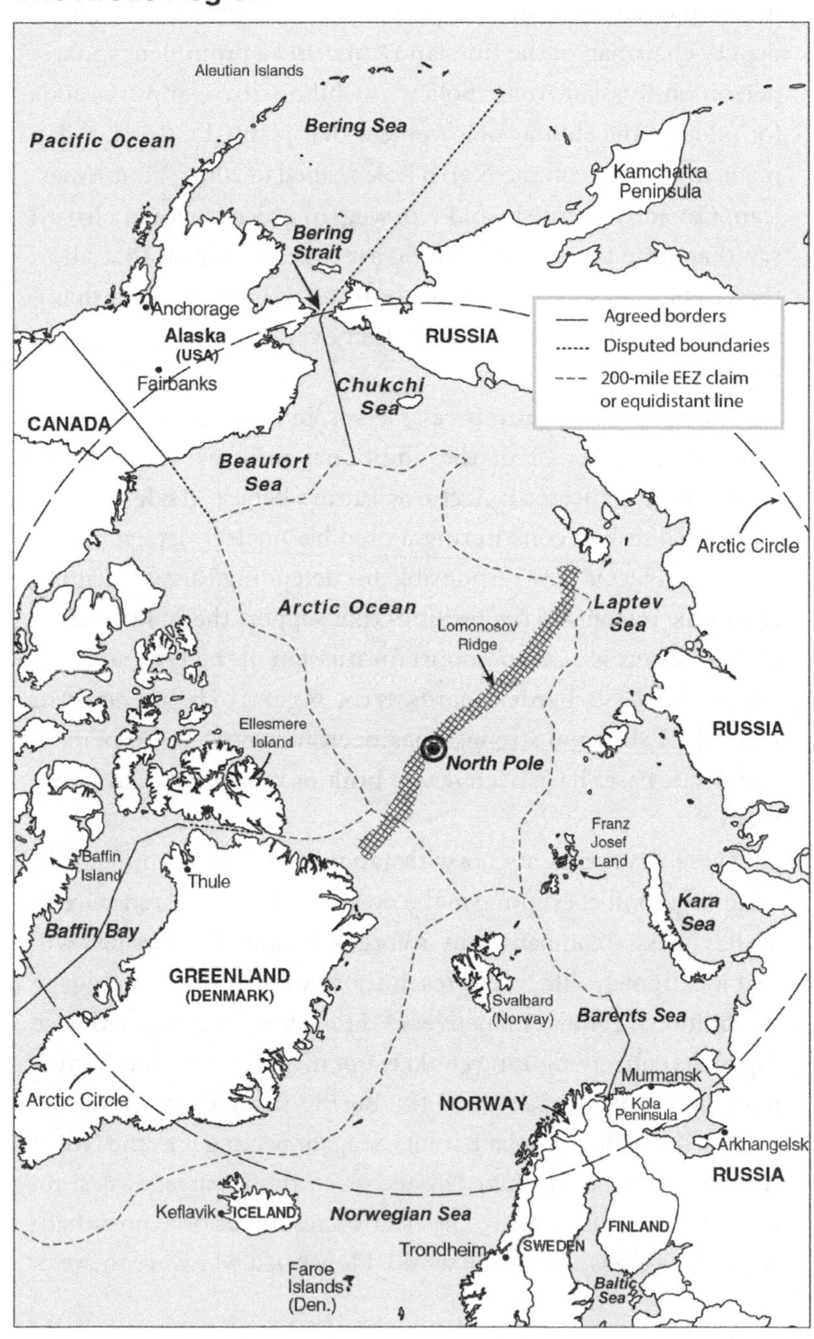

we should demonstrate our presence," said Artur Chilingarov, deputy chairman of the Russian Duma and a prominent spokesperson on Russian Arctic policy.[36] (Chilingarov is most famous for piloting the submersible vehicle that planted a Russian flag made of titanium on the North Pole seabed in 2007.[37]) But American, Canadian, Danish, and Norwegian officials would also all say that large parts of the Arctic are "theirs." Given that all of the Arctic states view their offshore territories in this fashion, the potential for friction and conflict over disputed resources is significant.

The protection of resource assets is, in fact, one of the major tasks assigned to all of the additional military forces being deployed in the Russian Arctic at Putin's behest. Aside from its traditional task of constituting a credible nuclear deterrent, the Northern Fleet is now responsible for defending Russian drilling rigs in the region and the facilities that support them. Protection of these assets is also an important mission of the Federal Security Service (FSB) border guards in the region; to better perform this role, FSB troop strength has been increased by 30 percent and Arctic bases have been newly built or rehabilitated to house them.[38]

These developments notwithstanding, it may be difficult to imagine a conflict erupting in the open waters of the Arctic Ocean itself. Unless accompanied by icebreakers, surface warships will find it extremely difficult to reach those waters, let alone engage in traditional combat maneuvers.[39] However, long before the ice cap melts entirely, fighting could erupt in and around the Arctic's main points of entry and exit: the Bering Strait, connecting it to the North Pacific, and the Barents Sea, connecting it to the North Atlantic. Without unimpeded access to those passageways, no country can gain access to the Arctic's resources or export them to markets elsewhere in the world. Hence, if a war were to break out over control of Arctic resource zones, it could well be fought in or near those nautical bottlenecks.

American strategists see the Bering Strait as a particularly likely site for such an engagement. This narrow strip of water—fifty-one miles across at its narrowest point—connects the North Pacific with the Chukchi Sea (an offshoot of the Arctic) while separating easternmost Siberia from Alaska. Shipping through the Bering Strait, both military and commercial, is bound to grow as the ice cap melts, increasing the strait's strategic significance. This is true both for the United States, which hopes to see an increase in energy extraction in Alaska's offshore waters, and for Russia, which seeks increased traffic through the Northern Sea Route.[40] In recognition of the strait's strategic significance, both countries have been strengthening their military capabilities in the immediate area. Russia has reinforced its Cape Schmidt and Wrangel Island bases in Chukotka, in far eastern Siberia; the United States is beefing up its forces at Eielson and Elmendorf air bases, located near Fairbanks and Anchorage, respectively.[41] In 2017, for example, the Air Force announced that it would deploy fifty-four advanced F-35 stealth fighters at Eielson, representing a significant increase in U.S. combat power.[42]

The Bering Strait area has also been the site of stepped-up training exercises and other demonstrations of military muscle. The Russians conducted a series of amphibious landings on Cape Vankarem, in the Chukchi Sea, as part of its massive "Vostok 2018" exercise involving some three hundred thousand troops.[43] On the Alaska side of the Chukchi Sea, the Department of Defense has been conducting a major combat exercise, called Northern Edge, every other year.[44] More worryingly, both sides routinely conduct air patrols over these waters to identify adversary capabilities and test defensive responses; on some occasions, these can lead to risky military encounters, as when the aircraft of one side approaches too close to the airspace of another. In May 2018, for example, two Russian Tu-95 "Bear" nuclear-capable bombers entered American airspace off Alaska's west coast and were turned away by two F-22 fighters from Elmendorf sent to intercept them.[45]

Considerable attention has also been paid by the major powers to the other primary access point to the Russian Arctic, the Barents Sea. Connecting the North Atlantic and the Norwegian Sea in the west to the Kara Sea (another Arctic offshoot) in the east, the Barents Sea is an essential lifeline to Russia's northernmost territories. At present, the West's primary strategic concern over the Barents Sea is focused on increased Russian submarine activity, as exemplified by a 2016 Pentagon decision to reoccupy the U.S. naval base at Keflavik in Iceland and to deploy P-8 Poseidon antisubmarine warfare patrol planes there.[46] In the future, however, these waters (and adjoining land areas) could become the site of a larger geopolitical struggle, as Russia increases its maritime traffic through the Barents Sea and bolsters its military capabilities in adjacent areas—precisely the scenario that underlay Exercise Cold Response 2016.

The strategic importance of the Barents Sea was accorded further emphasis in May 2018, when the Department of Defense reactivated the Navy's Second Fleet (it had been deactivated in 2011 to save funds) and gave it responsibility for U.S. and allied defense in the North Atlantic. Significantly, Admiral John Richardson, chief of naval operations, indicated that the Second Fleet's area of operations would extend right up to the entrance to Russia's naval enclave in the Barents Sea, an obvious threat to Moscow. "Second Fleet will approach the North Atlantic as one continuous operational space and conduct expeditionary fleet operations where and when needed," Richardson declared.[47] It is no wonder, then, that Russia's Northern Fleet has been stepping up its own combat preparations. In June 2018, it staged a major exercise, involving combat maneuvers in the Baltic Sea by some thirty-six warships—said to be its largest such drill in decades.[48]

Whatever the immediate cause of a great-power clash in the Barents or Bering Sea, any fighting that erupts there could easily escalate to high-intensity combat—and potentially to nuclear war. This risk is especially present in the areas facing Russia's naval facilities around Murmansk, the Northern Fleet's headquarters and home port for its ballistic missile–carrying submarines. Vladimir Putin has explicitly raised the prospect of nuclear escalation arising from future military engagements in this region. "I do not want to stoke any fears here," he said in a 2017 interview on Russia's interests in the Arctic, "but experts are aware that U.S. nuclear submarines remain on duty in northern Norway . . . and we need to have a clear idea of what is happening there. We must protect this shore accordingly, and ensure proper border guarding."[49] Combine this with Admiral Richardson's pledge to extend the area of operations of the Navy's Second Fleet right up to Russian territory in the Barents Sea, and it is not hard to conceive of a scenario in which a clash there initiates a catastrophic escalatory spiral.

For now, the likelihood of a major-power conflict erupting over the energy and mineral supplies of the Arctic would appear relatively low, given the difficulty of exploiting those resources and the apparent sufficiency of existing stockpiles to meet global needs. It is not impossible, however, to imagine a time in the relatively near future when global warming and widespread state failure have made the extraction of African and Middle Eastern oil and gas reserves nearly impossible, while Arctic reservoirs have become far more accessible. Climate scientists now believe that summer temperatures in large parts of the Middle East will average 110 to 120 degrees Fahrenheit for long stretches of time, making outdoor labor there nearly impossible.[50] At that point, the major industrial powers may be forced to abandon their reliance on African and Middle Eastern resources and turn to alternative sources. Under those circumstances, war in the Arctic over vital resource supplies becomes far more plausible.

Adding to this danger is the growing perception of the Arctic as a major arena for great-power competition. In the words of Secretary Pompeo, "We're entering a new age of strategic engagement in the Arctic, complete with new threats to the Arctic and its real estate."[51] As an expression of growing U.S. determination to counter its rivals in the area, the Navy announced in early 2019 that it would begin conducting "freedom of navigation operations" in Arctic waters, possibly by sending warships along the Northern Sea Route. This, in turn, has incensed Russian leaders, who perceive such operations as a potential threat to Russian sovereignty.[52] How all this will play out in the years ahead cannot be foreseen, but the disappearance of the ice cap may eliminate the region's historic immunity to friction and conflict.

## THE HIMALAYAN WATERSHED AND BEYOND

From the very beginning, American military analysts have viewed the Arctic as the region in which climate change is most likely to play a direct role in precipitating war among the great powers. However, as the planet warms, climate change is likely to have an influence on other great-power rivalries as well, although it may not be possible to pinpoint the scope and nature of this influence with the same precision. Many great-power rivalries—such as those between the United States and Russia, Russia and China, China and India, and so on—have persisted for decades, and would have been likely to continue even without global warming. Nevertheless, climate change will make itself felt in multiple situations, increasing the risk that long-simmering hostilities will erupt into full-scale war.

In the Arctic, the decisive factor in provoking conflict is likely to be a shortage of energy and mineral resources; in many other areas, it is a shortage of water and arable land. "There are few convincing reasons to suggest that the world will become more peaceful" in the coming decades, the British Ministry of Defence (MoD) observed in an assessment of the future strategic environment. "Pressure on resources, climate change, population increases and the changing distribution of power are likely to result in increased instability and likelihood of armed conflict," it stated. In this tortured landscape, climate-related struggles over vital sources of food and water may prove a major source of strife. Indeed, for some countries these contests "may be viewed as wars of survival."[53]

When considering potential climate-related "wars of survival" among the great powers, the problem of shared river systems often comes to the fore—a danger highlighted by the U.S. Intelligence Community's 2012 assessment, *Global Water Security*.[54] In many areas of the world, important, well-armed nations are highly dependent for their water supply on major river systems that are shared with one or more neighboring countries, that report noted. Iraq and Syria, for example, are both dependent on the waters of the Tigris and Euphrates Rivers, which originate in Turkey; Egypt is reliant on the Nile, tributaries of which arise in Ethiopia, Sudan, Uganda, and several other countries; Israel relies on the Jordan River, which has its headwaters in Syria and Lebanon. In some such cases, the countries involved have managed to share these critical systems in a peaceful, cooperative fashion; in others, however, they have fought over the allocation of water supplies.[55] To further complicate the picture, the population of these and many other countries dependent on transboundary river systems is expected to expand substantially in the years ahead, increasing water demand; at the same time, global warming is likely to reduce the water flow in many such rivers, diminishing supply. Together, these factors could increase the risk of friction and conflict over the remaining flow.[56]

In most of the cases where conflict might arise over shared rivers, only one country in the system can be termed a paramount power, while the others are typically less powerful states. Egypt, for example, is the only major power in the Nile River system, while Turkey is the dominant player in the Tigris-Euphrates basin. This does not mean that conflict over water will not erupt in those systems, only that such an encounter would not constitute a conflict between well-armed major powers. But there is one such system that is shared by two nuclear-armed powers which could conceivably fight over vital supplies of water: the Brahmaputra River, which originates in China and traverses much of northeastern India before merging with the Ganges and emptying into the Bay of Bengal via Bangladesh.

The fifth-largest river in the world by volume of water flow, the Brahmaputra starts on the northern slopes of the Himalayan Mountains and flows easterly for about a thousand miles across the southern Tibetan plateau before making a nearly 180-degree turn and crossing into the Indian state of Arunachal Pradesh; from there, it flows in a southwesterly direction for some nine hundred miles toward its confluence with the Ganges and thence to its exit into the Bay of Bengal. For China, the Brahmaputra is an important engine of hydroelectric power; it has already installed one dam on the river, at Zangmu, and announced plans for at least three more.[57] For India, the river is a valuable source of water for irrigation, especially in agriculture-dependent regions of the northeast. Leaders of both countries are fully aware of their counterparts' interests and concerns over the river but have

**The Brahmaputra River Basin**

made little effort to reach a mutual understanding—let alone any formal agreements—regarding its future development.[58]

Several factors make the future status of the Brahmaputra a matter of deep concern. To begin with, the river enters India through the state of Arunachal Pradesh, an area of northeastern India that abuts Chinese-controlled Tibet and is claimed by both countries. Beijing insists that this region was once part of the kingdom of Tibet, and so belongs to China; New Delhi claims it is a legitimate part of India under a 1914 treaty between Tibet and Great Britain. The two sides fought a war in this area in 1962, with India suffering significant battlefield setbacks but China agreeing to restore the status quo ante. The countries have not been able to resolve the ownership dispute in subsequent years, despite intermittent negotiations, and both continue to maintain substantial military forces in the region. To this day, discord over Arunachal Pradesh remains a continuing source of friction in Sino-Indian relations and a potential spark for violent conflict.[59]

Another potential source of friction between China and India arises from Chinese plans to divert water from the upper Brahmaputra and funnel it via a series of canals to northeastern China, where existing supplies are hugely inadequate. Such a plan, discussed in Chinese journals, would accompany the existing South-North Water Diversion Project (a mammoth undertaking to channel water from rivers in south China to water-scarce areas of the northeast), but would be constructed farther west, linking the Brahmaputra to the upper reaches of the Yellow River.[60] Some Chinese officials have even gone so far as to propose the use of nuclear explosive devices to build tunnels through the Himalayas as part of such a diversion scheme.[61] While dismissed by many Chinese experts as overly ambitious and costly, the notion of diverting water from the Brahmaputra has generated considerable anxiety in India, where experts fear that the resulting decline in water flow into the Indian section of the river would threaten agricultural productivity.[62] Given the centrality of farming in the Indian economy and political system, any Chinese move to proceed with such a diversion project could lead to conflict.[63]

Few analysts believe that a Sino-Indian war over the Brahmaputra is likely in the years immediately ahead. Both countries have strong motives for maintaining friendly (if not necessarily warm) relations between them, and water issues have not yet dominated the bilateral agenda. This, however, is where climate change enters the picture. The Brahmaputra, like most major rivers in Asia, originates in the Himalayan Mountains and draws much of its flow, especially in dry seasons, from the melting of Himalayan glaciers; these are replenished each winter by fresh snow and ice, ensuring steady runoff in summer. But now, with global temperatures rising, the glaciers are gradually retreating—and could, in the years to come, shrink substantially, depriving the Brahmaputra and other key rivers of essential dry-season water. According to the Intergovernmental Panel on Climate Change, the Himalayan glaciers began experiencing a significant loss of mass in the 1990s and are expected to lose volume at an ever-increasing pace in the decades ahead; this will produce added runoff at first, as the glaciers melt, but will ultimately result in a diminished water flow.[64]

For both China and India, the melting of the Himalayan glaciers will have momentous consequences. The major Himalayan-sourced rivers, including the Ganges, Brahmaputra, Indus, and Yangtze, are a critical source of drinking and irrigation water for hundreds of millions of people and essential to the economic vitality of both countries. Any significant long-term decline in the flow of these rivers would be highly disruptive, possibly triggering mass social disorder.[65] In a special 2009 report, the U.S. National Intelligence Council warned of India's vulnerability to climate change and resulting water scarcity. "In the longer term," it said, "glacial melting will reach a tipping point where increased river flows from runoff subside, replaced by serious water shortages as the smaller ice mass provides less water to feed India's rivers." Such a development, the NIC noted, "would threaten the sustainability of the agrarian economy across the northern Indian plain," possibly provoking widespread rural unrest.[66] In a parallel report on China, the NIC warned of similar risks in that country. China is already suffering from severe droughts and heat waves attributable to climate change, and the melting of the glaciers threatens a further reduction in water availability.

Areas of persistent drought, especially in the north and west, "may be prone to social unrest caused by water shortages."[67]

Under these more stressful conditions, the Chinese leadership, desperate to provide additional supply to China's water-starved northeast, might be more inclined to proceed with water diversion projects on the Brahmaputra and other shared river systems.[68] Coming at a time of equivalent water scarcity in India, such an effort is almost certain to trigger a harsh Indian response. "The most salient climate-related point of conflict [between China and India] could be China's move to divert the upstream waters of rivers originating in the Himalayan watershed," the NIC warned in its 2009 report on India. "If China was determined to move forward with such a scheme, it could become a major element in pushing China and India towards an adversarial rather than simply a competitive relationship. Border clashes related to control of the rivers are not out of the question."[69]

As with Arctic conflict scenarios, the potential for a war between India and China over the waters of the Brahmaputra may seem exaggerated at this point. But the risk is likely to become far more substantial once global temperatures have risen, food and water supplies have diminished, and senior officials have come under enormous pressure from their citizenry to address the resulting hardships. Under these circumstances, the impulse to use force in resolving water issues may prove greater than any inclination to exercise restraint. Indeed, when the CNA Corporation sought to test the potential for a peaceful resolution of Asian water disputes through a series of simulated crisis negotiations—with retired ambassadors and military officials from the affected countries assuming the roles of their serving compatriots—it discovered strong resistance to any form of cooperation. "Over the course of the game," the CNA reported, "it became clear that there was a substantial lack of trust between the country teams that clouded any strategic negotiations and discussions."[70] With distrust over water proving intense even at a time when relations between Beijing and New Delhi are relatively friendly, it is not hard to imagine how a future dispute over the diversion of the Brahmaputra might push one or both parties over the edge to actual combat.

Any conflict between China and India over the waters of the Brahmaputra might remain a localized affair, without provoking a full-scale mobilization of forces on both sides. Nevertheless, once combat begins, it is impossible to predict the succeeding chain of events. Both countries have been modernizing their military forces in recent years, and each has acquired a large array of nuclear-tipped ballistic missiles—many capable of striking their opponent's major cities. Both, moreover, have been adding to their naval capabilities, and so can extend any conflict that does erupt into international waters, including the Indian Ocean and the South China Sea. Once ignited, an Indo-Chinese conflict over vital resources could prove hard to contain.

Of almost equal concern is the potential for conflict between India and Pakistan over another Himalayan-sourced river, the Indus. Just as the Brahmaputra is a vital source of water for China and eastern India, the Indus is essential for Pakistan and western India. To further complicate the picture, several of the river's tributaries travel through Kashmir, a territory claimed by both countries as well as the site of a determined independence drive. Indian officials have repeatedly accused the Pakistanis of arming and assisting the militants in Kashmir, and after a bloody terror attack on Indian forces in February 2019, they threatened to divert the flow of water in those tributaries away from Pakistan and toward water-scarce areas in India—a step that might easily provoke a Pakistani military response.[71] Although New Delhi did not carry through with its threat on that occasion, we can only wonder if it will choose to do so in the future when tensions are at an even higher pitch and climate change has further reduced the river's flow.

A minor skirmish along the Indo-Chinese or Indo-Pakistani border might not prove an immediate cause for alarm in the United States, but a larger war between any of these countries would be. All three countries are armed with nuclear weapons, and India is viewed by Washington as a strategic counterweight to China. If India appeared likely to suffer a crushing defeat, that would be seen as a potential threat to American national interests and could conceivably precipitate U.S. military intervention. Even without American intervention and the use of nuclear weapons, a decisive loss by any of these parties would have profound consequences for American security. Where it might lead is anyone's guess, but the mere possibility of such combat has made this scenario a matter of substantial concern in Washington.[72]

THE HIMALAYAN WATERSHED and the Arctic represent two regions where it is possible to discern global warming's direct impact on the likelihood of armed conflict among major powers, and for this reason they have received considerable attention from American security analysts. But it would be a mistake to assume that these are the only two areas where such an outcome is possible. Every country, large and small, will experience the impacts of climate change, and in some cases these effects could be seen as constituting a threat to survival—thereby justifying the use of military force. Of course, climate change may not be the *principal* cause of conflict in these encounters, at least not at first; typically, the countries involved will have experienced many years of hostility and distrust, as is true of China and India in the Himalayan region and of Russia and the United

States in the Arctic. Nevertheless, warming could be the decisive factor—the "tipping point," as the National Intelligence Council puts it—that nudges a tense situation into outright war.

For the moment, American strategists see the outbreak of a climate-induced major-power war as a distant possibility: of low probability when compared to other warming-related military scenarios, such as humanitarian disasters and beleaguered governments in the developing world, but a serious concern nevertheless. And while the likelihood of such war is low today, it is bound to grow with time, as global temperatures continue their inexorable rise. It is for this reason that the military services have begun to think about and prepare for such an eventuality. Exercise Cold Response 2016 may be only partially related to such developments, but it affords a unique window into the future of climate-altered battlefields.

6

# THE HOMELAND AT RISK

## Domestic Climate Disasters and the Military's Strategic Predicament

When Tropical Storm Harvey attained hurricane status on August 24, 2017, and began to approach the Texas coast, America's civil and military authorities responded as they had to previous large storms. Texas governor Greg Abbott activated nine hundred members of the state's National Guard and ordered them to report to local bases and supply depots. The U.S. Northern Command—the joint-service headquarters responsible for homeland security and disaster response—went on high alert, securing access to bases throughout the Southeast and identifying active-duty contingents for possible deployment to Texas. These preparations gathered further momentum over the next few days as Harvey gained in ferocity, attaining Category 4 status by the time it made landfall at Rockport, Texas, on the morning of August 26. With Harvey's winds now approaching 130 miles per hour, Governor Abbott ordered the call-up of additional National Guard units, bringing their total deployed strength to three thousand uniformed men and women.[1]

Up to that point, the military's performance was largely identical to its response to other big hurricanes of previous years. However, it soon became obvious that this hurricane was not behaving like those earlier storms. Most ominously, Harvey failed to move inland and dissipate, as hurricanes traversing the Gulf of Mexico typically do. Instead, it remained stationary over the Texas coast, where it could suck up more moisture from the Gulf and deposit it on land. It hovered over Houston for five agonizing days, generating the heaviest continuous rainfall in American history and inundating the nation's fourth-largest city. Entire neighborhoods were submerged under several feet of murky water; hundreds of thousands of people were forced to abandon their homes while thousands of residents had to be rescued from the roofs or upper stories of their flooded houses. In many areas, the standing water exhibited the telltale hues of chemical pollution, an unsurprising consequence of Houston's status as a major refining and petrochemical center.[2]

By August 28, it was evident that the state and federal efforts to cope with the impacts of Harvey were woefully inadequate and that a far more robust mobilization would be required.[3] With the rain still falling, Governor Abbott mobilized the entire Texas Army National Guard—a force of some twelve thousand men and women—and ordered them deployed to the storm-affected areas.[4] At the same time, various active-duty military contingents were rushed into the disaster zone from elsewhere in the country. Northcom provided seventy-three helicopters, three C-130 Hercules cargo planes, and eight para-rescue teams. The U.S. Army mobilized some sixteen thousand soldiers for rescue and support operations, along with ninety helicopters and seven hundred wheeled vehicles; the Air Force deployed seven C-17 Globemaster cargo planes plus one of its E-3 Sentry airborne warning and control system (AWACS) planes, a super-sophisticated aircraft usually used to manage airspace over a major war zone. On top of all this, the Navy dispatched two large combat vessels—the USS *Kearsarge*, an amphibious assault vessel, and the USS *Oak Hill*, a dock landing ship—accompanied by an onboard contingent of several hundred Marines from the 26th Marine Expeditionary Unit, based at Camp Lejeune, North Carolina.[5]

But as these efforts were getting under way, the military was confronted with a new, entirely unprecedented challenge: a second hurricane, dubbed Irma, was barreling across the Atlantic, headed directly toward the U.S. Virgin Islands, the Commonwealth of Puerto Rico, and, it appeared, the American mainland. Irma first arose off the west coast of Africa as a tropical storm on August 30, while Harvey was still lashing northeastern Texas with heavy rains. By the following day, Irma was upgraded to a Category 2 hurricane; on September 5, when it smashed into the island of Barbuda in the eastern Caribbean, it was classified as Category 5, the very highest ranking. At this point, most meteorologists predicted that Irma—by then one of the most powerful hurricanes ever detected in the Atlantic—would continue moving westward, striking the Virgin Islands, Puerto Rico, and the northern shore of Cuba before turning in a northwesterly direction toward the Florida Keys and the southern tip of Florida itself.

The appearance of Irma produced enormous logistical challenges for American military officials. As in a battle where the enemy opens a second line of attack and the defenders must reorient to face the new assault, so the Pentagon was forced to confront the threat posed by Hurricane Irma while still addressing the aftereffects of Hurricane Harvey. This meant, first, redirecting any forces no longer needed in Texas to new assignments in Florida and the Caribbean, and, second, mobilizing a whole slew of additional capabilities—more or less doubling the outpouring of effort made to cope with Hurricane Harvey. To further complicate matters, thousands of active-duty and National Guard troops were also being mobilized to fight a spate of ferocious wildfires in the American West. In California, the first fire duty call-ups came on September 4, and soon some two thousand members of the state's National Guard were being dispatched to the fire lines—at a time when other members of the California guard were being called up for emergency duty in Florida to brace for Hurricane Irma.[6] All of a sudden, the armed forces found themselves engaged on multiple fronts simultaneously, much as they would be in a major war.

Within days of Irma's appearance, Governor Rick Scott of Florida, who had graciously sent members of the Florida National Guard to Texas to help with relief operations there, summoned the contingent back home and ordered all remaining members of the Florida guard—about eight thousand strong—to active duty.[7] The USS *Kearsarge* and USS *Oak Hill*, originally dispatched to the Houston area following Harvey's landfall, were given orders to sail toward Puerto Rico and the Virgin Islands, to be better positioned to provide emergency aid there.[8] To reinforce those ships, the Navy also sent the nuclear-powered aircraft carrier USS *Abraham Lincoln*, the guided-missile cruiser USS *San Jacinto*, the amphibious assault ship USS *Iwo Jima*, and the amphibious transport dock ship USS *New York*.[9] At the same time, Northcom moved some forty-five hundred active-duty personnel into southern Florida to help provide emergency services to civilians in need. Anticipating mass evacuations, the Defense Logistics Agency made preparations to serve twelve million meals.[10]

Irma struck southern Florida on September 10, producing massive damage in the Keys and the southwestern edge of the state, and leaving an estimated ten million people without power. With electricity out and many roads impassable, the Guard and military services were called upon to rescue stranded citizens and perform a wide variety of other relief operations. An estimated 20,700 DoD personnel were committed to these activities in the southeastern United States, while another 10,000 were performing similar tasks in Puerto Rico and the U.S. Virgin Islands.[11]

By the following week, the worst seemed to be over, with floodwaters receding in Texas and power being restored to most of Florida. Many of the Guard and active-duty units brought into those states from other parts of the country were preparing to leave or had already returned to their home bases. But on September 20, *another* Category 5 hurricane—Maria—struck U.S. territory, ripping across Puerto Rico and incapacitating vital services there. Local mayors in some rural parts of Puerto Rico described the conditions as "apocalyptic," with roads washed out, water and electricity lost, and scant food and fuel supplies available.[12] Once again the Department of Defense organized a major relief operation, mobilizing the Puerto Rican National Guard and deploying specialized relief units in the area. An amphibious naval group built around the USS *Kearsarge* was deployed to waters off Puerto Rico and used to support the Marines and Seabees engaged in immediate relief operations. All told, the initial response to Maria involved approximately four thousand Guard members and active-duty troops.[13]

Within a matter of days, those early-arriving forces had succeeded in reopening Puerto Rico's main airports, allowing for the delivery of the most urgent emergency supplies. It soon became apparent, however, that this would be no ordinary, quick-in-quick-out operation: the destruction wreaked by Maria proved to be much greater and more widespread than had been assumed in Washington. With all of Puerto Rico's ports obstructed by storm damage, the Marines sent to provide disaster relief supplies were forced to use their amphibious assault vessels to disembark. "The ships arrived on a devastated island," the DoD reported on September 28. "There were no usable seaports or airports. . . . All electricity was down on the island, and all roads were blocked."[14] On September 30, ten days after Maria struck the island, 95 percent of the population still lacked electrical power and 55 percent had no drinking water; food remained scarce, and many hospitals were closed or only partially functioning. The growing misery of the island's residents, combined with the slow pace of emergency food and water deliveries, led to urgent pleas for additional aid. "Puerto Rico, which is part of the United States, can turn into a humanitarian crisis," warned Ricardo Rosselló, the island's governor.[15]

Once again, as in the aftermath of Hurricane Harvey, senior Pentagon officials realized that their relief operations would have to be brought to an entirely new level. On September 28, Northcom dispatched the commander of its Land Component Forces, Army General Jeffrey S. Buchanan, to oversee all military support activities on the island. Upon his arrival, Buchanan promised that Puerto Rico would be provided with whatever assistance it needed to recover from Maria, and that military forces would remain for as long as necessary to ensure this occurred. "Our capability is building every single day, and we will keep building until we have fully met the needs of the people of Puerto Rico," he declared.[16] In the days that followed, Buchanan and his subordinates announced one new initiative after another, representing an ever-expanding DoD role in the recovery effort. Northcom, they reported, would provide an "enhanced logistics capacity," to be managed by a "sustainment brigade" tasked with improving commodity distribution and medical support. Another high-ranking officer, General Todd T. Semonite of the Army Corps of Engineers, was dispatched to oversee emergency power projects and infrastructure improvements.[17]

By October, it had become apparent that this would be unlike any disaster response operation the DoD had ever undertaken. In a press release dated October 27, five weeks after Hurricane Maria struck Puerto Rico, the Pentagon reported that 11,400 active-duty and Guard personnel were still engaged in relief operations on the island: working to repair vital electricity and communications links, clear roads, provide medical assistance, and distribute food and water to remote communities. At that point, three-quarters of Puerto Rico's population still lacked access to electricity and a quarter had no drinking water.[18] Foreseeing no swift reversal of those hardships, the Army Corps of Engineers began settling in for a long-haul operation: on October 30, General Semonite told reporters that restoring power to the entire island would take at least a year.[19] The DoD also established a central hub for air and ship deliveries at Joint Base Charleston, South Carolina, a huge complex of air and naval facilities capable of handling regular supply shipments from the mainland to distribution hubs in Puerto Rico.[20] From the Pentagon's perspective, there appeared to be no end in sight for the military relief effort.

## RISING TEMPERATURES, BIGGER STORMS, AND GROWING PENTAGON INVOLVEMENT

Ever since U.S. military and intelligence officials began pondering the impact of climate change on American national security, they have consistently assumed that the homeland would, in time, experience the same sort of punishing impacts from warming that they were witnessing in other countries around the world. The United States, they fully understand, is highly vulnerable to sea-level rise and extreme storm events on its Atlantic and Gulf coasts and to prolonged drought and recurring wildfires in its western states. While they also recognize that the United States is better prepared to cope with such challenges than less-fortunate nations in the developing world, they have never assumed that it is immune to severe shocks. And they presume that, as warming's impacts on the homeland become more frequent and severe, the armed forces will be called upon with ever greater frequency to assist local authorities in the aftermath of disasters.

For senior Pentagon officers, such a situation is the stuff of nightmares. In modern times, the American military has largely been configured as a "forward-deployed" organization, trained and equipped to counter the nation's adversaries where *they* reside, rather than at America's borders. Since the end of World War II, this has meant the deployment of hundreds of thousands of sailors, soldiers, Marines, and Air Force personnel on widely dispersed ships or at bases in Europe, Asia, the Middle East, and elsewhere, allowing them to attack and defeat enemy combatants on their home turf. But when all is said and done, the ultimate responsibility of America's armed forces is to defend the homeland, and it would be inconceivable for senior commanders to turn down a request for help from besieged states and communities under assault from invasive forces as powerful as Harvey, Irma, and Maria. As storms of this magnitude become more common, therefore, the Pentagon could reach a point where requests for disaster relief and reconstruction at home consume such a large share of the military's assets and personnel that they imperil its ability to sustain an invincible forward presence abroad.

The triple punch of Harvey, Irma, and Maria made the nightmare palpable. It may be some time before scientists can determine exactly how much global warming contributed to the severity of the three hurricanes, but there is no question that climatic conditions before and during these storms were highly unusual—and can be explained only through reference to global warming. Hurricanes draw their destructive energy from the oceans' warm waters, and the months leading up to the emergence of Harvey and its two powerful successors saw a pronounced increase in water temperatures in hurricane-breeding areas of the Atlantic Ocean and Gulf of Mexico.[21] Sea surface temperatures in the eastern Atlantic, where most hurricanes arise, were between 0.5 and 1.0 degree Celsius (0.9 to 1.8 degrees Fahrenheit) above average during the summer of 2017, an increase great enough to add substantial energy to any storms developing in the area.[22] Sea surface temperatures in the Gulf of Mexico were also running substantially above average for that time of year, by as much as 1.5 to 4.0 degrees Celsius (2.7 to 7.2 degrees Fahrenheit) above normal; that meant that Harvey, while approaching the coast of Texas, was able to acquire fresh energy and so inflict greater damage.[23]

Harvey, Maria, and the others were also distinctive for the extraordinary amount of rainfall they delivered. "The intensity of heavy rain, including heavy rain produced by tropical cyclones, increases in a warmer world," the U.S. Global Change Research Program noted in its *Fourth National Climate Assessment*, and that fact was fully corroborated by the 2017 hurricanes. "Both Harvey and Maria were distinguished by record-setting rainfall amounts," the assessment noted. "Harvey's multiday total rainfall likely exceeded that of any known historical storm in the continental United States, while Maria's rainfall intensity was likely even greater than Harvey's, with some locations in Puerto Rico receiving multiple feet of rain in just 24 hours."[24] The unusual atmospheric pressure system that kept Harvey trapped over Houston for five days, allowing that unprecedented drenching to persist, was also likely a product of climate change.[25]

Equally striking, of course, was the simple fact of three extremely powerful hurricanes striking one right after another—an occurrence without precedence in recorded history. As noted, the waters of the Atlantic Ocean were unusually warm at the time those storms originated, adding energy to all three. But scientists have also warned that other effects of climate change, such as shifting wind patterns, increase the risk of extreme storm events occurring in clusters. This was a major finding of the National Research Council's 2013 report titled *Climate and Social Stress*, and has been confirmed by additional research since.[26]

For the most part, members of the military establishment did not comment publicly on the role of climate change in generating Hurricanes Harvey, Irma, and Maria. Nevertheless, it could hardly have escaped their attention that the armed services had been obliged to marshal extraordinary forces to address three major hurricanes in a row—the first time they had ever been called upon to do so. The one senior official who did speak out at the time, Air Force General Joseph Lengyel, was uniquely qualified to assess the situation: as chief of the National Guard Bureau, he played a pivotal role in mobilizing Guard units from around the country to assist those called up in Texas, Florida, and Puerto Rico. "I do think that the climate is changing, and I do think that it is becoming more severe," he observed on September 19, 2017, as Hurricane Maria was barreling its way toward Puerto Rico. "I do think that storms are becoming bigger, larger, more violent."[27]

General Lengyel's comments, although unusual in his explicit connection of climate change to a specific set of events, are fully consistent with the thinking of the military and intelligence community regarding global warming's threats to the U.S. homeland. The earliest Intelligence Community statement on climate change, from 2008, had already sounded the alarm about numerous ways in which the United States would be affected as temperatures rise, including from extreme storm events, severe droughts, and raging wildfires.[28] The Department of Defense, in its *Quadrennial Defense Review* for both 2010 and 2014, also highlighted these dangers. "Climate-related changes are already being observed in every region of the world, including the United States and its coastal waters," the 2010 edition stated. Among these consequences, it indicated, were rising sea levels, more severe storm events, and melting permafrost.[29]

These concerns were already on the minds of senior officers when they faced their greatest domestic challenge prior to the triple punch of 2017: Superstorm Sandy of October 2012. That storm, the largest hurricane by diameter ever recorded in the Atlantic—and one widely attributed to global warming—produced an enormous storm surge that inundated homes and businesses, knocked out power stations and transmission lines, and flooded subway and railway tunnels throughout the New York metropolitan area. Power was completely lost in lower Manhattan, the nation's economic capital. Road transportation was affected as well: gas stations could not operate without electrical power, and once power was restored, oil companies could not resupply those stations with fuel because many oil terminals were destroyed.[30]

With local authorities overwhelmed by Sandy, the Department of Defense was called upon to assist in every way imaginable. As usual, National Guard and active-duty troops were involved in a wide range of disaster-relief operations: rescuing civilians from flooded homes and cars; delivering food, water, and medicine to hospitals lacking power; and clearing storm debris from roads, highways, and airfields. But that was just the beginning. Substantial effort was also devoted to what the military called "unwatering": pumping seawater out of railroad tunnels and other flooded facilities, including the World Trade Center reconstruction site. At the same time, Army and Navy engineers scrambled to rebuild damaged port facilities, such as the Caven Point Marine Terminal in Jersey City, to facilitate critical deliveries of food and fuel to the affected area.[31] At the behest of President Obama, the DoD also transferred millions of gallons of diesel fuel from its own stockpiles to commercial distributors in the area, adding an entirely new mission to the military's task list.[32]

For senior military leaders, the Pentagon's response to Hurricane Sandy gave new meaning to what it calls Defense Support of Civil Authorities (DSCA).[33] In a 2015 report to Congress on climate change and national security, the DoD highlighted the Sandy operation as an example of its expanded role in this regard. The storm "resulted in over 14,000 DoD personnel mobilized to provide direct support, and at least an additional 10,000 who supported the operation in various capacities in the areas of power restoration, fuel resupply, transportation infrastructure repair, water and meal distribution, temporary housing and sheltering, and debris removal." Operations this vast were likely to become more common in the future, the report noted, as temperatures rise, extreme storms like Sandy become more common, and "flood risk threatens more people than any other natural hazard."[34] A new era in DSCA operations, it appeared, was under way.

## "COMPLEX CATASTROPHES"

In the wake of Hurricane Sandy, the Department of Defense and its subordinate units conducted a series of reviews to evaluate the military's performance during the disaster and assess its capacity to address future disasters of this magnitude.[35] As one result of this effort, the secretary of defense at that time, Leon Panetta, directed the armed services to prepare for an entirely new category of disasters—events he labeled "complex catastrophes." Such calamities, he indicated in 2013, would exceed anything previously experienced by the United States, engulfing several states at once and overpowering local governance systems. In a follow-up statement, the DoD defined catastrophes of this magnitude as being characterized by "cascading failures of multiple, interdependent, critical, life-sustaining infrastructure sectors," resulting in "extraordinary levels of mass casualties, damage, or disruption severely affecting the population, environment, economy, public health, national morale, response efforts, and/or government functions."[36]

As senior Pentagon officials saw it, Sandy came very close to meeting those criteria. "The scope, scale and duration of Hurricane Sandy fell short of the threshold for a complex catastrophe," the DoD indicated in a 2013 report. "However, the cascading effects of the failures of critical infrastructure in the New York–New Jersey metropolitan area resembled those of a potential complex catastrophe: 8 million people out of power in severe cold; major transport disturbances due to inoperable ferries and flooded tunnels; severe disruptions of the East Coast fuel distribution system, including 2,500 inoperable gas stations; and regional commerce at a near standstill due to the closure of the Port of New York."[37]

In recognition of this outcome, and with an understanding

that global warming was likely to increase the future incidence of such events, the DoD called for a department-wide effort to better prepare for such contingencies. In particular, the Pentagon stressed the urgency of ensuring "unity of effort" among the various federal and state organizations deployed in the aftermath of such calamities. This focus emerged from the various assessments of the government's response to Sandy, which revealed a lack of coordination among state and federal officials on the scene and a resulting duplication of effort. To help overcome this challenge, the DoD issued a *Strategy for Homeland Defense and Defense Support of Civil Authorities*, mandating greater cooperation between the armed services and civilian agencies in disaster-relief operations. To prevent competing lines of command, the strategy called for the designation by the president of "dual-status commanders" who would be granted operational control over all National Guard and active-duty units called up to deal with a major disaster. In addition, the DoD pledged to conduct additional multiagency crisis-response training exercises and to transfer useful emergency preparedness equipment to state and local authorities.[38]

The swift and largely effective response by the Department of Defense and other government agencies to Hurricanes Harvey and Irma in Texas and Florida shows that by 2017, they had made considerable progress in improving their disaster-relief capabilities. Nevertheless, it is also apparent from the aftermath of Hurricane Maria in Puerto Rico that much more progress will be required as the magnitude of these disasters grows. For the 3.5 million residents of Puerto Rico, "complex catastrophe" does not even come close to describing the nightmare they experienced after the storm knocked out all power and water services, most cellular coverage, and the majority of the roads on the island. Without power, hospitals and clinics were obliged to run on diesel-powered generators alone, limiting services to the bare minimum, or were forced to close entirely. Most banks, gas stations, pharmacies, and food markets also closed, or operated on a cash-only basis, since electronic transactions could not be processed. Long lines formed at the few ATMs and gas stations still in operation, and looting—especially of diesel fuel—became widespread.[39] The military and Guard units sent to the island in the storm's aftermath were able to address some of its immense relief requirements, but were wholly unprepared for the magnitude of the crisis they faced.

As the crisis in Puerto Rico unfolded, the federal government's response to Maria's destruction became a source of widespread contention. Many on the island complained about slow and haphazard delivery of essential relief supplies. "This is not a good news story," said Carmen Yulín Cruz, the mayor of San Juan, on September 29. "This is a 'people are dying' story. This is a 'life or death' story. . . . This is a story of a devastation that continues to worsen."[40] President Trump, in responding to such criticism, insisted that federal agencies were making "tremendous strides" in addressing the island's needs.[41] But months after Maria plowed through Puerto Rico, much of the island remained without electricity and running water, and many remote communities suffered from inadequate health care. It was not until early 2018 that power was restored to most customers, and even then they suffered from periodic blackouts.

Nearly a year after Maria's assault, the island's government dramatically revised the official death toll from the storm, raising it from 64 people to 2,975. The new number was based on a study of death records compiled by researchers at George Washington University's Milken Institute School of Public Health.[42] Many of the victims, it is believed, were poor and elderly residents who perished when they lost access to essential medications and safe drinking water. Without electricity or access to telecommunications, they were unable to contact any government officials or loved ones for assistance. "We never anticipated a scenario of zero communication, zero energy, zero highway access," Governor Rosselló told reporters when releasing the new death total.[43] (Rosselló was forced to resign in August 2019 following a public outcry over ingrained government corruption.)

The U.S. Global Change Research Program, in its *Fourth National Climate Assessment*, saw Harvey, Irma, and Maria as harbingers of the sort of complex disasters this country can expect from severe climate events—where one problem, such as the loss of power, generates numerous other hazards. "Hurricane Harvey," it stated, "provides a clear example of how impacts from extreme weather events can cascade through tightly connected natural, built, and social systems exposed to severe climate-related stressors." That storm "knocked out power to 300,000 customers in Texas, with cascading effects on critical infrastructure facilities such as hospitals, water and wastewater treatment plants, and refineries." Maria produced a similar cascade, "including the complete failure of Puerto Rico's power grid and the loss of power throughout the U.S. Virgin Islands."[44]

In their assessments of Sandy, Harvey, and Maria, U.S. analysts repeatedly hark back to one unavoidable conclusion: America's critical infrastructure—its power grid, transportation systems, oil and natural gas distribution networks, water and sewage facilities, and so on—are highly vulnerable to the severe effects of climate change. Whether those effects are high winds, storm surges, flooding, or wildfires, such systems can be overwhelmed and incapacitated. And without reliable infrastructure, other vital services—health care, banking, food delivery—are also placed at risk, inviting looting, epidemics, and other social disorders.[45] Ensuring the safety of critical infrastructure is largely a civilian and private-sector responsibility in the United States—but as Maria demonstrated, the armed forces alone may prove capable of preserving essential services in a climate-altered world.

For the U.S. military, then, the lessons of 2017 are unmistakable: the United States, like all other countries on the planet, is vulnerable to the extreme effects of climate change, and these effects are likely to become more severe and destructive over time. As Harvey, Irma, and Maria demonstrated, moreover, these disasters will generate cascading effects within affected communities, triggering all sorts of disruptive and unpredictable outcomes. It is clear that the armed forces will be called upon again and again to provide emergency assistance in such situations, and that the magnitude and complexity of their responsibilities is bound to grow. This, in turn, will require ever more disaster preparedness and training for all branches of the armed forces—a prospect with far-reaching consequences for U.S. strategic planning.

## THE SPECTER OF "CLIMATE REFUGEES"

Providing emergency services in the wake of extreme weather events, especially those of the "complex catastrophe" variety, is likely to prove the military's most demanding homeland task arising from climate change. But as global conditions deteriorate, it could face other challenging domestic missions as well. One such contingency that has preoccupied senior officers ever since climate change first emerged as a strategic concern is the prospect of being forced to cope with huge numbers of "climate refugees" seeking entry into the United States from storm- or drought-ridden parts of Latin America and the Caribbean.[46]

As we have seen, the threat of a "mass migration event"

caused by a hurricane or other natural disaster in the Caribbean area has already prompted Southern Command to conduct a series of Joint Task Force-Migrant Operations exercises, aimed at stopping disaster-driven refugees from entering the United States and repatriating them to their home countries. But such sudden-onset migrations by sea are not the only scenario that worries American military and intelligence officials. They also anticipate that as global warming progresses, there could be a dramatic increase in the flow of migrants coming to America's southern border from Mexico and Central America in search of food, shelter, and economic opportunity. Any such increase would provoke great controversy in the United States, as a large part of the U.S. population has already demonstrated—through the ballot box and other means—that it is disinclined to absorb additional migrants from south of the border. Inevitably, officials fear, the U.S. military will be brought in to deal with the problem in one fashion or another.[47]

To what extent climate change will, in fact, generate vast waves of climate migrants is a matter of debate among scholars. Some analysts believe that severe drought and storm damage are already significant factors in driving south-to-north migration and will prove even more significant in the future. In one study, for example, scientists from Princeton University calculated that up to 10 percent of the adult population of Mexico—some 6.7 million people—will seek to cross into the United States as crop yields plummet due to rising world temperatures.[48] Other scholars have questioned the degree to which climate change will prove a significant factor in propelling migration; political and economic considerations, they argue, are the main drivers of large-scale population movement, so we shouldn't expect vast hordes of climate refugees.[49]

This debate was given fresh impetus in 2018–19, when tens

of thousands of migrants from impoverished and conflict-prone areas of Central America trudged across much of Mexico (many walking together in large groups, or "caravans") in the hope of receiving political asylum in the United States—even though President Trump insisted they would not be admitted. Most analysts assumed that the migrants were fleeing gang violence, hunger, and unemployment in their home countries; some, however, saw global warming as a factor in the migratory impulse.[50] The northern triangle area of Central America, comprising parts of Guatemala, El Salvador, and Honduras, is both the source of a majority of the migrants seeking entry into the United States and the site of a prolonged drought widely attributed to climate change.[51] With croplands devastated, migration becomes an attractive option for impoverished farmers, said Edwin J. Castellanos, dean of the Research Institute at the Universidad del Valle de Guatemala in Guatemala City. "Small farmers are already living in poverty; they're already at the threshold of not being able to survive," he stated. "So any changes in the situation may push them to have enough incentives to leave."[52]

Although the Department of Defense has not taken a public stance on the role of climate change in driving the 2018–19 surge in asylum seekers from Central America, senior officers are well aware of the connection among warming, drought, poverty, and migration. They can therefore surmise that rising world temperatures will produce more such migrant waves in the future, as additional areas of Mesoamerica suffer extreme drought, sea-level rise, and other climate extremes. Addressing this challenge is not a primary DoD function—that's the responsibility of the U.S. Customs and Border Protection (CBP) agency—but senior officers can readily see that the armed services, like it or not, will be called upon to reinforce the border and repel climate refugees.

The Pentagon's ambivalence about border-protection duty

was put to the test in the fall and winter of 2018–19, when President Trump ordered that thousands of active-duty soldiers be deployed along the U.S.-Mexican border to halt what he described as an onslaught of Central American migrants. "This is an invasion of our Country and our Military is waiting for you," he wrote on Twitter on October 29.[53] Initially, 2,000 troops were deployed to the southern border, then 3,000 more; some of those soldiers were rotated back to their home bases around Christmastime, but in February 2019 another 3,750 soldiers were sent to the border region, bringing total strength there to about 6,000.[54] These troops have been employed in a wide range of logistical and engineering tasks, such as the emplacement of temporary barriers, but are prohibited by law (under the Posse Comitatus Act of 1878) from engaging in law enforcement actions such as the apprehension of illegal immigrants.

When given an order by their commander in chief to carry out a mission, U.S. military officers automatically fall in line. And so it was in this case: when ordered by President Trump to do so, Pentagon officials obediently ordered active-duty soldiers from bases all across the country to redeploy in border areas of Texas, Arizona, and California. Nevertheless, it is also evident that there was considerable grumbling among senior officers over a move that, in the view of many, was unnecessary and wasteful. The Central American migrants were known to be unarmed and to include many destitute women and children, posing no threat to U.S. national security. Furthermore, many of the active-duty units reassigned to the border were being trained and equipped for combat missions in Europe or Asia, so the deployments undermined U.S. military readiness.[55] Few serving officers were willing to say as much in public, but in March 2019 the *Los Angeles Times* published two official memos sent from the commandant of the Marine Corps, General Robert Neller, to the secretary of defense, delineating the harm to readiness being caused by the border assignments. The deployments along the southwest border, Neller indicated, posed "unacceptable risk to Marine Corps combat readiness and solvency."[56]

Whatever their objections, it is likely that DoD officials will be required to deploy large contingents on the southern border for some time to come. President Trump initially suggested that he might order as many as fifteen thousand troops to the border zone, and in January 2019 extended the duration of the existing six thousand–strong deployment to at least September of that year.[57] Following a visit to the border with the president, Acting Secretary of Defense Patrick Shanahan told reporters in April 2019 that the DoD was preparing for the deployment of additional soldiers. "Our support is very elastic, and given the deterioration there at the border, you would expect that we would provide more support," he said.[58] This, in turn, has prompted discussion in Congress over the skyrocketing costs of these deployments—now estimated at $600 million by the end of September 2019—and their impact on U.S. combat readiness.[59]

However all this plays out, there are good reasons to believe that the specter of climate refugees will continue to haunt U.S. military officials for years to come. President Trump's tough stance on immigration may suppress south-to-north migration for a time, but the severe effects of climate change are likely to produce increased hardship and misery for many in Central America and the Caribbean, potentially leading to future waves of desperate migrants. Even if senior commanders believe that a rising China and resurgent Russia pose the greatest threat to U.S. security, they are likely to face unremitting demands to consign at least some of their combat assets to anti-migrant duties on the U.S.-Mexican border.

## THE PENTAGON'S STRATEGIC DILEMMA

In 2013, when the DoD released its first *Strategy for Homeland Defense and Defense Support of Civil Authorities*, noting that future climate catastrophes "would qualitatively and quantitatively exceed those experienced to date," and so generate an "unprecedented" requirement for DSCA operations, many senior officers must have felt a deep sense of foreboding. While fully prepared to engage in disaster-relief operations at home when called upon to do so, force commanders are naturally uneasy if such missions divert their units from their regular combat assignments, thereby lowering U.S. military readiness. The notion, then, that global warming will result in a growing number of DSCA and border-protection missions of ever-increasing complexity and duration could only be viewed as a matter of serious concern.

In the aftermath of Harvey, Irma, and Maria, what might have seemed a distant prospect in 2013 has become an inescapable reality. Not only was the DoD confronted with a series of extremely powerful storms in August and September 2017 but it was also obliged to undertake a variety of complex operations under diverse and highly challenging conditions. And according to climate science, this is not likely to prove a freak occurrence, but rather will tend to occur ever more frequently in the years ahead. In fact, the National Research Council has warned that "clustered" disasters like this will become increasingly common as global temperatures rise, posing mounting challenges for the U.S. military.[60] For Pentagon leaders, the key question thus becomes: At what point will defending the homeland from severe climate impacts erode the armed forces' ability to address conventional military threats arising overseas?

Historically, the Pentagon has largely regarded DSCA operations and their overseas equivalent—humanitarian assistance and disaster relief (HA/DR) missions—as a "lesser included case." This means that the military services do not structure their forces or equipment with such missions in mind, but rather employ whatever assets they have at hand when ordered to conduct them. Forces and equipment that can handle combat, they believe, will work well enough for noncombat relief operations. As former deputy undersecretary of defense Sherri Goodman put it to me, "You size your force to have tanks, carriers, and aircraft to conduct a major war, and whatever forces you need for *that* would be more than sufficient for the lesser included case of HA/DR or DSCA."[61] Even for major storms like Katrina, Sandy, and Harvey, the basic philosophy—use regular combat forces to provide emergency services on a short-term basis, then send the military units back to their home bases once civil authorities are able to replace them—has been the same.[62]

As the frequency and severity of the storms, droughts, wildfires, and other climate-related events has increased, however, that approach is coming under mounting strain. "What you increasingly find is that the stress on the force of having to do DSCA missions and HA/DR is taxing the ability to set the force to do the larger regional conflicts," Goodman told me. At some point, she suggested, the armed forces may have to begin earmarking substantial resources—troops, equipment, basing facilities—*specifically* for DSCA and HA/DR operations. That would represent a fundamental break with traditional Pentagon policy, which, as noted, does not view such operations as requiring independent funding and staffing. While such allocations might make sense given the increasing duration and complexity of DSCA operations, they could be viewed as draining resources from programs aimed at combating America's foreign enemies, and so would be considered anathema by many officers.

It is this disjunction that has troubled military officials ever since the prospect of a warming planet entered the discourse on American national security. Senior officers uniformly believe that defense of the homeland is their most sacred, ultimate responsibility; at the same time, current U.S. strategy requires them to contest America's adversaries where those adversaries reside, which often means deploying forces to distant battlefields far from home. When the world is relatively peaceful, commanders can contemplate the diversion of major force units from such overseas service to domestic relief operations without great anxiety. But as the number and complexity of those operations grows and the world turns more violent, the commanders could face some agonizing choices between homeland defense and foreign battle. Their predicament will grow even more acute as the U.S. military *itself* comes under assault from climate change—the topic of the next chapter.

7

# NO SAFE HARBORS

## The Climate Change Threat to American Military Facilities

As Hurricane Irma carved its destructive path toward the United States in September 2017, the Department of Defense began making plans to deploy active-duty troops to Florida and Georgia for emergency relief operations. At the same time as the Pentagon was moving some of its forces into the areas predicted to experience Irma's fury, however, it was also telling others to *leave*, fearing catastrophic damage to military facilities in the hurricane's path. With many key air and naval installations located in low-lying areas of the Atlantic and Gulf of Mexico coasts—and so highly vulnerable to the high winds and storm surges expected from Irma—tens of thousands of troops and their dependents were ordered to evacuate their bases.

On September 5, as Irma bore down on the Florida Keys with Category 4 winds, the commanding officer of Navy Region Southeast, Rear Admiral Babette Bolivar, issued a mandatory evacuation order for all nonessential personnel from Naval Air Station (NAS) Key West, a major hub for U.S. military operations in the Caribbean and Central America. Under Bolivar's order, approximately five thousand people—active-duty service members, DoD civilians, contractors, and family members—were told to abandon the base and make their way, as best they could, to a "designated safe haven" near Atlanta, Georgia.[1] "Please keep safety in mind when traveling to your safe haven," Bolivar said in her evacuation order. "The interstate highway and other roads will be congested with other Florida residents moving away from the storm."[2] Only about fifty to sixty essential personnel were left behind to staff critical security and communications systems, using a hurricane-reinforced hotel nearby as their base of operations.[3]

NAS Key West was not the only Pentagon facility to be issued mandatory evacuation orders as Hurricane Irma approached Florida. Nonessential personnel at NAS Jacksonville and Naval Station Mayport, on Florida's northeastern coast, were also told to flee the area and travel to a safe haven near Atlanta. NAS Jacksonville, one of the Navy's largest East Coast facilities, hosts a wide array of maritime surveillance and antisubmarine-warfare aircraft; the Mayport facility is the home port for numerous cruisers, destroyers, and other large surface ships. Just across the Florida border, in Georgia, nonessential personnel at Naval Submarine Base Kings Bay were also ordered to evacuate. Kings Bay is a major component of America's strategic nuclear capability, housing a pack of ballistic missile submarines. Along with personnel, the Navy ordered the evacuation of major military hardware: fearing wind and flood damage to ships and planes, it relocated critical assets to other locations. Jacksonville's P-3 Orion and P-8 Poseidon patrol planes were flown to Wright-Patterson Air Force Base in Ohio; most of the surface ships and submarines from Mayport and Kings Bay were sent far out to sea, where they were better positioned to weather the storm.[4]

The Air Force also chose to relocate large numbers of planes and flight crews from areas expected to be impacted by Irma. Joint Base Charleston in South Carolina relocated twenty-seven of its C-17 transport planes to airfields in California, Illinois, Louisiana, and Ohio. "Each airplane is worth about $213 million. That's a big bill to pay even if one of them gets damaged due to winds or due to storms," explained Colonel Jimmy Canlas, commander of the 437th Airlift Wing. Roughly four thousand Air Force personnel were relocated along with the aircraft, Canlas noted.[5] A similarly extensive evacuation was ordered at Shaw Air Force Base in Sumter, South Carolina, which redeployed fifty F-16 fighter planes of the 20th Fighter Wing along with their flight crews to facilities inland.[6]

After Hurricane Irma completed its destructive sweep through Florida, Georgia, and the Carolinas, the evacuations could start to be reversed. But recovery did not occur overnight. Although some of the bases reopened relatively quickly, allowing service personnel to return from their safe havens, others remained closed while extensive repair work was undertaken. Irma had weakened after it struck the Florida Keys and did not produce as much destruction as some had feared, but it flooded many coastal installations and destroyed or damaged numerous structures. NAS Key West, the hardest-hit facility of all, did not issue a recall order until September 22, more than two weeks after base personnel were required to evacuate. And even then, troops were warned to anticipate harsh conditions upon their return. "We need everyone to be prepared," said base commander Captain Bobby Baker. "Don't expect all services to be completely up. You may have to boil your water until told it is safe to drink."[7] Considerable off-base housing was damaged or destroyed by the storm, forcing some returning personnel to live in makeshift quarters while new residences were found for them. In the surrounding communities, schools, shopping, and medical facilities did not reopen until weeks after the storm's passage.

The aftermath of the 2017 storm thus found a very large part of the DoD's Atlantic fighting force either scattered at bases around the country or engaged in disaster relief operations. Fortunately, the United States was not engaged in a major war at that time, so the dispersal of such a large portion of America's combat capability did not expose the nation to military setback or to defeat on a crucial battlefield. It did, however, vividly demonstrate that the U.S. military was *itself* vulnerable to the effects of climate change, and that those vulnerabilities could result in a significant reduction in the armed forces' ability to undertake critical defense operations.

This danger was further highlighted in 2018, when extreme climate events again incapacitated major East Coast military facilities. Two events in particular—Hurricane Florence in September and Hurricane Michael in October—underscored the vulnerability of DoD installations to climate change.

Hurricane Florence emerged as a tropical storm off East Africa on August 30, and was elevated to a Category 4 hurricane, with winds exceeding 120 miles per hour, on September 5. As Florence approached America's Eastern Seaboard, worried officers ordered the evacuation of several key bases, including the Marine Corps Recruit Depot at Parris Island, South Carolina, the naval base at Norfolk, Virginia, and Langley Air Force Base, also in the Norfolk area. All major warships at Norfolk were moved out to sea, and the Air Force relocated its F-22 Raptor jets from Langley to Rickenbacker Air National Guard Base in Ohio.[8] Although Florence weakened somewhat as it approached the coast, it hovered over Virginia and the Carolinas for days (a consequence of the same "blocking effect" that was experienced with Hurricane Harvey off Houston a year earlier), causing widespread wind and flood damage at some low-lying bases. Repair work at just one of the affected facilities—Marine Corps Base Camp Lejeune in North Carolina—is estimated at $3.6 billion.[9]

Hurricane Michael, arising as a tropical depression in the southwestern Caribbean Sea about one month after Florence's emergence, gained strength quickly as it fed on the exceptionally warm waters of the Gulf of Mexico. Gathering power with unprecedented speed, it struck the Florida Panhandle on October 10 with peak winds of 160 miles per hour, making it the fourth most powerful hurricane to make landfall in the United States.[10] Almost directly in its path lay Tyndall Air Force Base, home of the 325th Fighter Wing and some forty-five hundred military personnel. When it became evident that Michael would pack a devastating punch, Air Force officials ordered the evacuation of all but a handful of essential personnel and the relocation of the fighter wing's F-22s to Wright-Patterson Air Force Base in Ohio. Most of the Raptors made it out in time, but seventeen of the notoriously temperamental jets—each costing a third of a billion dollars—were unable to undertake the journey. Instead, they were stored in hangars at Tyndall that were ripped apart by the storm, causing substantial damage to those seventeen planes.[11] Trump administration officials say that Tyndall will be entirely rebuilt, but it is unclear whether Congress will vote the necessary funds—estimated at $4.5 to $5 billion—and whether the Air Force will choose to station some of its most costly and sophisticated aircraft at such an exposed location.[12]

Climate change poses many varied threats to American national security. But for military commanders, none are more terrifying than its potential to directly undermine the military's capacity for carrying out its fundamental operations. This is an institution that prides itself, above all else, on being prepared at all times to carry out orders from the commander in chief pertaining to the nation's security. And being prepared, in this case, means having fully functioning bases at home to support operations conducted elsewhere. The fact that climate change might, in the years ahead, imperil that ability is the Pentagon's ultimate "all hell breaking loose" nightmare. And while this may once have seemed only a distant possibility, recent events show that this scenario could arise much sooner than many analysts initially assumed.

## "ON THE FRONT LINES OF CLIMATE CHANGE"

When first evaluating the impacts of climate change on American national security, U.S. military and intelligence analysts initially focused on threats arising abroad, such as resource-driven conflicts in the developing world; with time, however, concern over the vulnerability of domestic military bases to warming's effects has become ever more pronounced. By the time Donald Trump assumed office as president in 2017, this issue had become a major focus of congressional probes into the links between climate change and American national security.[13]

The military community's first detailed assessment of the risks of global warming, the CNA Corporation's 2007 report *National Security and the Threat of Climate Change*, mainly emphasized the threat of overseas resource wars. The CNA report did, however, suggest that global warming could pose a direct threat to the military, by increasing the exposure of key coastal facilities to powerful storms and flooding. That peril can only grow worse as global warming progresses and sea levels rise, potentially threatening the very survival of some installations.

An increase of one meter (3.3 feet) of sea-level rise, it noted, "would inundate much of Norfolk, Virginia, the major East Coast hub for the U.S. Navy."[14] Similarly, the first public statement on climate change from the Intelligence Community, its 2008 National Intelligence Assessment, spoke mainly of threats arising from climate-induced resource scarcities in the developing world, but also warned of the danger to America's coastal bases from rising seas and extreme storms: "A number of active coastal military installations in the continental United States are at a significant and increasing risk of damage, as a function of flooding from worsened storm surges in the near-term."[15]

By 2010, the danger from climate change to U.S. forces and installations was beginning to receive more focused attention from military officials. In the *Quadrennial Defense Review* released that year, the DoD openly addressed its own vulnerability to warming's effects. Referring to that National Intelligence Assessment, it reported that "in 2008, the National Intelligence Council judged that more than 30 U.S. military installations were already facing elevated levels of risk from rising sea levels." Rising temperatures were also limiting the utility of many key training areas, undermining the DoD's "operational readiness." In recognition of the mounting threat, it proclaimed a need to perform "a comprehensive assessment of all installations to assess the potential impacts of climate change on its missions and adapt as required." Every branch of the armed forces was instructed to identify its vulnerabilities to global warming and to undertake remedial action as necessary.[16]

Once these initiatives got under way, it quickly became apparent that the American military faced a huge and multilayered threat from climate change, with rising sea levels identified as the most acute danger. A 2011 study conducted by the National Research Council at the behest of the chief of naval operations,

*National Security Implications of Climate Change for U.S. Naval Forces*, found that fifty-six naval installations would be severely affected by a sea-level rise of a meter or more. Those low-lying bases, the report noted, were established "before climate change was recognized as a factor in their design and construction"—meaning they had no protection against rising seas and more powerful storm surges.[17] A subsequent report, released in 2013 by the Strategic Environmental Research and Development Program (SERDP)—a joint endeavor of the DoD, the Department of Energy, and the Environmental Protection Agency—amplified this message. "In many ways, coastal military installations have been on the front lines of climate change," the SERDP report stated. Not only are these bases facing rising sea levels, but they are also exposed to "tropical and extra-tropical storms, high tides, and high waves that can bring significant storm surge, flooding, heavy rain, and destructive winds."[18]

As a result of these and other such studies, the risk to military installations on America's Atlantic coast began to attract attention from the media and the political realm. These bases play a critical role in projecting American power abroad, by housing and servicing the planes, ships, and other equipment used to sustain NATO and conduct combat missions abroad. The more frequently they are flooded or otherwise forced out of commission by storm damage, the less prepared this country will be to fulfill its overseas military obligations—a concern voiced not only by senior military officers, but by many in Congress. Senator Tim Kaine of Virginia, whose state houses the Norfolk naval base and several other major coastal installations, was particularly outspoken about the danger. "Military readiness is already being impacted by sea-level rise," he declared in 2015, adding that the situation will get much worse as time goes on.[19]

Just how severe a peril the U.S. military will face from global warming will depend on the speed of warming and the extent to which American forces prepare for and adapt to a climate-altered world. International success in curbing the emission of greenhouse gases would, of course, reduce the level of threat, while failure in this regard would have the opposite effect. By the same token, a crash program undertaken *now* to protect U.S. bases and personnel from the anticipated effects of warming would have much greater impact than similar efforts initiated *later*, when global conditions have become far more inhospitable. On our current path, however, the threat to American forces and installations is bound to grow in coming years, undermining the foundations of U.S. national security strategy.

## INUNDATED COASTAL BASES

There is both a historical and a practical basis for the concentration of American military bases in highly vulnerable coastal areas. Historically speaking, the Eastern Seaboard of the United States was long thought to be at risk of enemy attack, an anxiety that goes back to the American Revolution and the War of 1812, when British forces seized and occupied major coastal cities. This resulted in the construction of numerous bases and fortifications around vital ports and waterways. Many of these historic installations—including those in Portsmouth, New Hampshire; Newport, Rhode Island; Norfolk, Virginia; and Charleston, South Carolina—have remained major military bases to this day. And from a practical standpoint, the Navy obviously needs ready access to the Atlantic for its combat vessels if it is to perform the global combat role envisioned by U.S. strategy. Accordingly, a substantial number of the Pentagon's largest and most important installations are located along the East Coast.

Of course, not all of these facilities are equally vulnerable.

Some are on reasonably high ground set back from the waterfront, and so are safe from high tides and storm surges. Many others, however, are situated in low-lying areas close to the ocean, and thus are at far greater risk of inundation. According to the 2013 SERDP report, about 10 percent of DoD costal installations and facilities are "located at or near sea level and are already vulnerable to flooding and inundation."[20] And that threat will become far more severe in coming years as the Greenland and Antarctic ice sheets melt, adding colossal volumes of water to the world's oceans. In its 2011 report for the U.S. Navy, the National Research Council calculated that by 2100, global sea levels will rise by 0.4 to 2 meters (1.3 to 6.6 feet), enough to imperil many low-lying coastal installations. Many subsequent studies, as noted earlier, suggest that the higher estimates are more likely to come true. But "sea-level rise even in the lower range projections will challenge the utility and perhaps even the viability of some shore-based facilities," the NRC warned.[21]

As the 2011 NRC report made clear, moreover, low-lying coastal installations must fear not only this increase in sea level—which will permanently inundate many bases unless they build seawalls and other costly infrastructure—but also the storm surges brought by the more intense hurricanes that are expected from global warming. These surges can add another fifteen to twenty feet to mean sea level at the storm's peak (and even more if they coincide with especially high tides), pushing seawater far inland and causing widespread damage to military structures and equipment. Even bases that escape complete inundation, therefore, could still experience severe flooding on a regular basis as the water line edges ever upward.[22]

In recognition of this looming peril, military and scientific experts have teamed up on several studies to assess the relative vulnerability of America's major coastal bases. One such study, by the Union of Concerned Scientists (UCS), was published in 2016 as *The US Military on the Front Lines of Rising Seas*; a second, by the Center for Climate and Security (CCS), was released that same year as *Sea Level Rise and the U.S. Military's Mission*. Both began from the same premise—that rising sea levels combined with increasingly severe storms will endanger many of America's key coastal installations—and both examined a constellation of such bases said to be especially vulnerable to climate-related effects.

Of the Pentagon's facilities said to be at risk from climate change, the one that has received the most attention is Naval Station Norfolk, the world's largest naval installation and the headquarters of the U.S. Atlantic Fleet, along with numerous other Navy commands. Located at Hampton Roads, the anchorage (or "roadstead") formed by the James River as it enters Chesapeake Bay, NS Norfolk is the home port for the nation's largest assemblage of major combat vessels, typically consisting of six aircraft carriers, six cruisers, twenty guided-missile destroyers, seven amphibious assault ships, and six submarines. Much of this critically important facility is already prone to flooding during high tides and storm surges; with global warming, the frequency and extent of the flooding will increase substantially. By the end of the century, according to calculations by the Union of Concerned Scientists, 60 percent of the installation's land area will be exposed to tidal flooding on a regular basis, and 95 percent of it will experience ten feet or more of flooding during a Category 4 hurricane. Long before this, however, "portions of NS Norfolk would be inundated with each high tide," essentially rendering them useless.[23]

The Hampton Roads area also houses several other major military facilities, including the Norfolk Naval Shipyard, which keeps all those warships in top operational condition, and Langley Air Force Base, home to America's largest contingent of F-22 Raptor fighter planes. Located on a spit of land protruding into Chesapeake Bay, Langley is only a few feet above sea level and already prone to periodic flooding during high tides and strong storms. As the sea levels rise, such flooding will become more frequent and cover ever larger areas of the base. By 2050, the UCS projects, low-lying areas of Langley will be flooded an average of 280 times per year, significantly interfering with base operations. By 2100, under some scenarios, 90 percent of Langley would experience daily flooding, rending it essentially useless for military operations.[24]

With its low-lying topography and proximity to the open ocean, the Norfolk complex is especially vulnerable to powerful hurricanes like those arising regularly in the Atlantic. Such storms "have the potential for serious, if not catastrophic damage, and it would certainly put the shipyard out of business for some amount of time," said Ray Mabus, former secretary of the Navy, regarding Norfolk Naval Shipyard.[25] This peril was brought into sharp focus in September 2018, when Hurricane Florence bore down on the Eastern Seaboard. Initial predictions had Florence making landfall very close to Hampton Roads, which prompted worried Navy officials to order the evacuation of all nonessential personnel at NS Norfolk and the hurried dispatch of all seaworthy vessels then anchored at the base—some thirty warships in all—far out into the Atlantic.[26] Although Florence shifted southward at the last minute, sparing Norfolk from a direct hit and striking North Carolina instead, it nevertheless produced widespread flooding and severe damage throughout the region, including at several key bases in the Carolinas.

Given its critical importance to American national security, Hampton Roads is bound to receive attention from government officials concerned about the impact of climate change on U.S.

military preparedness. Senator Kaine and other members of Virginia's congressional delegation have spoken repeatedly of Norfolk's vulnerability to climate effects and sought funds for additional seawalls and other defenses against rising seas.[27] As a result, huge sums are being allocated for the protection of Navy and Air Force facilities in the area—usually under the designation of "base modernization" or "weather protection," without climate change mentioned directly. In 2018, for example, the Navy announced a multiyear, $21 billion plan to repair and bolster facilities at NS Norfolk and several other endangered naval facilities.[28] Even spending at this level, however, is unlikely to save Norfolk from the future ravages of climate change.

What's more, as Pentagon analysts are well aware, NS Norfolk and its neighbors are hardly the only major installations at risk from global warming. Many other bases on America's Atlantic and Gulf of Mexico coasts face similar threats from intense storms and rising seas. Among those that stand out in this regard are the three major installations in coastal Florida and southeast Georgia that were affected by Hurricane Irma: Naval Air Station Key West, Naval Station Mayport, and Naval Submarine Base Kings Bay. Both the Union of Concerned Scientists and the Center for Climate and Security identified those three bases as exhibiting levels of vulnerability comparable to those found at Hampton Roads.

Naval Air Station Key West, as already noted, is home to several key military organizations. The base is situated entirely on low-lying islands, or keys, that are conspicuously exposed to high tides and storm surges. Today, even a Category 1 hurricane, the weakest on the hurricane scale, floods more than 80 percent of the base, and a larger storm is bound to flood almost all of it. Furthermore, because the keys are made of porous limestone, it is almost impossible to build seawalls or levees to hold back the seas, since the limestone allows water to seep upward through the ground. As the oceans rise, therefore, high tides and storm surges will engulf ever more of the base for longer periods of time. By 2070, the UCS predicts, "NAS Key West's currently flood-prone areas would be underwater 85 percent of the year." By 2100, virtually the entire base could be underwater during high tides.[29]

Naval Station Mayport and Naval Submarine Base Kings Bay, both located near Jacksonville, Florida, are two other vital bases at risk from rising seas and storm damage. Naval Station Mayport hosts the Navy's third-largest concentration of surface ships, behind only Norfolk and the San Diego area; Kings Bay houses the Navy's Atlantic complement of nuclear-powered submarines, including those carrying intercontinental ballistic missiles. Both facilities thus play essential roles in the implementation of U.S. national security strategy, with Kings Bay standing out in this regard as a critical node in the nation's strategic nuclear deterrence system.[30] Both, however, are vulnerable to the same perils as NAS Key West and the Hampton Roads area. By 2050, large areas of Mayport could be flooded at high tide every day, and some parts of the base would be underwater most of the time.[31] A similar picture obtains at Kings Bay, where low-lying areas are likely to become permanently submerged by 2070 and higher-elevation areas would be flooded during any major hurricane, impeding vital operations at the base. This, noted the Center for Climate and Security, "portends potentially catastrophic impacts to the readiness and responsiveness of our strategic nuclear submarine force."[32]

Other key bases on the U.S. Atlantic and Gulf coasts also face threats of this magnitude. In Florida, the precarious location of Tyndall Air Force Base, on a low-lying peninsula facing the Gulf, has already been mentioned. In addition to housing the F-22

Raptors of the 325th Fighter Wing, Tyndall also accommodated the wing's Air Operations Center, a major component of the Pentagon's nationwide air defense system. Like the Raptors, the operations center and its crew were relocated to another base as Hurricane Michael approached the coast, and it remains unclear if they will ever return to Tyndall.[33] Also affected by Michael was Eglin Air Force Base, situated some eighty miles to the west of Tyndall. Eglin, a major DoD installation with numerous tenants, houses the 33rd Fighter Wing, the 96th Test Wing (used to test and evaluate air-delivered munitions), and the 7th Special Forces Group. Although it did not suffer the extreme damage experienced by Tyndall, Eglin was also battered by the high winds and storm surge generated by Michael. With much of its territory located in low-lying areas adjacent to the Gulf, Eglin is likely to experience periodic flooding as sea levels rise and will remain vulnerable to the extreme effects of future hurricanes.[34]

The Marine Corps, too, relies on a constellation of East Coast bases that face significant risks from climate change. Three of its major facilities—Camp Lejeune in North Carolina, plus Marine Corps Recruit Depot Parris Island and Marine Corps Air Station Beaufort in South Carolina—are located in low-lying areas abutting the Atlantic, making them highly vulnerable to sea-level rise and major storm surges. When Hurricane Florence shifted course and headed to the Carolinas instead of the Norfolk area in September 2018, those bases were severely impacted; normal operations were suspended and nonessential personnel ordered to evacuate. Camp Lejeune, a major Marine training center, was especially hard hit by Florence, with some nine hundred buildings damaged or destroyed.[35] As sea levels rise, flooding of Lejeune's low-lying areas is likely to occur on a daily basis and large parts of it can expect to be fully inundated during future hurricanes.[36] Parris Island, the Marines' main East Coast recruit training facility, and MCAS Beaufort, home to six Marine F/A-18 fighter squadrons, are equally at risk of inundation. At present, a storm surge of five to ten feet induced by a Category 1 hurricane would cover some 90 percent of Parris Island; by 2100, almost the entire base would be covered by ten to fifteen feet of water. MCAS Beaufort faces similar risks.[37]

By and large, extreme climate effects pose a greater threat to America's East Coast facilities than to those on the West Coast, as the Eastern Seaboard is exposed to the constant menace of hurricanes and its coastal area itself tends to be relatively flat, facilitating coastal inundation. Nevertheless, some West Coast bases can also expect significant damage from the effects of climate change in the decades ahead. Of these, Naval Base Coronado, across the bay from San Diego, and Marine Corps Base Camp Pendleton, just up the coast from that city, are considered particularly vulnerable. The Coronado base houses Naval Air Station North Island, one of the Navy's major air combat facilities, while Camp Pendleton is one of the Marines' principal training sites, the West Coast counterpart to Camp Lejeune. Large parts of both bases are situated in low-lying areas and so are vulnerable to flooding during high tides and storm surges. With climate change, both the frequency and the extent of that flooding will increase.[38]

## INLAND FLOODING

Although the severe flooding expected from climate change is largely projected to transpire on the nation's coastlines as a result of rising seas and storm surges, it can also occur in inland areas because of heavy, prolonged rainfall that fills the nation's rivers and overwhelms dikes, levees, and dams. Scientists believe that a warmer atmosphere, combined with other climate shifts, will result in periodic bouts of intense rainfall in the Midwest and Great Plains, especially during springtime. Such deluges, if continued over several days, can cause streams and rivers to overflow their banks and flood surrounding areas for miles around. Such storms have always been a feature of the nation's interior, but in recent years they have become more frequent and more prolonged.[39] This was especially evident in 2019, when portions of the Missouri River and then the Arkansas—swollen from unprecedented spring rains—broke through restraining levees and inundated surrounding areas.

Although the majority of U.S. military facilities are situated on the coasts, to ensure access to the high seas and facilitate the projection of power to foreign battlefields, a fair number are located in the Midwest and Great Plains. Some of these, such as Fort Leavenworth, Kansas, are legacies of the Indian Wars, when the U.S. military established bases on what was then the frontier to help protect newly arrived settlers from Native American attacks; others are of Cold War vintage, built to house missiles and bombers intended for transpolar attacks on the Soviet Union. In many cases, these bases were established along the major river systems that once provided access to the West, especially the Missouri and its many tributaries. Fort Leavenworth, now a major officer-training school, and Offutt Air Force Base, Nebraska, headquarters of the U.S. Strategic Command, are among major DoD facilities located on the Missouri River.

As the climate changes and intense rainfalls become more common, these riverside bases are becoming increasingly vulnerable to flooding, just like their counterparts on the East and West Coasts. This peril was brought into sharp relief in March 2019, when a so-called bomb cyclone—a rapidly forming low-pressure area—brought severe winds and torrential rain to large parts of the High Plains and Upper Midwest. With the ground in most of these areas still frozen from winter, the rain had nowhere to go except into streams and rivers, which quickly reached record levels and, in many places, overflowed the dikes and levees meant to keep them confined, resulting in widespread flooding.[40]

Among the places most affected by the Missouri's flooding was Offutt Air Force Base, which houses the 55th Wing—the nation's premier assemblage of reconnaissance and electronic-warfare planes—as well as the Strategic Command's headquarters. When the Missouri overflowed its banks, one-third of Offutt's runway was covered with water, rendering it inoperable; in addition, many of the 55th Wing's hangars and service facilities were severely damaged. All of the wing's super-sophisticated aircraft had to be relocated to other bases, where most remain. The U.S. Strategic Command—the nation's nuclear war command center—continued to operate during the flood, but many of its key personnel were unable to report for duty because of flooded roads around the base.[41] The Air Force is now seeking $350 million in emergency funds for base cleanup and repair (surely just a small down payment on the billions of dollars that ultimately will be required to rebuild the base), but it is unclear when Offutt will be able to resume normal operations.[42]

Offutt was not the only base to be affected by the March 2019 storm. Camp Ashland, a Nebraska National Guard training site located about twenty-five miles west of Offutt on the Platte River (a Missouri tributary), was completely submerged by floodwaters and the 225 soldiers studying there had to be evacuated.[43] Fort Leavenworth escaped major damage, but parts of the base were inundated and the town of Leavenworth's wastewater treatment plant was disabled by the floodwaters, posing a serious public health risk to local residents, including military families.[44] All of those facilities, like others located along America's interior rivers, can expect more such inundation on a regular basis as the planet warms.

## EXTREME HEAT AND WILDFIRES

Rising seas, storm surges, and interior flooding may pose the greatest threat to American military readiness, but they are not the only consequences of climate change to do so. Heat and fire, too, are major menaces, threatening to immobilize troops and equipment and ravage major facilities. As global temperatures rise, these effects will gain in severity, further impeding the Pentagon's ability to carry out its core responsibilities.

As the Department of Defense acknowledged in its 2012 *Climate Change Adaptation Roadmap*, rising temperatures will directly affect U.S. military readiness in numerous ways. Simply by increasing the number of very hot days and extended heat spells, warming will force the cancellation or curtailment of outdoor training exercises, reducing troop proficiency. The usability of certain types of equipment, such as aircraft and helicopters, can also be curtailed by extremely hot weather. Very high temperatures, when combined with prolonged drought, typically produce abnormally dry conditions, which in turn will increase the risk of wildfires—an especially worrisome danger at the numerous Army, Marine Corps, and Air Force bases dotting the American Southwest. In Alaska, meanwhile, rising temperatures will thaw large areas of permafrost, threatening the viability of Army and Air Force installations built on top of it.[45]

All these effects are expected to become far more severe in the years ahead, as global temperatures continue to rise. However, many are already being witnessed *now*, as demonstrated by a 2014 study by the Government Accountability Office (GAO).

After visiting a representative sampling of domestic DoD installations, the GAO reported that "infrastructure across the United States is being adversely affected already by phenomena associated with climate change," including "extreme heat." At stake, it said, is the continued viability of numerous military facilities throughout the country.[46]

Many of the installations at greatest risk, the GAO surprisingly discovered, are located in Alaska, a major hub for defenses oriented toward Northeast Asia and the Arctic. These facilities, in many cases, were built on permafrost—the layer of frozen earth and water that underlies the northern rim of Eurasia and North America—and much of this surface is beginning to thaw as a result of climate change. As the atmosphere heats up, the Earth's surface warms as well, gradually thawing the permafrost and so converting it from a solid substance to unstable mush.[47] In fact, this thawing process has already begun, threatening the utility and even the survival of some Alaska bases. The GAO's 2014 report described multiple instances of problems caused by this peril. At one Alaska facility, Army officials reported that an especially warm winter had caused widespread permafrost thawing and "forced the DoD to halt training for approximately three weeks because the ground was too soft to traverse." With this expected to become a recurring problem, the GAO warned that permafrost thawing "may impact military readiness because the DoD could not easily find another location to replicate the training offered in this area."[48]

When permafrost thawing occurs at a seaside location, moreover, the ground there becomes highly vulnerable to coastal erosion, putting at risk any infrastructure installed on that land. The vulnerability of shoreline facilities is further amplified, of course, by the rising seas and increasingly severe storms connected with global warming. For the DoD, this poses a significant peril because many of the nation's early-warning radars—pointed across the Arctic Ocean toward Russia and North Korea—are located along Alaska's shorelines. During its visit to Alaska, the GAO survey team discovered that coastal erosion has already damaged some Air Force facilities and is expected to cause far more damage as climate change advances. As an example, they described one early-warning installation where "40 feet of shoreline has been lost as a result of erosion and the erosion has damaged half of the runway," preventing large planes from landing there. In the future, the GAO indicated, more such sites will be destroyed or become inaccessible.[49]

Continuing with its investigation of bases at risk, the GAO next looked at DoD facilities in California and the American West, where heat, drought, and fire posed the greatest climate-related risk to military readiness. Some of the Pentagon's largest and most important bases are located in this region, where rising temperatures and protracted droughts have created extremely hot and dry conditions—the perfect conditions for outbreaks of ferocious wildfires. The GAO was told of extremely dry conditions at some key bases, resulting in restrictions on certain military activities. Fearful of igniting fires, military officials have prohibited the use of live ammunition at some training operations during summer months, diminishing the realism of combat exercises. At one site visited by the GAO team, live-fire training was banned for two months as a result of the growing fire hazard.[50]

Many of the officers interviewed in the course of the GAO's investigation spoke of fire danger at their facilities. It was only after the GAO completed its report, however, that this peril became fully apparent: in the years since then, major fires have erupted on or near several key West Coast bases, demonstrating just how severe the threat has become. One such conflagration erupted at Camp Pendleton Marine Corps Base in May 2014, right around the time the GAO was submitting its report to Congress. The Tomahawk Fire, as it was called, broke out in the vicinity of Naval Weapons Station Fallbrook—a major repository for naval bombs and missiles—and then jumped to other areas of the base. As the fire spread, evacuations were ordered for children at two schools on the base and for residents of a nearby military housing complex. The fire was finally contained five days later, after scorching six thousand acres. In the end, Tomahawk did not cause any significant damage to military facilities, but it did come close to storage facilities for Navy ordnance at the Fallbrook site; had the fire ignited any of the munitions buildings, a far more calamitous outcome could have resulted.[51]

An even larger and potentially more dangerous fire erupted in September 2016 at Vandenberg Air Force Base, located on the California coast some fifty miles northwest of Santa Barbara. Vandenberg is a major Air Force installation, used to launch satellite-bearing rockets into space and to test other space-launch vehicles (including Elon Musk's SpaceX Falcon series of rockets). It also houses a battery of Ground-Based Midcourse Defense missile interceptors, intended to shoot down any ballistic missiles fired at this country by North Korea or another Asian adversary. The Canyon Fire, as this blaze was known, burned over twelve thousand acres and forced Air Force officials to cancel the launch of an Atlas V rocket carrying an Earth-imaging satellite. At one point, the fire edged close to several of Vandenberg's key launch facilities, including Space Launch Complex 3, where the Atlas V was being readied for flight, and Space Launch Complex 4, where ten Iridium mobile communications satellites were being prepped for a SpaceX rocket launch. More than a thousand firefighters from over fifty agencies were deployed to fight the flames. Ultimately, a shift in wind patterns sent the fire away from the launch facilities and toward uninhabited areas inland from the coast—a lucky break.[52]

Because so many of the DoD installations throughout the American West are located in areas that were relatively arid to begin with, and often experience extremely hot days in the summer, their vulnerability to prolonged heat waves and wildfires can only grow. Whether or not one of them will someday be completely overrun by a wildfire even more destructive than the Tomahawk and Canyon blazes cannot be foreseen, but the danger is real.

## OVERSEAS BASES UNDER THREAT

Most of the studies conducted by governmental and nongovernmental agencies on the U.S. military's vulnerability to the impacts of climate change have focused on domestic facilities. It is clear, however, that the vulnerabilities reported at home also extend to American military installations and troop deployments abroad. In fact, many of those overseas bases and deployments are even more exposed to the severe effects of climate change than are domestic installations—an unavoidable consequence of the fact that American military commitments are heavily concentrated in Asia, Africa, and the Middle East, where global warming has already taken a heavy toll on the environment.

For forces operating in the Asia-Pacific area, sea-level rise and extreme storm events are likely to pose the greatest dangers. America's military presence in this region is largely comprised of air and naval components, which rely on bases that are often located at or close to sea level in areas that are highly exposed to typhoons. This peril was highlighted by the General Accounting Office in a 2017 report on the vulnerability of the DoD's overseas facilities to climate change (a counterpart, of sorts, to its 2014 report on the vulnerability of domestic bases). Without specifying locations, the GAO reported that officials at some Pacific installations "stated that personnel must switch from their normal focus—supporting the operations and maintenance needs of the base—to focus instead on preparing for approaching extreme weather events, such as typhoons, and addressing the impacts of extreme weather events." Officials at one installation also reported "that their base typically experiences at least five typhoons annually and that they have noticed storms have been more severe over the past few years."[53]

While the GAO report did not identify the facilities their investigators visited in preparing the 2017 report, other studies have highlighted the vulnerability of several specific key DoD facilities in the Asia-Pacific region. One location that has received considerable scrutiny in this regard is the joint UK-U.S. military facility at Diego Garcia, a low-lying atoll in the Indian Ocean. Located south of India, approximately midway between Indonesia and the Arabian Peninsula, Diego Garcia constitutes a strategically important logistical base for American air and naval forces transiting between the Pacific and the Persian Gulf area. A Navy Support Facility at the base is used to replenish surface warships and missile-firing nuclear submarines; an Air Expeditionary Wing helps sustain long-range bomber operations, including strikes in Iraq and Afghanistan. Most of Diego Garcia does not exceed two meters in elevation and so, if current predictions prove accurate, will be fully submerged by the end of the century. Even before then, however, the base will become increasingly vulnerable to powerful storm surges, made ever more destructive by the collapse—due to climate-driven ocean acidification—of the coral reefs that now help protect the atoll from raging seas.[54]

Another strategic site at risk from sea-level rise is Kwajalein Atoll in the Marshall Islands, in the western Pacific Ocean.

Kwajalein is home to the Ronald Reagan Ballistic Missile Defense Test Site, a multibillion-dollar facility used to test the effectiveness of U.S. antimissile defense systems. Much of the island lies very close to sea level and is vulnerable to flooding from storm surges; as the oceans rise, more of the atoll will be inundated by such storms, and the community's freshwater supplies—derived from an underground aquifer—will be permanently swamped by seawater. A 2018 study commissioned by the Department of Defense concluded that Kwajalein is likely to become "uninhabitable" by midcentury due to this saltwater intrusion.[55]

Elsewhere in the region, the DoD faces a substantial climate threat to its cluster of air and naval bases in Japan. These installations, including the naval base at Yokosuka, on Japan's main island of Honshu, and Kadena Air Force Base, on Okinawa, are among the most important U.S. military facilities in Asia. Yokosuka, located at the mouth of Tokyo Harbor, hosts the aircraft carrier USS *Ronald Reagan* (America's only forward-deployed carrier) and its supporting vessels; Kadena is the largest Air Force facility in East Asia, housing the 18th Air Wing and a host of other units. Both of these bases, and many others nearby, are located on or close to the Pacific Ocean and are regularly menaced by typhoons.[56] As global warming proceeds, these facilities—like their counterparts in the eastern United States—will be exposed to rising seas and an ever-increasing risk of extremely powerful storms.

For U.S. forces in the Middle East and North Africa, the greatest impediments to military operations are likely to come from extraordinary heat, prolonged drought, and sandstorms. Research suggests that, as climate change proceeds, large parts of the Middle East and North Africa will regularly experience temperatures high enough to endanger human health.[57] The DoD is well aware of the risks to soldiers' health when conducting operations in extremely hot weather, and so takes elaborate precautions to prevent heatstroke and other heat-related ailments. Soldiers deployed in persistently hot countries like Iraq are warned to drink water regularly and to avoid excessive activity during the hottest hours of the day. Nevertheless, rising temperatures of the sort described in the studies cited above will pose a major threat to the health and survival of any U.S. military personnel deployed in these regions.

American military operations in the Middle East and North Africa are also being hindered by another consequence of climate change: an increase in the frequency of severe sandstorms, which impair mechanical equipment and interfere with sensors. With diminishing rainfall and rising temperatures, ever-larger areas of vegetation are being converted into dust bowls, providing the raw material for the blinding storms.[58] Such storms have already caused havoc for U.S. and allied forces operating in the Middle East. The U.S.-led campaign to destroy the Islamic State's "caliphate" in Iraq and Syria, for instance, was slow to get under way in 2014 partly because sandstorms "thwarted many surveillance missions needed to identify targets," reported Eric Schmitt of the *New York Times*.[59] The following year, Islamic State fighters used the cover of a sandstorm to stage an assault on the Iraqi provincial capital of Ramadi, forcing a retreat by government defenders.[60]

Assuming that American combat forces will continue to be sent to these areas in the years ahead, the military services will be forced to contend with high temperatures and frequent sandstorms to an ever greater extent. In part, this will require modifications to equipment: weapons, vehicles, and support systems will have to be reconfigured to cope with extreme heat and sand infiltration, while uniforms and body armor will have to be made lighter and more effective at diffusing heat. The problem of water scarcity will also have to be addressed, since deployed troops will increasingly be unable to rely on local sources (which may become nonexistent) and will have to bring their own water supplies, requiring elaborate logistical arrangements. Ultimately, however, warming will require a strategic recalibration: In the future, the very notion of deploying regular combat forces in certain areas of the world may become inconceivable.

## THE STRUGGLE TO ADAPT

Ever since climate change was designated as a significant threat to national security in the 2010 *Quadrennial Defense Review*, the armed services have been on notice to identify their vulnerabilities to global warming and to begin defending themselves from these perils. Officially, the terms used to describe such efforts are *adaptation* and *resiliency*: that is, the services have been told to adapt as necessary to the climate-related changes now occurring or soon to arrive, and to make themselves more resilient in the face of events such as severe hurricanes and typhoons. In doing so, the services are not acting out of some "altruism thing," but out of necessity, said John Conger, a former deputy undersecretary of defense and a key architect of these efforts. "There are mission reasons to do these kinds of things. . . . If sea level rise is going to impact infrastructure, if a runway gets flooded, that's a mission impact and that's the kind of thing you've got to pay attention to."[61]

To guide these endeavors, in 2012 the Department of Defense produced its first *Climate Change Adaptation Roadmap*, requiring every DoD component entity to appoint a senior official or team to oversee assessment and adaptation endeavors. Climate change, it said, was to be viewed not as some extraneous issue, but "rather as an aspect of overall management."[62] A second version of the *Climate Change Adaptation Roadmap*, released two years later, provided far more detail than the 2012 document and stipulated more aggressive adaptation and sustainability measures. It called on base commanders to integrate climate change projections into their Installation Master Plans and other fundamental operating blueprints, and enjoined every DoD component to "develop new climate-specific plans and guidance" for all future procurement activities.[63]

Seen from a distance, the 2012 and 2014 adaptation roadmaps were extraordinarily broad and ambitious. Not only were the military services directed to make climate change an integral aspect of their day-to-day planning and operations, but the military's entire basing infrastructure was to be assessed for climate-related vulnerabilities and then modified as necessary to overcome likely impacts. This, needless to say, is an incredibly demanding task—and a very expensive one. Nonetheless, many base commanders have taken these obligations seriously, doing what they can with the resources available to them to limit their installation's exposure to severe climate effects. These officers have been hampered, however, by a persistent lack of sufficient guidance and resources to undertake such efforts and by resistance from Republicans in Congress to anything that represents a response to global warming.[64]

In response to complaints that the two adaptation road maps provided insufficient guidance on steps going forward, the Office of the Secretary of Defense issued a new edict in January 2016: DoD Directive 4715.21, "Climate Change Adaptation and Resilience." The 2016 directive, possessing greater authority than the road maps, requires all defense organizations to incorporate climate change considerations into their planning in multiple respects, including "force structure, basing, military operations, capacity building, [and] stability operations."

Under the directive, officials at every U.S. military command and installation are enjoined to assess their organization's exposure to severe climate effects and take action as needed to overcome those risks.[65]

In some ways, DoD Directive 4715.21 represents the most elaborate blueprint of its kind issued by any U.S. government agency. If fully implemented, it will entail a thorough overhaul of training, weapons and equipment procurement, installation management, and the very roles and missions of the U.S. armed forces. But while it enjoys considerable support in the upper echelons of the DoD, the measure has run afoul of Republican politicians, who, for ideological reasons, oppose any governmental initiatives that arise from acknowledging the reality of climate change. Legislation introduced by Democrats to allocate funds for climate-related improvements to base infrastructure has largely gone nowhere. With the Trump White House and most Republicans in Congress firmly opposed to any measures taken in response to global warming, the military services have had to slacken these efforts or disguise them as something else altogether.[66]

Despite that Republican resistance, however, the Department of Defense still views climate change as an existential threat to its major stateside bases and continues to prescribe efforts to bolster their defenses against warming's severe impacts. This much was made clear by the Pentagon's January 2019 *Report on Effects of a Changing Climate to the Department of Defense*. As mentioned earlier, the document acknowledged that many key bases were at risk from flooding, wildfires, and other climate effects—a finding that generated numerous headlines. A less heralded finding of that report, however, was that the DoD is "updating various built and natural infrastructure design standards to better adapt to climate standards." As an example of such efforts, it noted that Navy commanders, in planning new facilities, "now incorporate adaptive planning measures from a variety of government agency sources, including the NAVFAC's [Naval Facilities Engineering Command's] *Climate Change Installation Adaptation and Resilience Planning Handbook*." Among the naval facilities to receive special attention are those in the Hampton Roads area, which was said to be "very vulnerable to flooding caused by rising sea levels and land subsidence." At nearby Langley Air Force Base, the report said, all new development must be "constructed at a minimum elevation of 10.5 feet above sea level with some projects planned for higher elevation due to high communication intensity and need for greater hardening."[67] Even if the White House sees no danger from climate change, senior military officials continue to perceive multiple threats to U.S. national security and an urgent need to prepare for its effects.

Regardless of the political wrangling, however, the DoD's vulnerability to climate change will only grow in the coming years, diminishing its capacity to perform vital defense missions. Piecemeal improvements to Naval Station Norfolk and other highly exposed facilities, such as the remedial efforts advocated by Senator Kaine, will offer temporary relief but will not protect these facilities from warming's future ravages. As the storms of 2017 and 2018 demonstrated, moreover, these climate assaults are ever more likely to occur in clusters, with U.S. forces obliged to address several civil emergencies simultaneously at a time when many of their own critical facilities are immobilized by extreme storm damage, diminishing their capacity to address both foreign and domestic emergencies. At some point, officers who view national security as a sacred obligation will have no choice but to confront those who persist in climate denial.

8

# GOING GREEN

## The Pentagon as Change Agent

As is customary when a U.S. warship departs on an extended deployment, hundreds of family members, well-wishers, and assorted dignitaries gathered at Naval Air Station North Island in California on January 20, 2016, to bid farewell to the USS *Stockdale*, a guided-missile destroyer with 320 crew members, as it sailed out of San Diego Bay. In accordance with the standard script for such events, speeches were delivered and tears were shed as the *Stockdale* set off on its six-month voyage. But this particular send-off was unusual in that the visiting dignitaries included both the secretary of the Navy, Ray Mabus, and the secretary of agriculture, Tom Vilsack. They were present to highlight an especially distinctive feature of the *Stockdale*'s voyage: instead of being fueled entirely by petroleum, as had always been the case in the past, the ship had been supplied with a blend of petroleum and liquefied beef fat from midwestern farmers.

As it sailed from San Diego, the *Stockdale* became the first U.S. naval vessel to be powered by alternative fuel while on operational duty—a major milestone in the Navy's efforts to reduce its reliance on fossil fuels.[1]

For Mabus, the longest-serving secretary of the Navy since Woodrow Wilson's day, provisioning the *Stockdale* with an innovative biofuel represented the culmination of years of effort. Excessive dependence on fossil fuels, he believed, had made the Navy vulnerable to unanticipated fuel price increases and the whims of unreliable, possibly unfriendly foreign oil producers. "We need an American home-grown source of alternative energy," he explained at the *Stockdale*'s departure ceremony. "We need one that is not subject to the wild price swings of conventional fuel. . . . We need ones that can't be used against us."[2] In pursuit of this objective, Mabus had explored a number of biofuels before settling on the petroleum–beef fat blend, chosen because it was cost-competitive with conventional fuels and thus complied with congressional requirements on that account.[3]

In fact, Mabus had arranged to supply not just one ship with an alternative fuel, but an entire fleet. After the *Stockdale* sailed off, it joined other members of the John C. Stennis Strike Group out in the Pacific. Built around the nuclear-powered carrier USS *John C. Stennis*, the strike group also included the guided-missile cruiser USS *Mobile Bay* and guided-missile destroyers USS *Chung-Hoon* and USS *William P. Lawrence*. Like the *Stockdale*, the other three escort ships were fueled by the petroleum–beef fat mix—and so, with the *Stennis* itself powered by nuclear engines, every ship in this flotilla was now running on some alternative to conventional petroleum, the first U.S. combat formation to achieve that distinction. In recognition of this achievement, Mabus christened this deployment of the Stennis Strike Group the "Great Green Fleet."[4]

For the next six months, the Great Green Fleet, accompanied by underway replenishment ships carrying the innovative fuel mix, sailed up and down the Western Pacific, engaging in a wide variety of practice drills and show-of-force operations. Among these were a series of joint maneuvers with the navies of other nations and so-called freedom of navigation patrols in the hotly contested South China Sea.[5] Along with the alternative fuel arrangements, the ships also undertook a variety of other energy-efficiency measures, such as installing stern flaps to improve fuel efficiency and drifting with ocean currents when their tasks allowed. Thanks to such practices, during one stretch of the deployment the *Lawrence* recorded a 40 percent lower fuel burn rate than it had during its operations the previous year.[6]

Although intended primarily as a test bed for these new technologies, the Great Green Fleet also had a geopolitical objective: to demonstrate U.S. leadership in the development of advanced energy systems and their application to military purposes. This was made explicit in the very title of the enterprise. As the Navy explained, "Secretary Mabus chose the name Great Green Fleet to honor President Theodore Roosevelt's Great White Fleet, which helped usher in America as a global power on the world stage at the beginning of the 20th Century."[7] The "Great White Fleet" was the name given by Roosevelt to a flotilla of sixteen battleships plus an array of supporting vessels—all painted stark white—that were deployed on an around-the-world, two-year-long mission in 1907.[8] Like that earlier voyage, the 2016 Great Green Fleet was intended to showcase America's mastery of advanced naval technologies—in this case, renewable energy—to emphasize its status as a major world power.[9]

None of these efforts, it should be noted at the outset, were specifically aimed at combating climate change. The U.S.

Department of Defense has been slow to embrace climate change *mitigation*—the enactment of steps to slow global warming by reducing the military's greenhouse gas (GHG) emissions—as distinct from measures toward adaptation and increased resiliency. Some officers have long regarded mitigation efforts as a distraction from the armed forces' principal responsibilities of homeland defense and the deterrence and defeat of foreign enemies. As senior officials have grappled with the impacts of climate change, however, they have increasingly realized that, as we have seen, rising temperatures threaten American security both by increasing chaos and conflict abroad and by directly endangering the homeland. Reducing their own GHG emissions, therefore, means that the military services could enhance American security by helping to diminish those threats.

At the same time, while acknowledging the strategic importance of reduced emissions, senior officers have also understood that undertaking any substantial energy transformations requires presenting such endeavors as a contribution to combat effectiveness. Even if sympathetic to Pentagon concerns about the long-term implications of a warming planet, many unit commanders would balk at major changes to their normal operating procedures if they thought that combat performance would suffer in the process. Accordingly, mitigating climate change has rarely been portrayed by the DoD as an end in itself—though some Pentagon documents do mention that as a vital objective. Rather, it has been largely pitched as a beneficial side effect of accomplishing other goals, such as reducing dependence on fossil fuels or lessening vulnerability to disruptions in the domestic electric grid. Given these nuances, it is worth looking closer at the genesis of the Great Green Fleet and related measures undertaken by the U.S. Navy under Secretary Mabus's oversight.

## THE GREAT GREEN FLEET IN PERSPECTIVE

The Great Green Fleet began to take shape in 2009, long before the *Stockdale* and its fellow warships set sail to the Western Pacific. That year, in an "Energy Message to the Fleet," Mabus declared that "energy reform must inform and shape every decision we make during research, development, and procurement of our systems, during training operations, and during daily life aboard ship." The Navy, he proclaimed, would undertake a historic mission: to transition from an essentially petroleum-driven force to one largely powered by alternative sources of energy.[10]

To realize this extraordinary vision, Mabus announced four specific "energy targets" for 2020. First, half of all energy consumed at shore-based installations had to come from renewable on-site sources, such as wind, solar, and geothermal; second, petroleum use by the Navy's fleet of fifty thousand "non-tactical" commercial vehicles would be cut in half through the acquisition of hybrid and all-electric cars; third, at least 40 percent of the Navy's *total* energy consumption would come from alternative sources. And fourth, as a capstone to all of this, the Navy would create a "green strike group" composed of nuclear vessels and ships powered by a biofuel mixture—the Great Green Fleet.[11]

Driving all this, Mabus indicated at the time, was the need to reduce the Navy's reliance on petroleum and kick-start the development of energy alternatives. For decades, petroleum—a widely available, easily transported, and relatively affordable substance—had been the fuel of choice for naval vessels. But that affordability could no longer be taken for granted. While the price of oil had long been fairly low and largely stable, in the twenty-first century crude oil prices had risen dramatically, with the cost climbing from an average of $19 per barrel in 2002 to

$74 per barrel in 2006 and a high of $133 per barrel in mid-2008.[12] With ship and aircraft fuel accounting for a large share of the Navy's operational budget, those increases—and the speed with which they occurred—proved a massive headache for Navy officials, who were forced to shuffle funds from one account to another in order to keep ships operating.

Even more worrying was the DoD's excessive dependence on unreliable and potentially unfriendly foreign oil suppliers. Secretary Mabus, who had served as ambassador to Saudi Arabia during the Carter administration, was forthright in expressing his anxiety about this dependency. "We simply buy too much fossil fuels from places that are either actually or potentially volatile, from places that may or may not have our best interests at heart," he later testified to Congress.[13] Increased use of renewable fuels, he believed, would liberate the Navy from its dependency on foreign oil suppliers, affording it greater freedom of action. "Diversifying our energy sources arms us with operational flexibility and strengthens our ability to provide presence, turning the tables on those who would use energy as a weapon against us."[14]

While such considerations largely motivated the effort to shift from fossil fuels to renewables, Navy officials were also aware of the growing specter of climate change, and understood that their reductions in fossil fuel consumption would translate into reduced carbon emissions. This commitment to the reduction of greenhouse gases was given further impetus in October 2009 when President Obama signed Executive Order 13514, "Federal Leadership in Environmental, Energy, and Economic Performance." Under this directive, all federal agencies, including the Department of Defense and the individual armed services, were required to "increase energy efficiency" and "measure, report, and reduce their greenhouse gas emissions from direct and indirect activities." As part of the effort, all government organizations were ordered to diminish their emissions by "reducing the use of fossil fuels" and "increasing agency use of renewable energy."[15]

With President Obama pushing for government-wide progress in this area, the Navy's increased use of renewable energy sources made good political sense. Nevertheless, as Mabus moved forward with his plans, he was always careful to present military preparedness—not environmental stewardship—as the primary goal of the enterprise. "The Great Green Fleet," he declared at the *Stockdale*'s 2016 departure ceremony, "shows how we are transforming our energy use to make us better warfighters, to go farther, stay longer and deliver more firepower. In short, to enable us to provide the global presence that is our mission."[16]

Ultimately, the Great Green Fleet arguably made only a minimal contribution to slowing the advance of global warming. The "alternative fuel" consumed by the *Stockdale* and other vessels of the 2016 fleet was composed of only 10 percent animal fat, with the remainder being ordinary petroleum. That's not exactly a giant step toward fossil fuel elimination. (Earlier Navy trials had used a fifty-fifty mixture, but that approach was shelved due to the biofuel's high cost.[17]) Still, the Great Green Fleet does represent a significant effort by a large and powerful organization to at least start transitioning from carbon-based fuels to climate-friendlier alternatives.

## THE FLIGHT FROM PETROLEUM

As the story behind the Great Green Fleet suggests, the Pentagon's steps toward climate change mitigation have been closely connected to the matter of its energy use in general—or, more specifically, to what it calls "energy security." As defined by the DoD, energy security means "having assured access to reliable supplies of energy and the ability to protect and deliver sufficient energy to meet operational needs."[18] From this perspective, the primary attraction of alternative fuels is not their role in reducing greenhouse gases but rather their utility in weaning the United States off its dependence on unreliable suppliers of petroleum. While the military has cited its efforts to develop renewable energy as evidence of its commitment to GHG reductions mandated by Obama's Executive Order 13514, those efforts had in fact begun earlier, and had initially been triggered by strategic, not environmental, considerations.

To appreciate the Pentagon's profound concern about energy security, it is necessary to go back to the early days of fighting in Iraq and Afghanistan. American forces there were routinely deployed in remote combat posts, and had to be provided with critical fuel supplies by tanker convoys that were often exposed to enemy ambushes.[19] In Afghanistan, for example, enemy attacks resulted in one Marine casualty for every fifty convoys and one Army casualty for every twenty-four convoys.[20] The way to reduce this danger, the Pentagon indicated, was to increase energy efficiency and place greater reliance on renewable sources of energy.[21]

This history was made vividly evident to me by Michael Breen, a former Army officer who saw extensive combat in Iraq. In 2004, Breen was serving with a group of armored vehicles stationed at a forward operating base (FOB) located south of Baghdad and near the cities of Fallujah and Karbala—an area that came to be known as the Triangle of Death because of all the ambushes conducted there by enemy forces. "We were totally dependent on liquid fuel not just for our vehicles but also for the generators that powered our small tactical power grid," he told me.

That fuel, "along with our water and other supplies, had to come in through a daily convoy. And every day, more or less, that convoy ran into trouble. And then we would send out a force of Bradley Fighting Vehicles, the quick reaction force, to essentially rescue the convoy and bring them in, which consumed the previous day's fuel delivery, or at least some of it." The same phenomenon, he said, was occurring all over Iraq, constituting "a major drain on the force."[22]

Other officers had similar experiences in Iraq and Afghanistan, prompting many to take up the cause of energy transformation. One figure who played an especially pivotal role in this respect was General Richard Zilmer of the Marine Corps, then commander of Multinational Force-West in Iraq's Anbar Province, one of the country's most hotly contested areas. In 2006, Zilmer sent an urgent message to the DoD in Washington, requesting the expedited development of "a self-sustainable energy solution"—presumably employing wind and solar power—to lessen his forces' reliance on vulnerable fuel convoys. By reducing the need for petroleum at outlying bases, he wrote, "we can decrease the frequency of logistics convoys on the road, thereby reducing the danger to our Marines, soldiers, and sailors."[23]

Zilmer's memo, and similar expressions of concern from soldiers in the field, prompted the DoD and the individual armed services to undertake crash programs to increase energy efficiency and develop better renewable energy systems. The Army, for example, directed its Rapid Equipping Force—a special unit created to speed the introduction of new technology on the battlefield—to develop and deploy renewable energy power systems for frontline troops. Out of this came Operation Dynamo, a project to swap gas-guzzling power generators at forward operating bases with energy-efficient replacements. Dozens of these alternative systems, which use a mix of solar and wind power to augment diesel generators, were sent to Army FOBs in Afghanistan.[24]

The Marine Corps went a step further, establishing a pilot combat station in Afghanistan, to test new energy technologies. Among these were the Solar Portable Alternative Communications Energy System (SPACES), a flexible solar panel that can be carried by an individual Marine and used to recharge radio batteries, and PowerShade, a larger solar tarp that fits over a standard Marine Corps tent and provides enough energy to power the tent's lighting system. Another system tested at ExFOB, the Ground Renewable Expeditionary Energy Network System (GREENS), used a portable 300-watt photovoltaic battery setup to deliver all the electricity needed for a platoon-size command center.[25]

Out of these experiences came a shared perception that excessive energy use and petroleum consumption had become a strategic liability for the American military. "As long as U.S. forces rely on large volumes of energy, particularly petroleum-based fuels, the vulnerability and volatility of supplies will continue to raise risks and costs for the armed forces," a 2011 DoD report indicated. To overcome this liability, the military services would have to reduce oil demand by improving efficiency and developing a range of nonpetroleum alternatives.[26] Or, as General James Mattis famously put it after serving as commanding general of the 1st Marine Division in Iraq, the services should cooperate to "unleash us from the tether of fuel."[27]

## OPERATIONAL ENERGY

The battlefield-driven concerns over excessive reliance on petroleum made their way fairly quickly to the upper echelons of officialdom at the Department of Defense. In 2006, the undersecretary of defense for Acquisition, Technology, and Logistics commissioned the Defense Science Board (DSB), a federal advisory committee, to establish a task force that would identify "opportunities to reduce fuel demand by deployed forces." In its final report, *More Fight—Less Fuel*, the DSB task force chastised the military services for their profligate use of energy on the battlefield, urging them to adopt a range of measures aimed at reducing petroleum use and accelerating the introduction of alternatives. These included, for example, proposals for developing synthetic fuels that could be generated at forward operating locations using kitchen waste and local vegetation.[28]

The same sort of concern over military energy security and the need for alternatives generated considerable interest in Congress. In 2009, American lawmakers authorized the establishment of a new high-level Pentagon position, the assistant secretary of defense for Operational Energy Plans and Programs, to better focus efforts on these priorities. *Operational energy* (OE), as defined by the DoD, is "the energy used by military forces in execution of their day-to-day missions." The assigned role of the new assistant secretary, it decreed, was to assess the existing energy-use behavior of the services and provide guidance to the secretary of defense and other top officials on how to "promote the energy security of military operations."[29]

In attempting to fulfill its mandate, the new OE office adopted an overriding focus on expediting the development of alternative fuels. "Most military operations depend on a single energy source, petroleum, which has economic, strategic, and environmental drawbacks," an early presentation declared. Accordingly, "the Department needs to diversify its energy sources and protect access to energy supplies in order to have a more reliable and assured supply of energy for military missions."[30] To speed up this transition, the OE office proposed a wide range of initiatives aimed at the increased use of alternative fuels in air, sea, and ground combat systems.

Alongside this effort, each of the military services undertook its own initiatives to reduce reliance on petroleum and increase energy efficiency. Air Force secretary Michael B. Donley took the lead in 2008 with the release of a memorandum calling for immediate action in "reducing aviation, ground fuel, and installation energy demand." High priority was also placed on utilization of renewable energy at Air Force ground installations, and on the development of alternative aviation fuels "derived from domestic sources produced in a manner that is greener than fuels produced from conventional petroleum."[31] In 2009, this was followed by Navy secretary Mabus's "Energy Message to the Fleet," outlining the ambitious goals described earlier, including the eventual launching of the Great Green Fleet. The Army, not to be outdone, came up with its own "Green Warrior Convoy," a procession of combat and supply vehicles powered by innovative propulsion systems. Announcing the plans in a 2012 speech on energy security, President Obama explained that "the convoy will test and demonstrate the Army's advanced vehicle power and technology including fuel cells, hybrid systems, battery technologies and alternative fuels."[32]

In the twenty-aughts, virtually all these initiatives were presented as measures to enhance energy security and to escape the tyranny of petroleum. By the twenty-teens, however, the topic of energy security was fused with concerns about climate change to create a combined energy/climate policy. "Although they produce distinct types of challenges," the DoD's 2010 *Quadrennial Defense Review* stated, "climate change, energy security, and economic stability are inextricably linked." This is so, the QDR explained, because increases in energy efficiency and the use of renewables contribute both to improved security and to diminished greenhouse gas emissions. "The Department is increasing its use of renewable energy supplies and reducing energy demand to improve operational effectiveness, reduce greenhouse gas emissions in support of U.S. climate change initiatives, and protect the Department from energy price fluctuations," it stated.[33]

In accordance with this stance (and Obama's Executive Order 13514), the Department of Defense announced ambitious goals to increase the use of renewable energy sources while decreasing both fossil fuel consumption and GHG emissions. The DoD's 2010 Strategic Sustainability Performance Plan stated that "the Department not only commits to complying with environmental and energy statutes, regulations, and Executive Orders, but [intends] to go beyond compliance where it serves our national security needs." This exemplary intent was demonstrated by the plan's major objectives for 2020, which included a 34 percent reduction in the DoD's net GHG emissions and a 30 percent reduction in petroleum consumption by non-tactical vehicle fleets. The goals also included having 18 percent of all energy used at fixed installations come from renewable energy sources.[34]

By the middle of the twenty-teens, the military services were making significant progress toward achieving these ambitious objectives, as documented in the DoD's *Fiscal Year 2016 Operational Energy Annual Report* (the most recent available). The Air Force, for example, was developing next-generation aircraft engines with a 25 percent increase in fuel efficiency. The Navy, in addition to the innovations associated with the Great Green Fleet, had begun the installation of hybrid-electric drive power systems on its *Arleigh Burke*–class missile destroyers; these systems take over from the ship's main propulsion systems when cruising at low speeds, saving energy. The Army, for its part, was speeding the deployment of advanced fuel-efficient generators like those developed under Operation Dynamo.[35] It had also set up a Ground Systems Power and Energy Lab in Warren, Michigan, a major facility devoted to the development and testing of energy-efficient propulsion systems for combat vehicles.[36]

Turning around an organization as large as the U.S. Department of Defense—the nation's largest single consumer of energy—is no easy task. Nevertheless, in response to all the motivations described above, the armed forces have made credible progress in their drive to reduce oil use, curb GHG emissions, and increase use of renewables. According to the DoD's *Fiscal Year 2016 Operational Energy Annual Report*, total petroleum consumption by the DoD's operating forces declined by nearly 20 percent over the preceding five-year period, from approximately 112 million barrels in FY 2011 to 86 million in FY 2016.[37] Further reductions in fossil fuel use were accomplished through phasing out oil-powered vehicles in the services' non-tactical fleets of cars and trucks. All this, combined with other energy-saving efforts, resulted in a substantial drop in the DoD's carbon emissions, putting it on track to achieve its ambitious 2011 objectives.[38]

## TOWARD NET ZERO AT DOMESTIC BASES

When the Department of Defense first undertook energy reform in a systemic manner, it was largely driven by events on the battlefield, particularly the perils encountered while trying to deliver oil supplies to frontline forces in Iraq and Afghanistan.

This led, as we have seen, to a department-wide focus on "operational energy," or the safe delivery of vital fuels to troops in the field. As that effort was getting under way, however, the Pentagon was confronted with a second major threat to its energy security: disruptions in electrical power supply to its bases in the United States. Most domestic U.S. military installations rely on the commercial grid for their electrical supply and, as climate change advances, those networks have suffered more and more breakdowns from demand overload and intense storm activity. To address this problem, the stateside bases have increasingly been seeking energy self-sustainability—an impulse often conjoined with the Pentagon's commitment to reducing greenhouse gases.

"DoD's reliance on the commercial grid to deliver electricity to more than 500 major installations places the continuity of critical missions at risk," the department warned in its Strategic Sustainability Performance Plan for 2011. "In general, installations lack the ability to manage their demand for and supply of electrical power, making them potentially vulnerable to intermittent or prolonged power disruption caused by natural disasters, attacks, or sheer overload of the grid."[39] With global warming increasing the frequency and ferocity of extreme storm events, the number of extended disruptions to the electrical grid has skyrocketed in recent years. According to research by the Pew Charitable Trusts, the frequency of such weather-related disturbances jumped from less than a dozen per year in the early 1990s to about 75 in 2010 and 135 in 2011.[40]

By that point, concerns about grid reliability and ever-increasing climate impacts had combined to make energy security at stateside bases a major Pentagon priority. The obvious solution, in the eye of most beholders, was to reduce dependence on the commercial grid and to boost facility self-sufficiency through the expansion of on-site renewable energy. The more that bases could rely on their own sources of energy, senior officers concluded, the less vulnerable they were to grid breakdowns. "The Department is committed to renewable energy not only because it is dedicated to showing leadership in sustainability," the 2011 sustainability plan explained, "but because it improves resilience and thus mission readiness."[41] In addition, by increasing the military's use of renewables, such initiatives also helped advance the DoD's obligation under Executive Order 13514 to reduce greenhouse gas emissions. All of a sudden, American military bases became giant laboratories for the large-scale utilization of alternative energy.

As these endeavors got under way, the Department of Defense and the individual services established ambitious goals for increased facility self-reliance through conservation measures and the expedited installation of renewable energy. In its 2011 plans, the DoD set a department-wide goal of reducing the energy intensity of its bases (that is, the energy use per square foot of facility space) by 37.5 percent in 2020 relative to 2003. At the same time, it decreed that 20 percent of all electricity consumed at those facilities by 2020 had to come from renewable energy sources.[42] Given that the DoD then owned some 202,000 buildings at 4,337 sites in the United States, occupying a total of 1.8 billion square feet, these initiatives represented an enormous commitment to energy efficiency and the installation of renewables at a time when other sectors of American society were moving at a much slower pace in reducing their carbon emissions.[43]

By the end of fiscal year 2015 (the most recent year for which comprehensive data is available), the Pentagon could report substantial progress in the achievement of its goals. All told, energy intensity at stateside DoD installations had fallen by 20 percent over 2003 levels, while the energy supplied by renewables had been increased by 12.4 percent. As a result of these and other efforts, net greenhouse gas emissions by the DoD had been reduced by 12 percent over 2003 levels—a decline much greater than that achieved by many other large organizations and the nation as a whole.[44]

Among the individual services, the Navy was farthest along in this drive to reduce reliance on fossil fuels, reflecting Secretary Mabus's zeal on this front. It had installed or placed contracts for over a gigawatt of renewable energy, enough to supply approximately 250,000 homes.[45] As part of this effort, in 2014 the Navy had signed an agreement with Sempra U.S. Gas and Power to supply fourteen California installations with 210 megawatts of electricity from a mammoth solar facility near Phoenix, Arizona, representing the largest purchase of renewable energy ever made by a federal entity. The Arizona plant, Mesquite Solar 3, went into operation in 2016 with a giant array of 650,000 photovoltaic panels.[46]

As the Navy charged ahead, the other services were proceeding with plans of their own. In 2012, both the Army and the Air Force announced that they each would install at least a gigawatt of renewable energy by 2025.[47] By 2016, the Army had installed 159 megawatts toward its goal, representing approximately 12 percent of its total facility electricity consumption, and had another 300 MW in the final stages of development. In 2017, it inaugurated its largest renewable project yet, a hybrid wind-solar system at Fort Hood, Texas, that is expected to supply about half of the base's power needs.[48] The Air Force was lagging a bit, with only 7 percent of its electricity obtained from renewables, but was moving swiftly to catch up with the other services.[49] Among the major projects being undertaken by that service in pursuit of its gigawatt objective are a 16.4 MW solar array at Davis-Monthan Air Force Base in Tucson, Arizona, and a 28 MW solar power project now under construction at Vandenberg Air Force Base, California.[50]

Alongside these ambitious efforts to embrace renewable energy, a parallel push in many instances has been to strive for "net zero" installations, or bases that produce as much energy on-site as they consume—thus making them entirely independent of the commercial grid and other external energy sources. This goal arose out of the notion of "islanding," or making military bases into self-reliant entities, an approach recommended by the Defense Science Board task force on energy in its 2008 report.[51] The islanding concept attracted considerable interest from senior commanders, who wanted to minimize their exposure to breakdowns in the commercial electrical grid while also speeding the transition to renewable energy. Secretary Mabus, for example, embraced this objective in his 2009 proclamation on energy reform. "By 2020," he declared, "we will make half of our installations net-zero energy consumers, using solar, wind, ocean, and geothermal power generated on base."[52]

The Army has pursued the "net zero" concept with particular enthusiasm, seeking to make its bases independent not only of external energy inputs but also of outside water supplies. "Net Zero is . . . operationally necessary, financially prudent, and mission essential," Army officials stated in 2011.[53] To launch their Net Zero drive, Army officials designated seventeen bases to serve as test sites, including Fort Bliss, Texas; Fort Carson, Colorado; Fort Riley, Kansas; and the U.S. Military Academy at West Point, New York. Commanders of all these facilities pledged to undertake a variety of measures aimed at reducing their dependence on external sources of energy and water.[54] By 2016, those endeavors were reported to have achieved considerable progress in reducing water and energy use and in installing renewable sources of energy at the selected sites, but were still far from achieving the ultimate goal of net zero. Nevertheless, the Army insisted that those pilot efforts would prove valuable as the service strives to convert *every one* of its bases to net zero status.[55]

Exactly how all these energy initiatives will proceed during the Trump era is unclear. The president and many of his top aides have certainly made no secret of their disbelief in—or disregard for—the science of climate change and have sought to impede any efforts to accelerate the installation of renewable energy. Nevertheless, many of the plans for such installations at major military installations are well advanced and are not likely to be reversed. Moreover, many senior officers and technical personnel have come to view energy reform as a contribution to organizational resiliency, and thus a boon to combat effectiveness. "To do something other than continue these programs would be a mistake," said Joe Bryan, the Navy's deputy assistant secretary for energy, in January 2017. "My expectation is that will be recognized no matter where people are on the political spectrum."[56]

## GIRDING FOR COMBAT IN A CLIMATE-ALTERED WORLD

Programs such as the Great Green Fleet and the Army's Net Zero initiative may reshape operations on American warships and at military bases, but they have relatively little impact on infantry battalions and other combat units deployed in foreign combat zones. Slowly but surely, however, senior leaders are coming to realize that they must also equip U.S. forces to survive and prevail on a climate-altered planet. In many of the places where American soldiers may be obliged to fight in the years ahead, local sources of water, food, and energy are likely to be scarce or nonexistent, requiring deployed troops to carry all such essentials with them. Global warming will add to this problem by further diminishing the availability of water and other critical resources in many areas of the world. Higher temperatures, prolonged heat waves, blinding sandstorms, and other climate impacts will add further challenges to soldiers in the field.

Preparing the armed forces for the climate-altered battlefields of the future was one of the principal objectives of the *Climate Change Adaptation Roadmaps* issued by the Department of Defense in recent years. As the planet warms, the 2014 edition indicated, many of the weapons and support systems carried by soldiers into battle will have to be modified or replaced to ensure their effective use under changing conditions. "Climate change impacts," that version noted, "may affect the supplies, equipment, vehicles, and weapons systems the Department buys, where and from whom we buy them, how they are transported and distributed, and how and where they are stockpiled and stored." The road map further indicated that global warming could mean "reduced or changed availability and access to food and water sources to support personnel" once deployed abroad. To address these potential dangers, the DoD and its component organizations were enjoined by the road map to integrate climate considerations into all future procurement decisions.[57]

In responding to these instructions, the individual services have, for the most part, tended to focus on modifications to their energy systems and stateside installations—where change can be implemented more swiftly and easily—rather than on the problems likely to hit frontline forces. Here and there, however, some DoD components have started working on the task of preparing for deployment on a climate-altered planet. For the most part, this has entailed the creation or designation of special units to test and refine tactics and equipment for employment in hotter, drier, and more resource-constrained conditions.

Perhaps unsurprisingly, the military service that has moved most vigorously in this direction is the Marine Corps. The smallest and lightest (in terms of reliance on heavy weapons) of the services, the Marines are often called upon for rapid engagement in what are called "expeditionary" operations: inserting military forces into the territory of a foreign country, whether invited or not, and sustaining them there independent of local facilities or resources.[58] Since the start of the twenty-first century, the Marines have repeatedly been called upon to perform such missions, and, under prevailing international conditions, are likely to receive more such calls in the future. Because of that, the Marine Corps is paying close attention to changes in the global environment and how these might affect tactics, training, and equipment. To jump-start this effort, in 2009 the commandant of the Marine Corps, General James F. Amos, established the Marine Corps Expeditionary Energy Office (E2O) and charged it with devising novel solutions to the energy and resource constraints the Marines will face on future battlefields.[59] (The E2O operation subsumed the Marines' ExFOB project described earlier and gave it a permanent identity.)

Two years after its formation, the E2O issued an *Initial Capabilities Document for USMC Expeditionary Energy, Water, and Waste,* describing how one branch of the U.S. military is preparing to deploy and fight in this new era. Future operations, it suggested, "are likely to occur in areas that present challenges due to distance, rough terrain, and climatic extremes," and that, in most cases, will lack "energy and water resources and infrastructure." In these harsh environments, the document stated, the Marines will be compelled to minimize their reliance on extended supply lines for energy and other basic commodities and to increase their capacity for generating vital resources on-site.[60] With this as a starting point, the *Initial Capabilities Document* called for multiple projects to develop technologies needed to field a self-sufficient expeditionary force for the deployments of the future. On its list of "task descriptions," energy autonomy was identified as the top priority: "Reduce the need for fuel resupply by harvesting the required energy, in place, from natural and man-made sources," it decreed. Water was also high on the list: "Produce potable and non-potable water on site. . . . These systems shall be energy efficient and where possible leverage renewable energy sources."[61]

To follow through on these and other tasks identified in the document, the Expeditionary Energy Office has collaborated with active-duty Marine units in conducting field tests of some of its innovative projects. In 2016, for example, the E2O conducted an Energy Capability Exercise at the Marines' Twentynine Palms combat training center in Southern California, showcasing an updated version of its GREENS solar array and other portable solar systems. A press release from the event noted that "the Marine Corps is striving to make itself leaner, meaner, and 'greener' as it takes a look at energy use across the Corps, equating the efficient use of vital resources with increased combat effectiveness."[62]

None of the other services have gone quite as far as the Marines in this direction, but all have made at least some forays toward it. In 2015, for example, the Department of the Army released its Energy Security and Sustainability (ES2) Strategy, intended to "foster a more adaptable and resilient force that is prepared for a future defined by complexity, uncertainty, and rapid change." Among the challenges Army forces will face in this future world, the strategy indicated, are "global resource constraints" and the effects of climate change. To prepare for these challenges, the Army must free itself from reliance on elaborate supply lines and learn to obtain vital resources on-site.[63]

In accordance with this vision, the Army is devising and testing a wide variety of systems intended for deployment on the resource-constrained battlefields of the future. One of its more novel experiments, now being developed at the Army's Natick Soldier Research, Development and Engineering Center, involves wearable energy-harvesting systems that allow soldiers on the march to power their radios or recharge batteries just by walking. The devices being tested include backpack solar panels and a "knee harvester" that collects kinetic energy from each stride. Such technologies have the potential to "fulfill a need for instant power generation on long-range missions when displaced from traditional resupply methods," said Sergeant Arthur H. Jones, an infantryman who participated in some of the tests.[64]

## COLLABORATION WITH ALLIES

From the very beginning of its engagement with climate change, the Department of Defense has proclaimed that efforts to address this challenge must encompass not only America's armed forces but also those of its friends and allies. This reflects the belief, so forcefully stated by Admiral Locklear in his 2013 appearance before the Senate Armed Services Committee, that America's security relies on the cooperation of key foreign partners and that many of these states are at severe risk from warming's punishing effects. From this perspective, it is therefore essential that the United States work with the militaries of those countries on building resilience to climate change and reducing their own reliance on fossil fuels.

The Pentagon's collaborative approach to overcoming warming's effects was first articulated in its *Quadrennial Defense Review* for 2010. "In some nations," it stated, "the military is the only institution with the capacity to respond to a large-scale natural disaster. Proactive engagement with these countries can help build their capability to respond to such events." Accordingly, it said, America's armed services have been conducting "environmental security cooperative initiatives" with foreign military organizations, aimed at sharing "best practices" for installation management and relief operations, among other activities.[65]

By 2015, such collaborative efforts were said to be well under way. In its report to Congress titled *National Security Implications of Climate-Related Risks and a Changing Climate*, the DoD noted that each of the geographic combatant commands had undertaken joint projects with allied militaries aimed at enhancing climate resiliency. "Although activities vary," it indicated, "all GCCs are working with partner nations to increase partner abilities to reduce risks and implications from environmental impacts and climate change, including severe weather and other hazards." Depending on the location, such efforts were said to include training in disaster management, the installation of emergency operations centers, and the construction of dams for hydroelectric power.[66]

Further details on these endeavors can be obtained from the annual posture statements provided by the GCC commanders to the House and Senate Committees. In 2015, for example, General John F. Kelly told the Senate Armed Services Committee that over the course of the previous year, Southcom had "funded the construction of 172 humanitarian projects in the region, building disaster relief warehouses, emergency operations centers, and emergency shelters."[67] Africom, for its part, has tended to emphasize preparedness for pandemics and other humanitarian disasters, given its experience with the Ebola epidemic of 2014–16 and its belief that climate change will engender more such calamities. In 2015, Africom helped establish the West Africa Disaster Preparedness Initiative in collaboration with Economic

Community of West African States (ECOWAS), the Kofi Annan International Peacekeeping Training Centre, and the Republic of Ghana National Disaster Management Organization. Under that program, each of the fifteen members of ECOWAS has received disaster preparedness training from Africom and partner organizations.[68]

Although public discussion of such collaborative endeavors has tended to be muted in recent years, reflecting the Trump administration's aversion to climate change discourse, it is evident that military leaders continue to uphold the importance of military-to-military (MIL-to-MIL) collaboration in tackling the challenges posed by global warming. In its 2019 *Report on Effects of a Changing Climate to the Department of Defense,* for example, the Pentagon informed Congress that "DoD is continuing to work with partner nations to understand and plan for future potential mission impacts" of planetary warming. This is "a global issue," it noted, and so "the department has funded cost-effective climate-related MIL-to-MIL engagements" between the combatant commands and partner militaries.[69]

Exactly what all the endeavors and experiments described in this chapter will lead to in the years ahead is impossible to predict. From all signs, though, the efforts are gathering momentum and beginning to make inroads into the institutional culture of the armed services. Even as President Trump and his senior advisers have sought to reverse many of the climate-related policies initiated by his predecessor, the armed services—driven by their own vision of what the future holds—are proceeding in their efforts to prepare for combat on a climate-altered world. And although these efforts, as indicated above, are primarily intended to enhance the services' combat effectiveness, many of the initiatives—ranging from the Great Green Fleet to the Marines' portable solar arrays—also result in reduced greenhouse gas emissions and so help slow down the onrush of climate change.[70]

As global temperatures soar and vital resources dwindle, the Pentagon's drive to enhance energy security and reduce its "logistics footprint" could provide a useful model for the rest of society to emulate as it struggles to prevent runaway climate change. Even if the efforts are motivated by other considerations, such as enhanced combat mobility, they represent a significant contribution to climate change mitigation. Given the immense size of the U.S. military establishment and its proven ability to embrace technological innovation, the Department of Defense is one of the few institutions in American society with the capacity to make a real difference in slowing the pace of warming.

Equally significant, perhaps, is the military's emphasis on collaborative efforts to overcome the damaging effects of global warming. As Admiral Locklear told Congress in 2013, U.S. national security relies on the cooperation of partner nations, and that can only be assured if those states are adequately defended against the future ravages of climate change—a task best undertaken when nations cooperate in overcoming warming's severe effects. This is the approach followed by the Obama administration when helping to negotiate the Paris Climate Agreement in December 2015, but which has largely been abandoned by the Trump White House since then. That the DoD continues to view climate change as a "global issue" and to advocate cooperative action in overcoming its harmful effects should be considered the starting point for America's future foreign relations.

# CONCLUSION

In January 2018, when the U.S. Department of Defense adopted a new National Defense Strategy, climate change was not identified as a significant threat to American security.

This was, of course, a moment when the nation's commander in chief was regularly expressing skepticism about the reality of global warming and was staffing key government agencies with officials who shared his views. Not keen to display outright defiance to the president, most military officers have chosen to abide by his preferences, and so have excluded talk of climate change and its disastrous effects from public discussion. This does not mean, however, that they are unaware of warming's threat to national and international security. Indeed, in late 2017, when the strategy document was being composed, many top military officers were still dealing with the aftermath of Hurricanes Harvey, Irma, and Maria. Though some pundits and politicians sought to disavow any link between the trio of devastating hurricanes and climate change, those closer to the scene were drawing an opposite conclusion: global warming is altering the planet in manifold ways, and the military will be called upon again and again to deal with the harsh and chaotic consequences.

The 2018 strategy document, composed by policy analysts in Washington, D.C., reflects the consensus military view that Russia and China will pose the greatest potential threat to U.S. security in the coming years. The military, it states, "acknowledges an increasingly complex global security environment," shaped in large part by "the re-emergence of long-term, strategic competition between nations." Few serving officers would question this as an overarching principle. But many also see a more complicated reality, in which climate change is undermining the capacity of some key allies to assist American forces in times of mutual peril and the U.S. homeland itself is under assault from multiple climate threats. Many weaker states, they fear, will collapse under the pressures of a changing climate and inadequate resources, leading to widespread chaos, conflict, and human dislocation. Some officers, moreover, foresee a time when extreme conditions will thoroughly disrupt relations among the major powers, possibly triggering new conflicts or turning allies one against the other.

In confronting the specter of global warming, American officers have come to understand how a wide range of climate effects will intrude upon and reshape their roles as military professionals. These begin with an increase in severe storms and humanitarian disasters, both at home and abroad, requiring their participation in emergency relief operations. Such operations, they recognize, will become ever more complex and challenging as global warming intersects with other factors—such as poverty, resource scarcity, ethnic animosity, and governmental corruption—to cause "complex emergencies," involving looting, pandemics, and social unrest. When, as is bound to occur, civil authorities collapse under such pressures, the armed forces will be obliged to maintain order and perform other functions of government. And these contingencies will arise not just one at a time, allowing the military to regroup between deployments, but increasingly in clusters (as with Harvey, Irma, and Maria), steadily eroding military readiness.

For many senior officers, these scenarios foreshadow a future of ever-increasing danger and disruption—what I have termed the climate ladder of escalation. On the lowest rungs of this ladder, involving occasional domestic and foreign emergency relief operations, the armed services are essentially lending some portion of their regular forces for temporary duty in a noncombat role before swiftly returning them to their original functions. At each higher rung, however, the demands on the services become more extensive and the risk of involvement in armed violence that much greater. As humanitarian aid missions turn into complex emergencies with dueling ethnic militias and a disintegrating government, any U.S. forces sent to the disaster site will have to be prepared to defend themselves along with the aid workers on the scene and possibly large parts of the population. As state failures spread and waves of desperate climate refugees pour across international borders—provoking yet more new bouts of violence—the military could face even more demanding and hazardous contingencies.

As temperatures continue to rise, moreover, entire new battlefields and conflict situations could emerge, drawing the armed forces farther up that ladder of escalation. The first locale where this might occur is the Arctic, where the prospect of a "whole new ocean" preoccupies the Navy. With the polar ice cap shrinking year by year, a vast seascape—once largely immune to human activity—is becoming accessible to ships of all sorts, including oil-drilling vessels and the warships of other nations, America's strategic competitors among them. The Arctic region is believed to harbor nearly one-third of the world's untapped oil and natural gas reserves—some located in disputed waters—and energy firms from many countries seek to reap this bounty. For the U.S. military, managing this situation will require the rehabilitation of bases originally constructed during the Cold War to guard against Soviet bombers and the establishment of new ones to oversee drilling operations and foreign naval activity. Similar challenges could arise elsewhere in the world where climate change has altered the landscape, generating fresh disputes over access to water supplies or other critical resources.

Ultimately, the U.S. military could face an "all hell breaking loose" scenario—a situation in which the armed forces are confronted with multiple warming-related crises abroad while the homeland itself is suffering from severe climate effects *and* many of the military's own facilities are immobilized by rising seas or other climate impacts. With governments collapsing in many areas of the world, global trading systems—for food, energy, and other vital commodities—will begin to break down, producing widespread chaos and flight. In this terrifying scenario, the military will be stretched far beyond its deployable capacity and senior commanders will be forced to make heart-wrenching decisions about which emergencies can be accorded attention and which will have to be ignored, at whatever cost in human life and the national interest.

An "all hell breaking loose" scenario would, no doubt, prove the American military's greatest nightmare. This is so not because senior officers fear injury or death in battle—they are fully prepared to face that risk in some future clash with China or Russia, if ordered to do so—but rather because they dread institutional collapse under the weight of multiple deployments in impossible conditions. American officers are loyal above all else to the unfailing integrity of the military services (which they view as the ultimate bulwark against America's adversaries), so anything that might undermine institutional integrity is perceived as an existential threat. Climate change, by multiplying the risks to world stability while placing the military itself in danger, constitutes just such a threat.

In recognition of this peril, the senior military leadership has taken numerous steps to prepare the armed services for the advent of climate change. This may not be apparent in the 2018 edition of the National Defense Strategy—hardly surprising, given the president's iconoclastic views on the matter—but it is evident throughout various DoD documents cited in this volume and in the testimony of senior officers. In fact, the military has devised a multifaceted, deeply ambitious strategy for addressing the challenges posed by climate change—a strategy well worth wider public appreciation. This strategy begins with a rigorous understanding of warming's deleterious impacts on human societies and how those effects are likely to exacerbate existing propensities for chaos and conflict. On this basis, it envisions constructive action on three crucial fronts: better preparing the military's own forces and installations to withstand the harsh impacts of climate change; reducing the DoD's reliance on carbon-emitting fossil fuels; and, not least, cooperating with the militaries of other nations in adopting similar measures.

To guide these efforts, the American military leadership has devised its own distinctive analysis of the climate change threat to U.S. and world security. In contrast to scientific and environmental assessments, which tend to begin with warming's threat to vulnerable wildlife and natural habitats, the military's analysis begins with the threat to human systems—both physical (energy infrastructure, medical facilities, communication and transportation networks) and organizational (governments, public services, community organizations). From this perspective, climate change presents its greatest harm not by hastening the extinction of endangered species but by decimating the vital systems upon which our communal life depends. When those systems fail, chaos and conflict ensue, triggering waves of human migrations and the violent resistance they often provoke. "Destruction and devastation from hurricanes can sow the seeds for instability," former secretary of defense Chuck Hagel once explained. "Droughts and crop failures can leave millions of people without any lifeline, and trigger waves of mass migration."[1]

With this analysis as a starting point, the U.S. military has focused its efforts on adapting to the effects of climate change and mitigating its consequences. These endeavors—spelled out in the Pentagon's *Climate Change Adaptation Handbooks* of 2012 and 2014 and in DoD Directive 4715.21, "Climate Change Adaptation and Resilience," from 2016—emphasize the protection of the military's own infrastructure against the ravages of climate change and the development of a climate-conscious institutional culture among combat forces, enabling them to better cope with future challenges. Every military installation and organization is directed to identify its vulnerabilities to extreme climate effects and to take whatever steps are deemed necessary to overcome those vulnerabilities. Similarly, all new weapons and equipment acquired by the armed services are to be designed to withstand climate extremes and to operate in a resource-constrained environment. At the same time, the services are instructed to reduce their own carbon footprint, both by increasing their reliance on renewable sources of electricity and by replacing petroleum-fueled vehicles with ones powered by alternative fuels. And, to better address these challenges on a global basis, the services are further enjoined to encourage the militaries of other countries to undertake comparable measures and to help them in their implementation.

While much of the material contained in the two Adaptation Handbooks and the 2016 directive (as well as in similar handbooks produced by the individual services) is specifically aimed at military facilities and organizations, it has obvious implications for nonmilitary communities. For example, military installations located in low-lying coastal regions have been instructed to locate new facilities away from flood-prone areas, to employ hurricane-proof construction methods, and to emplace critical equipment (such as electronics communications gear) on upper stories rather than lower—protocols that should be required for *all* new construction in these regions. Similarly, the Army's drive for "net zero" bases—facilities that draw all their energy and water from on-site sources—could be fruitfully emulated by towns and cities seeking to reduce their contribution to global warming and to guard against its harsh effects.

Equally insightful is the U.S. military's emphasis on cooperation with the militaries of friendly nations in addressing the perils of climate change. From the very beginning, senior officials have stressed the need to work with other countries in reducing their own climate change vulnerabilities, thereby enhancing regional and international stability.[2] In accordance with this precept, U.S. services have collaborated with foreign militaries in preparing for extreme events, for example, by stockpiling emergency relief supplies, conducting joint disaster relief drills, and helping to harden critical facilities. Although modest in comparison to what is actually needed to protect the world from warming's severe effects, these endeavors demonstrate a basic understanding that human survival at this perilous moment will require international collaboration of just this sort.

Senior officers may not say much about all this in public as long as their commander in chief scoffs at such talk—although even now, hints of this alternative outlook make their way into the public space from time to time. In April 2019, as this paragraph was being composed, the Air Force chief of staff, General David L. Goldfein, told the Senate Armed Services Committee, "We have to respond militarily very often to the effects, globally, of climate change."[3] At about the same time, General Thomas Waldhauser, commander of the U.S. Africa Command, told Mike Cerre of *PBS NewsHour* that "the climate and environment challenges on the continent really do start to contribute to security challenges."[4] In time, perhaps under a new administration, these voices will be heard more widely, and we will all benefit from these officers' valuable insights. Until then, hopefully, this book can provide a useful synthesis of the U.S. military's analysis of the consequences of climate change, and the measures it is taking to guard against those consequences and reduce their severity.

# NOTES

## INTRODUCTION

1. White House, "Presidential Executive Order on Promoting Energy Independence and Economic Growth," March 28, 2017, https://www.whitehouse.gov/presidential-actions/presidential-executive-order-promoting-energy-independence-economic-growth/.
2. U.S. Department of Defense (DoD), "DoD Directive 4715.21, Climate Change Adaptation and Resilience," January 14, 2016, https://dod.defense.gov/Portals/1/Documents/pubs/471521p.pdf.
3. See Tara Copp, "Pentagon Is Still Preparing for Global Warming Even Though Trump Said to Stop," *Military Times*, September 12, 2017, https://www.militarytimes.com/news/your-military/2017/09/12/pentagon-is-still-preparing-for-global-warming-even-though-trump-said-to-stop/; and Ben Wolfgang, "Despite Sea Change at White House, Pentagon Steps Up Climate Change Preparations," *Washington Times*, June 3, 2018, https://m.washingtontimes.com/news/2018/jun/3/pentagon-climate-change-plans-avoid-trump-politics/.
4. See Caitlin Werrell and Francesco Femia, "Chronology of U.S. Military Statements and Actions on Climate Change and Security: 2017–2018," Center for Climate and Security, October 2, 2018, https://

climateandsecurity.org/2018/10/02/chronology-of-u-s-military-statements-and-actions-on-climate-change-and-security-2017-2018/.

5. As cited in Caitlin Werrell and Francesco Femia, "Chairman of the Joint Chiefs: Climate Change a Source of Conflict Around the World," Center for Climate and Security, November 6, 2018, https://climateandsecurity.org/2018/11/06/chairman-of-the-joint-chiefs-climate-change-a-source-of-conflict-around-the-world/.
6. DoD, *National Defense Strategy of the United States of America* (Washington, D.C.: DoD, 2018).
7. On the question of risk and U.S. military planning, see John D. Steinbruner, Paul C. Stern, and Jo L. Husband, eds., *Climate and Social Stress: Implications for Security Analysis* (Washington, DC: National Research Council, National Academies Press, 2013), pp. 25–27.
8. As quoted in Margery A. Beck, Ellen Knickmeyer, and Robert Burns, "Floods Suggest National Security Threat from Climate Change," AP News, March 22, 2019, https://www.apnews.com/6d929a38194c4d10b4fc360dfc676b1f.
9. DoD, *Climate-Related Risk to DoD Infrastructure: Initial Vulnerability Assessment Survey*, January 2018, pp. 1–2, https://climateandsecurity.files.wordpress.com/2018/01/tab-b-slvas-report-1-24-2018.pdf.
10. Ibid., p. 7.
11. Reuters, "Climate Change Threatens Half of US Bases Worldwide, Pentagon Report Finds," *Guardian*, January 31, 2018, https://www.theguardian.com/us-news/2018/jan/31/climate-change-threatens-us-military-bases-pentagon.
12. As cited in Chris Mooney and Missy Ryan, "Pentagon Revised Obama-Era Report to Remove Risks from Climate Change," *Washington Post*, May 10, 2018, https://www.washingtonpost.com/news/energy-environment/wp/2018/05/10/pentagon-revised-obama-era-report-to-remove-risks-from-climate-change/.
13. See Tara Copp, "Dozens of Lawmakers Warn Defense Department: Don't Whitewash Climate Change Report," *Military Times*, July 25, 2018, https://www.militarytimes.com/news/your-military/2018/07/25/scores-of-lawmakers-warn-defense-department-dont-whitewash-climate-change-report/. The lawmakers' letter of July 16, 2018, can be accessed at https://partner-mco-archive.s3.amazonaws.com/client_files/1532536932.pdf.
14. See Umair Irfan, "Hurricane Michael Showed How Woefully Unprepared the Military Is for Extreme Weather," Vox, October 16, 2018, https://www.vox.com/2018/10/15/17978902/hurricane-michael-panama-city-tyndall-air-force-f22-climate-change; and Dave Philipps,

"Bulwark of Coastal Bases, Under Threat from More Menacing Storms," *New York Times*, October 18, 2018.

15. Norman Seip, "Our Military Bases Are Not Ready for Climate Change," *The Hill*, November 2, 2018, https://thehill.com/opinion/national-security/414540-our-military-bases-are-not-ready-for-climate-change.
16. Ibid.
17. DoD, *Report on Effects of a Changing Climate to the Department of Defense*, January 2019, https://media.defense.gov/2019/Jan/29/2002084200/-1/-1/1/CLIMATE-CHANGE-REPORT-2019.PDF.
18. See Copp, "Pentagon Is Still Preparing for Global Warming Even Though Trump Said to Stop."
19. Ibid.
20. DoD, *Climate-Related Risk to DoD Infrastructure*, pp. 3–6.
21. DoD, "Secretary of Defense Speech, Conference of Defense Ministers of the Americas," Arequipa, Peru, October 13, 2014, https://dod.defense.gov/News/Speeches/Speech-View/Article/605617/.

## 1. A WORLD BESIEGED

1. U.S. Senate, Committee on Armed Services (SASC), *Department of Defense Authorization of Appropriations for Fiscal Year 2014 and the Future Year's Defense Program*, April 9, 2013, p. 422, https://www.armed-services.senate.gov/imo/media/doc/pacom_fullcomm_hearing_040913.pdf.
2. Ibid., p. 434.
3. Ibid., pp. 440–43.
4. Ibid., p. 435.
5. Ibid.
6. Ibid., pp. 435–36.
7. Ibid., p. 436.
8. CNA Corporation (CNA), *National Security and the Threat of Climate Change* (Alexandria, VA: CNA, 2007), p. 6.
9. Ibid., p. 9.
10. Ibid., p. 3.
11. Ibid., p. 44.
12. Ibid., pp. 7, 37.
13. National Intelligence Council (NIC), *National Intelligence Assessment on the National Security Implications of Global Climate Change to 2030*, Statement for the Record of Dr. Thomas Fingar before the House Permanent Select Committee on Intelligence and House Select Committee on Energy Independence and Global Warming, June 25, 2008, pp. 4–5, https://fas.org/irp/congress/2008_hr/062508fingar.pdf.

14. DoD, *Quadrennial Defense Review Report*, February 2010 (Washington, DC: DoD, 2010), p. 85.
15. DoD, *Department of Defense 2014 Climate Change Adaptation Roadmap* (Washington, DC: DoD, 2014), p. 1.
16. White House, *National Security Strategy*, February 2015, p. 12, https://obamawhitehouse.archives.gov/sites/default/files/docs/2015_national_security_strategy_2.pdf.
17. John F. Kelly, "Posture Statement of General John F. Kelly, United States Marine Corps, Commander, United States Southern Command, Before the Senate Armed Services Committee," March 13, 2014, Washington, D.C., pp. 29–30, https://www.armed-services.senate.gov/imo/media/doc/Kelly_03-13-14.pdf.
18. "Statement of General Thomas D. Waldhauser, United States Marine Corps, Commander, United States Africa Command, Before the Senate Committee on Armed Services," February 7, 2019, https://www.armed-services.senate.gov/imo/media/doc/Waldhauser_02-07-19.pdf.
19. U.S. Department of Defense (DoD), *National Security Implications of Climate-Related Risks and a Changing Climate*, May 27, 2015, pp. 7–8, http://archive.defense.gov/pubs/150724-congressional-report-on-national-implications-of-climate-change.pdf.
20. Ibid., p. 8.
21. Ibid.
22. Ibid., p. 7.
23. Ibid., pp. 4–5.
24. Ibid., p. 14.
25. DoD, *Report on Effects of a Changing Climate to the Department of Defense*, p. 15.
26. Intergovernmental Panel on Climate Change (IPCC), *Global Warming of 1.5°C*, Summary for Policymakers (Geneva, Switzerland: IPCC, 2018).
27. DoD, *National Security Implications of Climate-Related Risks*, pp. 4–5.
28. Statement of Rear Admiral David W. Titley before the House Budget Committee on the Costs of Climate Change, July 24, 2019, https://budget.house.gov/sites/democrats.budget.gov/files/documents/Titley_Testimony.
29. See, for example, Steinbruner et al., *Climate and Social Stress*, pp. 121, 135.
30. These risks are thoroughly addressed in USGCRP, *Fourth National Climate Assessment*.
31. DoD, *National Security Implications of Climate-Related Risks*, p. 4.
32. See Jeffrey Lewis, "Yoda Has Left the Building," *Foreign Policy*, October 24, 2014, https://foreignpolicy.com/2014/10/24/yoda-has-left-the-building/.

33. Peter Schwartz and Doug Randall, "An Abrupt Climate Change Scenario and Its Implications for United States National Security," October 2003, https://eesc.columbia.edu/courses/v1003/readings/Pentagon.pdf.
34. Steinbruner et al., *Climate and Social Stress*, p. 73.
35. See DoD, *Report on Effects of a Changing Climate to the Department of Defense.*
36. DoD, *2014 Climate Change Adaptation Roadmap*, foreword.

## 2. HUMANITARIAN EMERGENCIES

1. Thomas Parker, Sean P. Carroll, Gregg Sanders, Jason E. King, and Imes Chiu, "The U.S. Pacific Command Response to Super Typhoon Haiyan," *Joint Force Quarterly*, no. 82 (3rd quarter, July 2016), p. 55.
2. On Tacloban's exposure to storm surge, see "Tacloban: City at the Centre of the Storm," BBC News, November 12, 2013, http://www.bbc.com/news/world-asia-24891456. See also Keith Bradsher, "Philippines Remains Haunted by the Chaos of a Devastating Storm in 2013," *New York Times*, September 15, 2018.
3. See Keith Bradsher, "Struggle for Survival in City Shattered by Typhoon," *New York Times*, November 12, 2013; and Andrew R. C. Marshall and Stuart Grudgings, "Desperate Philippine Typhoon Survivors Loot, Dig Up Water Pipes," Reuters, November 12, 2013, http://www.reuters.com/article/uk-philippines-typhoon-idUKBRE9A70I120131113.
4. As quoted in Paula Hancocks, Ivan Watson, and Matt Smith, "Typhoon Haiyan Leaves 1,774 Dead, 'Hideous' Destruction," CNN, November 11, 2013, http://www.cnn.com/2013/11/11/world/asia/typhoon-haiyan/.
5. Kate Hodal, "Typhoon Haiyan: Survival, Loss, and Humanity in Obliterated City of Tacloban," *Guardian*, November 11, 2013, https://www.theguardian.com/world/2013/nov/11/typhoon-haiyan-city-tacloban1.
6. See Keith Bradsher, "At a Hospital, Survivors Face Quiet Despair," *New York Times*, November 14, 2013; and Bradsher, "Death After the Typhoon: 'It Was Preventable,'" *New York Times*, November 16, 2013.
7. As quoted in Marshall and Grudgings, "Desperate Philippine Typhoon Survivors Loot." On the looting, see also Bradsher, "Philippines Remains Haunted by the Chaos of a Devastating Storm in 2013."
8. See Tania Branigan and Kate Hodal, "Typhoon Haiyan: Frustration at Slow Pace of Relief Effort," *Guardian*, November 15, 2013, https://www.theguardian.com/world/2013/nov/14/typhoon-haiyan-relief-effort-stalls-philippines.

9. Ibid. See also Andrew Jacobs, "Philippines' President Faces Growing Anger," *New York Times*, November 14, 2013; and Joyce Pangco Panares, "Govt Slow Response Hit," *Manila Standard*, November 14, 2013, http://manilastandard.net/news/headlines/133454/govt-slow-response-hit.html.
10. "Curfew, Armored Vehicles in Tacloban," Agence France-Presse, November 12, 2013, http://www.rappler.com/nation/43516-curfew-armored-vehicles-tacloban.
11. As quoted in Panares, "Govt Slow Response Hit."
12. U.S. Agency for International Development (AID), "President Obama Speaks on Typhoon Haiyan," November 14, 2013, https://www.usaid.gov/news-information/videos/president-obama-speaks-typhoon-haiyan.
13. Tyrone C. Marshall Jr., "Pentagon Acts Swiftly to Assist Typhoon-Stricken Ally," American Forces Press Service, November 12, 2013, http://www.public.navy.mil/surfor/Pages/PentagonActsSwiftlytoAssistTyphoon-strickenAlly.aspx.
14. U.S. Department of the Navy, "Joint Task Force 505 Activates for Operation Damayan," JTF 505 News Release, November 18, 2013, http://www.navy.mil/submit/display.asp?story_id=77735.
15. Parker et al., "The U.S. Pacific Command Response to Super Typhoon Haiyan," p. 54.
16. See Andrew Jacobs, "Typhoon Response Highlights Weaknesses in Philippine Military," *New York Times*, November 20, 2013.
17. Parker et al., "The U.S. Pacific Command Response to Super Typhoon Haiyan," p. 54.
18. As cited in *The Age of Consequences* (2017), a film by Jared P. Scott, from the official film transcript, p. 14.
19. IPCC, *Climate Change 2014: Impacts, Adaptation and Vulnerability, Part A: Global and Sectoral Aspects*, Report of Working Group II (New York: Cambridge University Press, 2014), p. 370.
20. As cited in John Vidal and Damian Carrington, "Is Climate Change to Blame for Typhoon Haiyan?," *Guardian*, November 13, 2013, https://www.theguardian.com/world/2013/nov/12/typhoon-haiyan-climate-change-blame-philippines.
21. Lijing Cheng, John Abraham, Zeke Hausfather, and Kevin E. Trenberth, "How Fast Are the Oceans Warming?," *Science*, vol. 363, no. 6423 (January 11, 2019), pp. 128–29.
22. As quoted in Elfy Scott, "The Ocean Is Warming Much Faster Than We Thought, According to a New Study," BuzzFeed News, January 10, 2019, https://www.buzzfeed.com/elfyscott/the-ocean-is-warming-much-faster-than-we-thought-according.

23. IPCC, *Climate Change 2014: Impacts, Adaptation and Vulnerability,* Part A, p. 372.
24. Ibid., p. 373.
25. Ibid., pp. 368–69.
26. Robert M. DeConto and David Pollard, "Contribution of Antarctica to Past and Future Sea-Level Rise," *Nature*, vol. 531 (March 31, 2016), pp. 591–97.
27. U.S. IndoPacific Command, "Atlantic Council Roundtable," with Admiral Samuel J. Locklear III, March 6, 2014, https://www.pacom.mil/Media/Speeches-Testimony/Article/565158/atlantic-council-roundtable/.
28. As quoted in John Conger, "Commander of US Forces in the Indo-Asia Pacific Affirms Climate Change Threat," Center for Climate and Security, February 14, 2019, https://climateandsecurity.org/2019/02/14/commander-of-us-forces-in-the-indo-asia-pacific-affirms-climate-change-threat/. On Super-Typhoon Yutu and U.S. relief operations in the Marianas, see "Typhoon Relief Efforts Continue on Tinian and Saipan," Marine Executive, November 9, 2018, https://www.maritime-executive.com/article/typhoon-relief-efforts-continue-on-tinian-and-saipan.
29. U.S. Indo-Pacific Command, "Atlantic Council Roundtable," March 6, 2014.
30. See IPCC, *Global Warming of 1.5°C*, esp. chap. 3.
31. IPCC, *Climate Change 2014: Impacts, Adaptation and Vulnerability*, Part A, pp. 709–54.
32. IPCC, *Climate Change 2014: Impacts, Adaptation and Vulnerability*, Part B, pp. 1524–26, 1623–29.
33. CNA, *National Security and the Threat of Climate Change*, p. 34.
34. See Michael Le Page, "Hurricane Irma's Epic Size Is Being Fueled by Global Warming," *New Scientist*, September 6, 2017, https://www.newscientist.com/article/2146562-hurricane-irmas-epic-size-is-being-fuelled-by-global-warming/.
35. For a roundup of Irma's impacts on these and other islands, see Claire Phipps, "Irma's Destruction: Island by Island," *Guardian*, September 10, 2017, https://www.theguardian.com/world/2017/sep/07/irma-destruction-island-by-island-hurricane.
36. As quoted in Lisa Friedman, "As Another Storm Churns On, Islands Already Hurting Seek Aid at U.N.," *New York Times*, September 20, 2017.
37. Terri Moon Cronk, "Southcom Commander: Military Hurricane Assistance Fast, Flexible," Department of Defense, Defense Media Activity, September 21, 2017, http://www.southcom.mil/MEDIA/NEWS

-ARTICLES/Article/1320668/southcom-commander-military-hurricane-assistance-fast-flexible/.

38. U.S. Southern Command (Southcom), "Joint Task Force Completes Support to Relief Mission in Caribbean," Southcom, October 5, 2017, http://www.southcom.mil/News/PressReleases/Article/1335971/release-joint-task-force-completes-support-to-relief-mission-in-caribbean/.
39. CNA, *National Security and the Threat of Climate Change*, p. 22.
40. DoD, *National Security Implications of Climate-Related Risks*.
41. Ibid.
42. Ibid.
43. "Statement of General Thomas D. Waldhauser," February 7, 2019.
44. IPCC, *Climate Change 2014: Impacts, Adaptation and Vulnerability*, Part B, pp. 1222–25.
45. U.S. Africa Command Public Affairs, "U.S. Africa Commander's 2018 Posture Testimony to the House Armed Services Committee," March 7, 2018, https://www.africom.mil/media-room/transcript/30469/gen-thomas-d-waldhauser-at-hasc-hearing-on-national-security-challenges-and-u-s-military-activities.
46. See Norimitsu Onishi and Jeffrey Moyo, "'90 Percent' of City Lost after a Cyclone in Africa," *New York Times*, March 19, 2019; and Onishi, "Whipped by Wind, Buried by Floods," *New York Times*, March 21, 2019.
47. Nicholas Scott, "CJTF-HOA Sends Disaster Relief to Mozambique," U.S. Africa Command, March 28, 2019, https://www.hoa.africom.mil/story/22618/cjtf-hoa-sends-disaster-relief-to-mozambique.
48. DoD, *National Security Implications of Climate-Related Risks*, p. 8.
49. For discussion, see Bert B. Tussing, "The Role of the Military in Civil Support," in Carolyn Pumphrey, ed., *Global Climate Change: National Security Implications* (Carlisle, PA: Strategic Studies Institute, U.S. Army War College, 2008), pp. 347–53.
50. See "Amphibious Ships Replace USS George Washington in Philippines," DoD News, November 22, 2013, http://archive.defense.gov/news/newsarticle.aspx?id=121216.
51. IPCC, *Climate Change 2014: Impacts, Adaptation and Vulnerability*, Part A, pp. 372–73, 776–77.
52. Steinbruner et al., *Climate and Social Stress*, pp. 87–91.
53. "Maoist Rebels Extend Truce in Philippine Disaster Areas," Reuters, November 24, 2013, https://www.reuters.com/article/us-philippines-typhoon-rebels/maoist-rebels-extend-truce-in-philippine-disaster-areas-idUSBRE9AN03Z20131124.
54. DoD, *National Security Implications of Climate-Related Risks*, p. 8.

55. See Azam Ahmed and Kirk Semple, "A Devastated Island's Cry: 'All the Food Is Gone,'" *New York Times*, September 11, 2017.
56. CNA, *National Security and the Threat of Climate Change*, p. 22.
57. John Podesta and Peter Ogden, "The Security Implications of Climate Change," *Washington Quarterly*, vol. 31, no. 1 (Winter 2007–08), p. 133.
58. As quoted in Cronk, "Southcom Commander: Military Hurricane Assistance Fast, Flexible."
59. Podesta and Ogden, "The Security Implications of Climate Change," p. 132.
60. See Michael E. Mann, "The Weather Amplifier," *Scientific American*, March 2019, pp. 43–49.
61. Steinbruner et al., *Climate and Social Stress*, pp. 68–70, 73.
62. Ibid, p. 68.
63. NIC, *National Intelligence Assessment on the National Security Implications of Global Climate Change to 2030*, p. 16.

### 3. STATES ON THE BRINK

1. For background on the conflict in Mali, see International Crisis Group (ICG), *Mali: Avoiding Escalation*, Africa Report no. 189, July 18, 2012, https://d2071andvip0wj.cloudfront.net/189-mali-avoiding-escalation.pdf. See also Dona J. Stewart, *What Is Next for Mali: The Roots of Conflict and Challenges to Stability* (Carlisle, PA: Army War College Press, 2013).
2. Reuters, "Islamist Militants in Mali Continue to Destroy Centuries-Old Shrines of Sufi Saints," *New York Times*, July 2, 2012.
3. ICG, *Mali: Avoiding Escalation*, pp. 10–17.
4. Ibid., pp. 18–23. See also Adam Nossiter, "Soldiers Overthrow Mali Government in Setback for Democracy in Africa," *New York Times*, March 23, 2012.
5. Alexis Arieff, *Crisis in Mali*, Congressional Research Service (CRS), CRS Report to Congress, R42664 (Washington, DC: CRS, January 14, 2013), https://www.fas.org/sgp/crs/row/R42664.pdf. On U.S. involvement in the conflict, see Mark Mazzetti and Eric Schmitt, "Mali Militants: U.S. Confronts a Hazy Threat," *New York Times*, January 17, 2013.
6. See Jean-Hervé Jezequel, "Mali's Peace Deal Represents a Welcome Development, But Will It Work This Time?," *Guardian*, July 1, 2015, https://www.theguardian.com/global-development/2015/jul/01/mali-peace-deal-a-welcome-development-but-will-it-work-this-time.
7. See, for example, Sewell Chan, "Three United Nations Soldiers Are Killed in a Northern Mali Peacekeeping Mission," *New York Times*, November 25, 2017.

8. See Eric Schmitt, "With U.S. Help, France Expands Fight Against Terrorism in Africa," *New York Times*, May 13, 2017; and Schmitt, "Deep in the Desert, a Murky U.S. War Ramps Up," *New York Times*, April 22, 2018.
9. For background on this incident, see Rukmini Callimachi et al., "A Risky Patrol, an Ambush and New Agony over 'an Endless War,'" *New York Times*, February 18, 2018.
10. For discussion, see Arieff, *Crisis in Mali*.
11. Stewart, *What Is Next for Mali*, pp. 28–29.
12. U.S. Africa Command (Africom), Media Room, "U.S. Africa Commander's 2018 Posture Testimony to the House Armed Services Committee," March 7, 2018, http://www.africom.mil/media-room/transcript/30469/.
13. ICG, *Mali: Avoiding Escalation*, pp. 7–11.
14. CNA, *National Security and the Accelerating Risks of Climate Change* (Alexandria, VA: CNA, 2014), p. 13.
15. Ibid.
16. Tussing, "The Role of the Military in Civil Support," p. 353.
17. CNA, *National Security and the Threat of Climate Change*, pp. 6, 24.
18. Ibid., p. 31.
19. U.S. Joint Forces Command (USJFCOM), *The Joint Operating Environment 2010* (Suffolk, VA: USJFCOM, 2010), foreword, https://fas.org/man/eprint/joe2010.pdf.
20. Ibid., pp. 50–52.
21. "Statement of General Thomas D. Waldhauser," February 7, 2019.
22. NIC, *National Intelligence Assessment on the National Security Implications of Global Climate Change to 2030*, pp. 4–5.
23. Ibid., pp. 5, 8–9.
24. Office of the Director of National Intelligence (ODNI), *Global Water Security*, Intelligence Community Assessment, ICA 2012-08, February 2, 2012, https://www.dni.gov/files/documents/Special%20Report_ICA%20Global%20Water%20Security.pdf.
25. Ibid., pp. 1–2.
26. Ibid., p. 3.
27. CNA, *The Role of Water Stress in Instability and Conflict* (Alexandria, VA: CNA, 2017), pp. 15–28.
28. See "Riots, Instability Spread as Food Prices Skyrocket," CNN, April 14, 2008, http://www.cnn.com/2008/WORLD/americas/04/14/world.food.crisis/.
29. ODNI, *Global Food Security*, Intelligence Community Assessment, ICA 2015-04, September 2015, pp. 1–5, https://www.dni.gov/files

/documents/Newsroom/Reports%20and%20Pubs/Global_Food_Security_ICA.pdf.

30. Ibid., p. 9. For background on land-grabbing, see Klare, *The Race for What's Left* (New York: Metropolitan Books, 2012), pp. 183–208.
31. DoD, "National Security Implications of Climate-Related Risks and a Changing Climate," pp. 3–4.
32. For discussion on these risks, see Stephen P. Cohen, "The U.S.-Pakistan Strategic Relationship and Nuclear Safety/Security," Brookings Institution, June 12, 2008, https://www.brookings.edu/testimonies/the-u-s-pakistan-strategic-relationship-and-nuclear-safetysecurity/. See also Shaun Gregory, "The Terrorist Threat to Pakistan's Nuclear Weapons," *CTC Sentinel*, Combating Terrorism Center at West Point, July 2009, https://ctc.usma.edu/the-terrorist-threat-to-pakistans-nuclear-weapons/.
33. For background, see K. Alan Kronstadt, *Pakistan-U.S. Relations: Issues for the 114th Congress* (Washington, DC: Congressional Research Service, May 14, 2015). See also Richard Haass, *A World in Disarray* (New York: Penguin Books, 2017), pp. 128–30, 183–85. Some of this aid was suspended in 2018 by President Trump, who claimed the Pakistanis were not doing enough to curb Taliban forces based in areas along the Pakistan-Afghanistan border. See Mujib Marshal and Salman Masood, "U.S. Cuts Off Pakistan, Gambling in Afghan War," *New York Times*, January 6, 2018.
34. Steinbruner et al., *Climate and Social Stress*, p. 122. The NRC's *Climate and Social Stress* report uses the same terminology—"countries of security concern"—as the IC assessments cited in this chapter. Unlike the ICAs, though, the NRC report identifies several countries by name that would plausibly fall into this category, devoting particular attention to Pakistan.
35. Ibid., pp. 122–23.
36. See IPCC, *Climate Change 2014*, Report of Working Group II, Part A, p. 243.
37. Steinbruner et al., *Climate and Social Stress*, pp. 123–25.
38. See "Pakistan: Tales of Self-Harm," *Economist*, January 12, 2019, pp. 17–19.
39. Jeffrey Goldberg and Marc Ambinder, "The Pentagon's Secret Plans to Secure Pakistan's Nuclear Arsenal," Nuclear Threat Initiative, November 9, 2011, https://www.nti.org/gsn/article/the-pentagons-secret-plans-to-secure-pakistans-nuclear-arsenal/.
40. BP, *Statistical Review of World Energy, June 2019* (London: BP, 2019), pp. 14, 16.

41. For background, see Lauren Ploch Blanchard and Tomas F. Husted, *Nigeria: Current Issues and U.S. Policy* (Washington, DC: Congressional Research Service, March 11, 2016).
42. Ahmad Salkida, "Africa's Vanishing Lake Chad," Africa Renewal Online, April 2012, https://www.un.org/africarenewal/magazine/april-2012/africa%E2%80%99s-vanishing-lake-chad.
43. CNA, *The Role of Water Stress in Instability and Conflict*, pp. 32–33.
44. See Paul Carsten and Ahmed Kingimi, "Islamic State Ally Stakes Out Territory Around Lake Chad," Reuters, April 29, 2018, https://www.reuters.com/article/us-nigeria-security/islamic-state-ally-stakes-out-territory-around-lake-chad-idUSKBN1I0063.
45. Emmanuel Akinwotu, "In Nigeria, a Deadly Competition for Land and Water Widens Divisions," *New York Times*, June 26, 2018.
46. ICG, *Herders Against Farmers: Nigeria's Expanding Deadly Conflict*, Report no. 252, September 19, 2017, https://www.crisisgroup.org/africa/west-africa/nigeria/252-herders-against-farmers-nigerias-expanding-deadly-conflict.
47. Ibid. See also Akinwotu, "In Nigeria, a Deadly Competition for Land and Water Widens Divisions."
48. See Aryn Baker, "Nigeria's Military Quails When Faced with Boko Haram," *Time*, February 10, 2015, https://time.com/3702849/nigeriasarmy-boko-haram.
49. See Dionne Searcey, "Nigerians Fed Up Waiting for 'Fruit' Brace for Election Day," *New York Times*, February 15, 2019; and Searcey and Emmanuel Akinwotu, "For Nigeria's Voters, Fighting Boko Haram Outweighs Graft," *New York Times*, February 12, 2019.
50. Blanchard and Husted, *Nigeria: Current Issues and U.S. Policy*, pp. 21–22.
51. See Meghann Myers, "Army Troops, Special Forces Train Nigerian Infantry for Fight Against Boko Haram, ISIS," *Army Times*, February 23, 2018, https://www.armytimes.com/news/your-army/2018/02/23/special-forces-troops-train-nigerian-infantry-for-fight-against-boko-haram-isis/.
52. BP, *Statistical Review of World Energy, June 2019*, pp. 14, 16.
53. For background, see Christopher M. Blanchard, *Saudi Arabia: Background and U.S. Relations*, CRS Report to Congress, RL33533 (Washington, DC: CRS, September 21, 2018), https://fas.org/sgp/crs/mideast/RL33533.pdf.
54. Catherine A. Theohary, *Conventional Arms Transfers to Developing Nations, 2008–2015*, CRS Report to Congress, R44716 (Washington, DC: CRS, December 19, 2016), Table 11, p. 36, https://fas.org/sgp/crs/weapons/R44716.pdf.

55. See Julie Hirschfeld Davis, "For Prince and President, Many Issues on the Table," *New York Times*, March 15, 2017; and Ben Hubbard and Thomas Erdbrink, "Siding with the Saudis," *New York Times*, May 22, 2017.
56. See Hazel Sheffield, "Saudi Arabia Is Running Out of Water," *Independent*, February 19, 2016, https://www.independent.co.uk/news/business/news/saudi-arabia-is-running-out-of-water-a6883706.html.
57. On the Saudis' land-grabbing activities, see Klare, *The Race for What's Left*, pp. 183–89.
58. For background, see Blanchard, *Saudi Arabia: Background and U.S. Relations*, pp. 4–12.
59. James A. Russell, "Saudi Arabia: The Strategic Dimensions of Environmental Insecurity," *Middle East Policy*, vol. 23, no. 2 (Summer 2016), p. 44.
60. "Climate Change in the Arab World: Too Hot to Handle," *Economist*, June 2, 2018, pp. 43–44.
61. Jeremy S. Pal and Elfatih A. B. Eltahir, "Future Temperature in Southwest Asia Projected to Exceed a Threshold for Human Adaptability," *Nature Climate Change*, letter, published October 26, 2015, vol. 6 (2016), pp. 197–200.
62. As quoted in Damian Carrington, "Extreme Heatwaves Could Push Gulf Climate Beyond Human Endurance, Study Shows," *Guardian*, October 25, 2015, https://www.theguardian.com/environment/2015/oct/26/extreme-heatwaves-could-push-gulf-climate-beyond-human-endurance-study-shows.
63. Ibid.
64. See Nicholas Kulish and David D. Kirkpatrick, "Arrests Reveal Blending of Kin and Kingdom," *New York Times*, November 8, 2017.
65. See Mark Mazzetti and Ben Hubbard, "Saudi Prince Ran Brutal Campaign to Stifle Dissent," *New York Times*, March 18, 2019.
66. As quoted in Stephen Weisman, "Reagan Says U.S. Would Bar a Takeover in Saudi Arabia That Imperiled Flow of Oil," *New York Times*, October 2, 1981.
67. For background on these events, see Klare, *Blood and Oil* (New York: Metropolitan Books, 2005), pp. 45–55.
68. DoD, *National Security Implications of Climate-Related Risks*, p. 6.

### 4. GLOBAL SHOCK WAVES

1. Andrew E. Kramer and Kevin Drew, "Wildfires Ravaging Heat-Seared Russia," *New York Times*, August 7, 2010.

2. James Brooke, "Russia Wildfires Rage Amid Record Heat," VOA News, August 2, 2010, http://www.voanews.com/a/russia-wildfires-rage-amid-record-heat-99850004/123211.html.
3. Ariana Eunjung Cha and Janine Zacharia, "Russia Bans Grain Exports Because of Fire and Drought, Sending Prices Soaring," *Washington Post*, August 6, 2010.
4. As quoted in Brooke, "Russia Wildfires Rage Amid Record Heat."
5. "Russia to Impose Temporary Ban on Grain Exports," BBC News, August 5, 2010, http://www.bbc.com/news/business-10879138.
6. Andrew E. Kramer, "Russia, Crippled by Drought, Bans Export of Grain," *New York Times*, August 6, 2010.
7. See Damien McElroy, "Russian Heatwave Kills 5,000 as Fires Rage out of Control," *Telegraph*, August 6, 2010, http://www.telegraph.co.uk/news/worldnews/europe/russia/7931206/Russian-heatwave-kills-5000-as-fires-rage-out-of-control.html.
8. James Hansen, Makiko Sato, and Reto Ruedy, "Perceptions of Climate Change," *PNAS Plus* (Web), March 29, 2012, http://www.pnas.org/content/109/37/E2415.full.pdf.
9. Cha and Zacharia, "Russia Bans Grain Exports Because of Fire and Drought."
10. See Adam B. Ellick, "Pakistan Floods Bring on Fears of Lasting Toll," *New York Times*, August 17, 2010.
11. See Troy Sternberg, "Chinese Drought, Bread, and the Arab Spring," *Applied Geography*, vol. 34 (May 2012), pp. 519–24, https://www.sciencedirect.com/science/article/abs/pii/S0143622812000161.
12. See "Riots in Mozambique: The Angry Poor," *Economist*, September 9, 2010, https://www.economist.com/middle-east-and-africa/2010/09/09/the-angry-poor.
13. World Bank, *Improving Food Security in Arab Countries* (Washington, DC: World Bank, 2009), p. xi.
14. Liam Pleven and Matt Bradley, "Mideast Staggered by Cost of Wheat," *Wall Street Journal*, May 19, 2011.
15. See Sarah Johnstone and Jeffrey Mazo, "Global Warming and the Arab Spring," in Caitlin E. Werrell and Francesco Femia, *The Arab Spring and Climate Change* (Washington, DC: Center for American Progress, February 2013), pp. 15–22.
16. Ibid., p. 18.
17. For discussion of these events, see Haass, *A World in Disarray*, pp. 155–77.
18. NIC, *NIA on the National Security Implications of Climate Change to 2030*, p. 7.
19. Steinbruner et al., *Climate and Social Stress*, pp. 71–72.
20. Ibid., pp. 76–87.

21. Ibid., pp. 37–39.
22. Ibid., pp. 68–70.
23. On the impacts of climate change on global food supplies, see IPCC, *Climate Change 2014*, Report of Working Group II, Part A, pp. 485–534.
24. Steinbruner et al., *Climate and Social Stress*, pp. 76–78.
25. Ibid., p. 45.
26. NIC, *Global Food Security*, pp. 2–3.
27. Ibid., p. i.
28. ODNI, "Worldwide Threat Assessment of the U.S. Intelligence Community," Statement for the Record, February 13, 2018, https://www.dni.gov/files/documents/Newsroom/Testimonies/2018---ATA–Unclassified-SSCI.pdf.
29. BP, *Statistical Review of World Energy, June 2019*, pp. 16, 20. Projections from International Energy Agency (IEA), *World Energy Outlook 2017* (Paris: IEA, 2017), pp. 163, 186.
30. BP, *Statistical Review of World Energy, June 2019*, p. 20.
31. Ibid., pp. 16, 29, 34, 38.
32. For background, see Daniel Yergin, *The Prize: The Epic Quest for Oil, Money, and Power* (New York: Simon and Schuster, 1991), pp. 588–646, 676–714; and Michael Palmer, *Guardians of the Gulf* (New York: Free Press, 1992), pp. 99–111.
33. Jimmy Carter, State of the Union Address, Washington, D.C., January 23, 1980, https://www.jimmycarterlibrary.gov/assets/documents/speeches/su80jec.phtml.
34. See Palmer, *Guardians of the Gulf*, pp. 112–92.
35. See annual posture statement of the commander, U.S. Central Command, https://www.centcom.mil/MEDIA/Transcripts/.
36. For discussion of these impacts, see IPCC, *Climate Change 2014*, Report of Working Group II, Part A, pp. 664–72. See also U.S. Department of Energy (DoE), *U.S. Energy Sector Vulnerabilities to Climate Change and Extreme Weather* (Washington, DC: DoE, 2013).
37. Steinbruner et al., *Climate and Social Stress*, pp. 78–80.
38. Ibid., p. 79.
39. DoE, *U.S. Energy Sector Vulnerabilities to Climate Change and Extreme Weather*, p. 6.
40. Steinbruner et al., *Climate and Social Stress*, pp. 79–80.
41. UN Environment Programme (UNEP), "Impacts of Summer 2003 Heat Wave in Europe," Environment Alert Bulletin, GRID-Europe, March 2004, http://www.unisdr.org/files/1145_ewheatwave.en.pdf.
42. Steinbruner et al., *Climate and Social Stress*, p. 80.
43. Andrew K. Githeko, Steve W. Lindsay, Ulisses E. Confalonieri, and Jonathan A. Patz, "Climate Change and Vector-Borne Diseases: A

Regional Analysis," *Bulletin of the World Health Organization*, vol. 78, no. 9 (January 2000), pp. 1136–47.

44. M. Pascual, J. A. Ahumada, L. F. Chaves, X. Rodó, and M. Bouma, "Malaria Resurgence in the East African Highlands: Temperature Trends Revisited," *Proceedings of the National Academy of Sciences*, vol. 103, no. 15 (April 11, 2006), pp. 5829–34, http://www.pnas.org/content/103/15/5829.full.pdf.
45. Harry Cockburn, "Climate Change to Expose Half of World's Population to Disease-Spreading Mosquitoes by 2050, Study Finds," *Independent*, March 6, 2019, https://www.independent.co.uk/environment/climate-change-disease-mosquitoes-zika-virus-yellow-fever-dengue-spread-a8809996.html.
46. U.S. Global Change Research Program (USGCRP), *Fourth National Climate Assessment*, vol. 2, Impacts, Risks, and Adaptation in the United States (Washington, DC: U.S. Government Printing Office, 2018), vol. 2, p. 545.
47. IPCC, *Climate Change 2014*, Report of Working Group II, Part A, pp. 718–20.
48. USGCRP, *Fourth National Climate Assessment*, vol. 2, p. 545.
49. Steinbruner et al., *Climate and Social Stress*, p. 107.
50. Ibid., pp. 81–82.
51. See Alina Bradford, "Ebola: Causes, Symptoms & Treatment," Live Science, March 28, 2016, https://www.livescience.com/48311-ebola-causes-symptoms-treatment.html.
52. World Health Organization (WHO), *Health Worker Ebola Infections in Guinea, Liberia and Sierra Leone*, Preliminary Report, May 21, 2014, http://www.who.int/hrh/documents/21may2015_web_final.pdf.
53. Alexandra Zavis and Christine Mai-Due, "Clashes Erupt as Liberia Seals Off Slum to Prevent Spread of Ebola," *Los Angeles Times*, August 20, 2104, https://www.latimes.com/world/africa/la-fg-africa-liberia-ebola-quarantine-curfew-20140820-story.html.
54. White House, Office of the Press Secretary, "Remarks by the President on the Ebola Outbreak," September 16, 2014, Centers for Disease Control and Prevention, Atlanta, Georgia, https://obamawhitehouse.archives.gov/the-press-office/2014/09/16/remarks-president-ebola-outbreak.
55. DoD, *Operation United Assistance: The DoD Response to Ebola in West Africa*, Joint and Coalition Operational Analysis (JCOA), January 6, 2016, p. v.
56. White House, "Remarks by the President on the Ebola Outbreak."
57. White House, Office of the Press Secretary, "Fact Sheet: U.S. Response to the Ebola Epidemic in West Africa," September 16, 2014, https://

obamawhitehouse.archives.gov/the-press-office/2014/09/16/fact-sheet-us-response-ebola-epidemic-west-africa. See also DoD, *Operation United Assistance.*

58. Steinbruner et al., *Climate and Social Stress*, pp. 81–82.
59. CNA, *National Security and the Threat of Climate Change*, p. 18.
60. DoD, "Secretary of Defense Speech, Conference of Defense Ministers of the Americas," October 13, 2014.
61. CNA, *National Security and the Threat of Climate Change*, p. 16.
62. For discussion, see IPCC, *Climate Change 2014*, Report of Working Group II, Part A, pp. 766–71. See also Steinbruner et al., *Climate and Social Stress*, pp. 112–17.
63. See Michael Werz and Max Hoffman, "Climate Change, Migration, and Conflict," in Werrell and Femia, *The Arab Spring and Climate Change*, pp. 36–37. See also William Wheeler and Ayman Oghanna, "After Liberation, Nowhere to Run," *New York Times*, October 30, 2011.
64. See Alison Smale, "Migrants Race North as Hungary Builds a Fence," *New York Times*, August 25, 2015.
65. See Michael S. Schmidt and Sewell Chan, "NATO Will Send Ships to Aegean to Deter Human Smuggling," *New York Times*, February 12, 2016; and "Migrant Crisis: NATO Deploys Aegean People-Smuggling Patrols," BBC News, February 11, 2016, http://www.bbc.com/news/world-europe-35549478.
66. See Colin P. Kelley et al., "Climate Change in the Fertile Crescent and Implications of the Recent Syrian Drought," *Proceedings of the National Academy of Sciences*, vol. 112, no. 11 (March 17, 2015), pp. 3241–46, http://www.pnas.org/content/pnas/112/11/3241.full.pdf.
67. John Wendle, "Syria's Climate Refugees," *Scientific American*, March 2016, p. 52.
68. See, for example, Jan Selby et al., "Climate Change and the Syrian Civil War Revisited," *Political Geography*, vol. 60 (2017), pp. 232–44, https://www.sciencedirect.com/science/article/pii/S0962629816301822.
69. CNA, *National Security and the Threat of Climate Change*, p. 32.
70. Kelly, "Posture Statement of General John F. Kelly," March 13, 2014, p. 29.
71. As quoted in Chris Moore, "Exercise at GTMO Tests Army South, SOUTHCOM's Abilities to Deploy, Set Up Joint Task Force," U.S. Army, February 20, 2013, https://www.army.mil/article/96783/exercise_at_gtmo_tests_army_south_southcoms_abilities_to_deploy_set_up_joint_task_force.
72. 12th Air Force (Air Forces Southern) Public Affairs, "AFSOUTH Trains for Humanitarian Crisis, Joint Operations," U.S. Air Force,

March 2, 2015, http://www.af.mil/News/Article-Display/Article/572252/afsouth-trains-for-humanitarian-crisis-joint-operations/.

73. See, for example, this report on Integrated Advance 2017: Carol Rosenberg, "It's Only a Drill: Guantánamo Trains for a Caribbean Migrant Crisis," *Miami Herald*, March 1, 2017, http://www.miamiherald.com/news/nation-world/world/americas/guantanamo/article135673913.html.
74. USGCRP, *Fourth National Climate Assessment*, vol. 2, p. 608.
75. Ibid., pp. 608–13.

## 5. GREAT-POWER CLASHES

1. Supreme Headquarters Allied Powers Europe (NATO), "Exercise Cold Response 2016 Wraps Up in Norway," press release, March 9, 2016, http://www.shape.nato.int/2016/exercise-cold-response-2016-wraps-up-in-norway.
2. For background on Cold Response 2016 and comments on the underlying scenario, see "U.S. to Assume Higher Profile in Nordic Exercises," *Defense News*, February 27, 2016, https://www.defensenews.com/2016/02/27/us-to-assume-higher-profile-in-nordic-exercises/; Crista Mary Mack, "U.S. Army Warms Up with Norwegian Cold Weather Training Exercise," U.S. Army, March 4, 2016, https://www.army.mil/article/163535/US_Army_warms_up_with_Norwegian_cold_weather_training_exercise; and Kirstin Merrimarahajara, "Norwegian, Marine Planning Effort Epitomizes Cold Response Spirit," U.S. Marine Corps, February 23, 2016, http://www.marines.mil/News/News-Display/Article/671134/norwegian-marine-planning-effort-epitomizes-cold-response-spirit/.
3. As quoted in Dan Lamothe, "What Happens When Marines Go to Norway? 'The Fast and the Furious' on Ice. In Tanks," *Washington Post*, February 18, 2016, https://www.washingtonpost.com/news/checkpoint/wp/2016/02/18/what-happens-when-marines-go-to-norway-the-fast-and-the-furious-on-ice-in-tanks.
4. See Lamothe, "What Happens When Marines Go to Norway?"; and Lamothe, "The Pentagon Is Adding to Its Arsenal of Weapons in Norway's Caves," *Washington Post*, August 12, 2014, https://www.washingtonpost.com/news/checkpoint/wp/2014/08/12/the-pentagon-is-adding-to-its-arsenal-of-weapons-in-norways-caves/. For a closer look inside the caves, see Christopher P. Cavas, "Cave-Dwellers: Inside the U.S. Marine Corps Prepositioning Program-Norway," *Defense News*, September 20, 2015, https://www.defensenews.com/digital-show-dailies/modern-day-marine/2015/09/20/cave-dwellers-inside-the-us-marine-corps-prepositioning-program-norway/.

5. For background, see Heather A. Conley and Caroline Rohloff, *The New Ice Curtain: Russia's Strategic Reach to the Arctic* (Washington, DC: Center for Strategic and International Studies, 2015).
6. Ibid., pp. 7–9, 69–75.
7. DoD, *Report to Congress on Strategy to Protect United States National Security Interests in the Arctic Region* (Washington, DC: DoD, 2016), pp. 6–7.
8. For background on the struggle over Arctic resources, see Klare, *The Race for What's Left*, pp. 70–99. On China's interests in the Arctic, see Heather Conley, *China's Arctic Dream* (Washington, DC: Center for Strategic and International Studies, 2018).
9. See Jennifer A. Francis, "Arctic Meltdown," *Scientific American*, April 2018, pp. 48–53. On ice-free summers, see IPCC, *Special Report: Global Warming of 1.5 °C*, chap. 3, "Impacts of 1.5°C of Global Warming on Natural and Human Systems," p. 178, https://www.ipcc.ch/site/assets/uploads/sites/2/2019/02/SR15_Chapter3_Low_Res.pdf.
10. Sherri Goodman, interview with the author, Washington, D.C., May 15, 2017.
11. As cited in CNA, *National Security and the Threat of Climate Change*, p. 33.
12. U.S. Navy, *U.S. Navy Arctic Roadmap*, October 2009, https://apps.dtic.mil/dtic/tr/fulltext/u2/a516591.pdf.
13. White House, "Arctic Policy," National Security Presidential Directive 66/Homeland Security Presidential Directive 25, January 12, 2009, https://fas.org/irp/offdocs/nspd/nspd-66.htm.
14. U.S. Navy, *U.S. Navy Arctic Roadmap*, October 2009.
15. DoD, "Secretary of Defense Speech, Halifax International Security Forum," Halifax, Nova Scotia, November 22, 2013, http://archive.defense.gov/speeches/speech.aspx?speechid=1821.
16. DoD, *Arctic Strategy* (Washington, DC: DoD, 2013), https://dod.defense.gov/Portals/1/Documents/pubs/2013_Arctic_Strategy.pdf.
17. DoD, *Report to Congress on Strategy to Protect United States National Security Interests in the Arctic Region.*
18. Ibid., p. 7.
19. As cited in "'America's Got to Up Its Game in the Arctic': Mattis," Reuters, June 25, 2018, https://www.reuters.com/article/us-usa-military-arctic/americas-got-to-up-its-game-in-the-arctic-mattis-idUSKBN1JL2W4.
20. Rebecca Kheel, "330 Marines to Deploy to Norway Amid Tensions with Russia," *The Hill*, October 24, 2016, https://thehill.com/policy/defense/302586-330-us-marines-headed-to-norway-amid-tensions-with-russia.

21. Andrew Wong, "China: We Are a 'Near-Arctic State' and We Want a 'Polar Silk Road,'" CNBC, February 14, 2018, https://www.cnbc.com/2018/02/14/china-we-are-a-near-arctic-state-and-we-want-a-polar-silk-road.html.
22. Ibid. See also Jeff Stein, "China Goes Polar," *Newsweek*, January 19, 2015, https://www.newsweek.com/china-goes-polar-300554.
23. Heather Wilson and David Goldfein, "Air Power and the Arctic: The Importance of Projecting Strength in the North," *Defense News*, January 9, 2019, https://www.defensenews.com/opinion/commentary/2019/01/09/air-power-and-the-arctic-the-importance-of-projecting-strength-in-the-north/.
24. Michael R. Pompeo, "Looking North: Sharpening America's Arctic Focus," Remarks, Rovaniemi, Finland, May 6, 2019, https://www.state.gov/looking-north-sharpening-americas-arctic-focus/.
25. U.S. Navy, *U.S. Navy Arctic Roadmap 2014–2030*, pp. 6, 8, 14–15.
26. Ibid., p. 15.
27. U.S. Geological Survey (USGS), "Circum-Arctic Resource Appraisal: Estimates of Undiscovered Oil and Gas North of the Arctic Circle," USGS Fact Sheet 2008-3049, 2008, https://pubs.usgs.gov/fs/2008/3049/fs2008-3049.pdf.
28. See Klare, *The Race for What's Left*, pp. 70–99.
29. Ibid., pp. 151, 163. See also Miguel Martin, "China in Greenland: Mines, Science, and Nods to Independence," China Brief, March 12, 2018, https://jamestown.org/program/china-greenland-mines-science-nods-independence/.
30. Daniel R. Coats, "Worldwide Threat Assessment of the U.S. Intelligence Community," Statement for the Record, Senate Select Committee on Intelligence, May 11, 2017, https://www.dni.gov/files/documents/Newsroom/Testimonies/SSCI%20Unclassified%20SFR%20-%20Final.pdf.
31. Pompeo, "Looking North: Sharpening America's Arctic Focus," May 6, 2019.
32. See Ariel Cohen, "Russia in the Arctic: Challenges to U.S. Energy and Geopolitics in the High North," in Stephen J. Black, ed., *Russia in the Arctic* (Carlisle, PA: Strategic Studies Institute, Army War College, 2011), pp. 17–21; and Matthias Schepp and Gerald Traufetter, "Riches at the North Pole: Russia Unveils Aggressive Arctic Plans," *Der Spiegel*, January 29, 2009, http://www.spiegel.de/international/world/riches-at-the-north-pole-russia-unveils-aggressive-arctic-plans-a-604338.html.
33. "Vladimir Putin: The Arctic Is an Extremely Important Region, Which Will Ensure the Future of Russia," from interview on Direct

Line TV, at Arctic.ru, June 16, 2017, https://arctic.ru/analitic/20170616/629407.html.

34. For background, see Congressional Research Service (CRS), *Changes in the Arctic: Issues for Congress*, Report to Congress, R41153 (Washington, DC: CRS, Library of Congress, March 4, 2019), pp. 15–17, 22–24, 30–31, 95–96, https://fas.org/sgp/crs/misc/R41153.pdf.
35. See U.S. Navy, *U.S. Navy Arctic Roadmap 2014–2030*, pp. 14–15. See also Klare, *The Race for What's Left*, pp. 93–98.
36. As quoted in Cohen, "Russia in the Arctic," p. 15.
37. See Klare, *The Race for What's Left*, pp. 1–3.
38. Conley and Rohloff, *The New Ice Curtain*, pp. 70–73, 77–78. See also Marlène Laruelle, "Russian Military Presence in the High North: Projection of Power and Capabilities," in Blank, ed., *Russia in the Arctic*, pp. 63–90.
39. For discussion, see Michael D. Bowes, *Impact of Climate Change on Naval Operations in the Arctic* (Alexandria, VA: Center for Naval Analyses, 2009).
40. U.S. Navy, *U.S. Navy Arctic Roadmap 2014–2030*, p. 6.
41. See CRS, *Changes in the Arctic*, pp. 70–75, 79–80.
42. "USAF to Deploy 54 F-35A Fighter Jets to Eielson Air Force Base, Alaska by 2022," DefPost, October 19, 2017, https://defpost.com/usaf-deploy-54-f-35a-fighter-jets-eielson-air-force-base-alaska-2022/.
43. Agence France-Presse, "Russia Begins Its Largest Ever Military Exercise with 300,000 Soldiers," *Guardian*, September 11, 2018, https://www.theguardian.com/world/2018/sep/11/russia-largest-ever-military-exercise-300000-soldiers-china.
44. U.S. Pacific Command, "Alaskan Command Announces Exercise Northern Edge 2017, May 1–12," April 24, 2017, http://www.pacom.mil/Media/News/News-Article-View/Article/1158423/alaskan-command-announces-exercise-northern-edge-2017-may-1-12/.
45. "U.S. Fighter Jets Intercept Russian Bombers in International Airspace off Alaska," Reuters, May 12, 2018, https://www.reuters.com/article/us-usa-airspace-intercept/u-s-fighter-jets-intercept-russian-bombers-in-international-airspace-off-alaska-media-idUSKBN1ID04V.
46. Steven Beardsley, "Navy Aircraft Returning to Former Cold War Base in Iceland," *Stars & Stripes*, February 9, 2016, https://www.stripes.com/news/navy-aircraft-returning-to-former-cold-war-base-in-iceland-1.393156.
47. Sam LaGrone, "CNO: New 2nd Fleet Boundary Will Extend North to the Edge of Russian Waters," *U.S. Naval Institute News*, August 24, 2018, https://news.usni.org/2018/08/24/cno-new-2nd-fleet-boundary-will-extend-north-edge-russian-waters.

48. Thomas Nilsen, "Alarm-Drill: 36 Russian Warships Sail Out to Barents Sea," *Barents Observer*, June 13, 2018, https://thebarentsobserver.com/en/security/2018/06/36-russian-warships-sails-out-barents-sea.
49. "Vladimir Putin: The Arctic Is an Extremely Important Region."
50. See Pal and Eltahir, "Future Temperature in Southwest Asia Projected to Exceed a Threshold for Human Adaptability."
51. Pompeo, "Looking North: Sharpening America's Arctic Focus," May 6, 2019.
52. Ben Kesling, "Cold War Games: U.S. Is Preparing to Test the Waters in Icy Arctic," *Wall Street Journal*, January 11, 2019, https://www.wsj.com/articles/cold-war-games-u-s-is-preparing-to-test-the-waters-in-icy-arctic-11547243592. On the Russian response, see Pavel K. Baev, "Putin Lauds Arctic Cooperation While Boosting Regional Militarization," Eurasia Daily Monitor, April 15, 2019, https://jamestown.org/program/putin-lauds-arctic-cooperation-while-boosting-regional-militarization/.
53. UK Ministry of Defence (MoD), *Global Strategic Trends—Out to 2040*, 4th ed. (London: MoD, 2010), pp. 14, 16.
54. NIC, *Global Water Security*, pp. 1–3.
55. For background, see Brahma Chellaney, *Water, Peace, and War* (Lanham, MD: Rowman & Littlefield, 2013), pp. 1–57; and Michael T. Klare, *Resource Wars* (New York: Metropolitan Books, 2001), pp. 138–89.
56. NIC, *Global Water Security*, pp. 1–3.
57. On the Brahmaputra's geography and China's dam-building plans, see Mark Christopher, *Water Wars: The Brahmaputra River and Sino-Indian Relations* (Newport, RI: Naval War College, 2013).
58. For background, see Nilanthi Samaranayake, Satu Limaye, and Joel Wuthnow, *Water Resource Competition in the Brahmaputra River Basin: China, India, and Bangladesh* (Arlington, VA: CNA, 2016).
59. Ibid., pp. 28, 46–48.
60. These plans were first discussed in *Tibet's Waters Will Save China*, a 2005 book by Li Ling, a former officer in China's People's Liberation Army. For discussion, see Samaranayake, Limaye, and Wuthnow, *Water Resource Competition in the Brahmaputra River Basin*, p. 23.
61. See Christopher, *Water Wars: The Brahmaputra River and Sino-Indian Relations*, pp. 18–19.
62. Samaranayake, Limaye, and Wuthnow, *Water Resource Competition in the Brahmaputra River Basin*, pp. 15–16, 21–24, 39, 43–46. For an Indian perspective on the issue, see Brahma Chellaney, *Water: Asia's New Battleground* (Washington, DC: Georgetown University Press, 2011).
63. See, for example, Brahma Chellaney, "China's Hydro-Hegemony," *New York Times*, February 7, 2013, http://www.nytimes.com/2013/02

/08/opinion/global/chinas-hydro-hegemony.html; and Sudha Ramachandran, "Water Wars: China, India and the Great Dam Rush," *The Diplomat*, April 3, 2015, http://thediplomat.com/2015/04/water-wars-china-india-and-the-great-dam-rush/. See also Sunil S. Amrith, "The Race to Dam the Himalayas," *New York Times*, December 2, 2018.

64. IPCC, *Climate Change 2014*, Report of Working Group II, Part A, pp. 242–43. See also Henry Fountain, "Glaciers Are Retreating. So Is a Reservoir for Asia," *New York Times*, January 20, 2019.
65. For an assessment of these consequences, see Philippus Wester, Arabinda Mishra, Aditi Mukherji, and Arun Bhakta Shrestha, eds., *The Hindu Kush Himalaya Assessment* (Cham, Switzerland: Springer, 2019).
66. NIC, *India: The Impact of Climate Change to 2030: Geopolitical Implications* (Washington, DC: NIC, 209), pp. 10–11.
67. NIC, *China: The Impact of Climate Change to 2030* (Washington, DC: NIC 2009), pp. 17–22, 33–34.
68. See Samaranayake, Limaye, and Wuthnow, *Water Resource Competition in the Brahmaputra River Basin*, p. 23.
69. NIC, *India: The Impact of Climate Change to 2030*, p. 25.
70. Catherine M. Trentacoste, E. D. McGrady, Shawna Cuan, and Nilanthi Samaranayake, *Bone Dry and Flooding Soon: A Regional Water Management Game* (Arlington, VA: CNA, 2014), p. iv.
71. See Jeffrey Gettleman, "India Threatens to Divert Water from Pakistan after a Suicide Attack," *New York Times*, February 22, 2019.
72. As evident, for example, by the NIC's 2009 reports on climate change and India (funded by the Central Intelligence Agency) and the CNA Corporation's 2014 crisis simulations.

## 6 THE HOMELAND AT RISK

1. DoD, Defense Media Activity, "Texas Guard Moves Ahead of Hurricane Harvey's Landfall," August 25, 2017, https://www.defense.gov/News/Article/Article/1289693/texas-guard-mobilizes-ahead-of-hurricane-harveys-landfall/; and Cheryl Pellerin, "DoD Moves Troops, Search-Rescue Units, Aircraft, Vehicles to Texas," DoD, Defense Media Activity, August 28, 2017, https://www.defense.gov/News/Article/Article/1292459/dod-moves-troops-search-rescue-units-aircraft-vehicles-to-texas/. See also Renuka Rayasam, "Texas Governor Says 3,000 Guard Troops Activated in Response to Harvey," *Politico*, August 27, 2017, http://www.politico.com/story/2017/08/27/hurricane-harvey-texas-national-guard-242079.
2. See Lisa Friedman and John Schwartz, "Warm Gulf Fuels the Rain and Gives It Nowhere to Go," *New York Times*, August 29, 2017; and

Sabrina Shankman, "6 Questions About Hurricane Irma, Climate Change and Harvey," Inside Climate News, September 10, 2017, https://insideclimatenews.org/news/06092017/hurricane-irma-harvey-climate-change-warm-atlantic-ocean-questions.

3. See Richard Sisk, "Government Response Overwhelmed by Texas Flooding: FEMA Chief," Military.com, August 28, 2017, http://www.military.com/daily-news/2017/08/28/government-response-overwhelmed-texas-flooding-fema-chief.html.
4. Office of the Texas Governor, "Governor Abbott Activates Entire Texas National Guard in Response to Hurricane Harvey Devastation," press release, August 28, 2017, https://gov.texas.gov/news/post/governor-abbott-activates-entire-texas-national-guard-in-response-to-hurric.
5. Jim Garamone, "More Than 13K Troops, DoD Civilians Aiding Harvey Lifesaving, Recovery Efforts," Defense Media Activity, September 1, 2017, https://www.defense.gov/News/Article/Article/1298174/more-than-13k-troops-dod-civilians-aiding-harvey-lifesaving-recovery-efforts/. See also Oriana Pawlyk and Richard Sisk, "Military Response in High Gear as Texas Floodwaters Recede," Military.com, September 1, 2017, http://www.military.com/daily-news/2017/09/01/military-response-high-gear-texas-floodwaters-recede.html.
6. See California National Guard, "Army National Guard Members Fight Western US Fires as Others Head for Hurricane Irma," U.S. Army, September 8, 2017, https://www.army.mil/article/193435/army_national_guard_members_fight_western_us_fires_as_others_head_for_hurricane_irma; and Edward Siguenza, "California Army National Guard Unit Brings 1900-plus Soldiers to Wildfire Relief Support," U.S. Army, October 30, 2017, https://www.army.mil/article/196104/california_army_national_guard_unit_brings_1900_plus_soldiers_to_wildfire_relief_support.
7. Oriana Pawlyk and Richard Sisk, "National Guard Moves Focus as Hurricane Irma Looms," Military.com, September 5, 2017, http://www.military.com/daily-news/2017/09/05/national-guard-moves-focus-hurricane-irma-looms.html.
8. DoD, "DoD Leans Forward to Support Preparation and Response Efforts for Hurricane Irma," press release, September 7, 2017, https://www.defense.gov/News/News-Releases/News-Release-View/Article/1302556/dod-leans-forward-to-support-preparation-and-response-efforts-for-hurricane-irma/.
9. Ibid. See also DoD, "DoD Continues Hurricane Irma Response Operations," Defense Media Activity, September 10, 2017, https://www.defense.gov/News/Article/Article/1304802/dod-continues-hurricane-irma-response-operations/.

10. DoD, "DoD Continues Hurricane Irma Response Operations."
11. DoD, "Pentagon Provides Update on Hurricane Irma Relief Operations," Defense Media Activity, September 12, 2017, https://www.defense.gov/News/Article/Article/1308113/pentagon-provides-update-on-hurricane-irma-relief-operations/.
12. See Nicole Chavez, "Hurricane Maria: Puerto Rico Officials Describe 'Apocalyptic' Conditions," CNN, September 24, 2017, http://www.cnn.com/2017/09/24/americas/hurricane-maria-puerto-rico-aftermath/index.html. See also Frances Robles, Lizette Alvarez, and Mary Williams Walsh, "Ordinary Life 'Beyond Reach' in Puerto Rico," *New York Times*, September 23, 2017.
13. DoD, "Northcom Providing Disaster Relief Following Hurricane Maria," press release, September 21, 2017, https://www.defense.gov/News/Article/Article/1320480/northcom-providing-disaster-relief-following-hurricane-maria/.
14. Jim Garamone, "Service Members Work with Puerto Rican, Federal Agencies to Help Island Recover," Defense Media Activity, September 28, 2017, https://dod.defense.gov/News/Article/Article/1328916/service-members-work-with-puerto-rican-federal-agencies-to-help-island-recover/.
15. As quoted in Frances Robles, Lizette Alvarez, and Nicholas Fandos, "In Battered Puerto Rico, Governor Warns of a Humanitarian Crisis," *New York Times*, September 26, 2017.
16. As quoted in Jim Garamone, "Military in Puerto Rico Will Stay Until 'All Needs Are Met,' DoD Liaison Says," Defense Media Activity, September 29, 2017, https://www.defense.gov/News/Article/Article/1330284/military-in-puerto-rico-will-stay-until-all-needs-are-met-dod-liaison-says/.
17. DoD, "DoD Accelerates Hurricane Relief, Response Efforts in Puerto Rico."
18. Terri Moon Cronk, "Power Restoration Remains Top Concern in Puerto Rico, U.S. Virgin Islands," Defense Media Activity, October 27, 2017, https://www.defense.gov/News/Article/Article/1356447/power-restoration-remains-top-concern-in-puerto-rico-us-virgin-islands/.
19. Terri Moon Cronk, "Power Restoration in Puerto Rico Could Take Up to a Year, Corps Chief Says," Defense Media Activity, October 20, 2017, https://www.defense.gov/News/Article/Article/1349844/power-restoration-in-puerto-rico-could-take-up-to-a-year-corps-chief-says/.
20. William O'Brien, "Joint Base Charleston Becomes Supply Center for Hurricane Maria Recovery," DoD, October 26, 2017, https://www

.defense.gov/News/Article/Article/1354816/joint-base-charleston-becomes-supply-center-for-hurricane-maria-recovery/.

21. See USGCRP, *Fourth National Climate Assessment*, vol. 2, p. 95.
22. See Shankman, "6 Questions About Hurricane Irma, Climate Change and Harvey."
23. Robinson Meyer, "Did Climate Change Intensify Hurricane Harvey?," *The Atlantic*, August 27, 2017, https://www.theatlantic.com/science/archive/2017/08/did-climate-change-intensify-hurricane-harvey/538158/.
24. USGCRP, *Fourth National Climate Assessment*, vol. 2, p. 95.
25. See Meyer, "Did Climate Change Intensify Hurricane Harvey?" On "blocking highs" of the sort that trapped Harvey in place over Houston for five days (and later blocked Hurricane Florence over the Carolinas), see Jennifer Frances, "How Arctic Warming Could Have Steered Hurricane Florence Towards the U.S.," Carbon Brief, September 17, 2018, https://www.carbonbrief.org/how-arctic-warming-could-have-steered-hurricane-florence-towards-the-us.
26. See "Big Storm Clusters Are on the Increase—What This Means for Hurricane Hotspots," The Conversation, March 12, 2019, https://theconversation.com/big-storm-clusters-are-on-the-increase-what-this-means-for-hurricane-hotspots-112584.
27. As quoted in Caitlin Werrell and Francesco Femia, "U.S. National Guard Chief: Climate Change 'Part of Our Job Jar,'" Center for Climate and Security, September 20, 2017, https://climateandsecurity.org/2017/09/20/u-s-national-guard-chief-climate-part-of-our-job-jar/#more-14689.
28. NIC, *National Security Implications of Global Climate Change to 2030*, p. 15.
29. DoD, *Quadrennial Defense Review 2010*, p. 84.
30. On the energy consequences of Sandy, see DoE, *Energy Sector Vulnerabilities to Climate Change and Extreme Weather*, p. 6.
31. U.S. Northern Command (Northcom), "USNORTHCOM Hurricane Sandy Response Support—Nov. 1," news release, November 1, 2012, http://www.northcom.mil/Newsroom/Article/563652/usnorthcom-hurricane-sandy-response-support-nov-1/.
32. American Forces Press Service, "DoD Gets Energy Department Fuel to Aid Superstorm Relief," news release, November 2, 2012, http://archive.defense.gov/news/newsarticle.aspx?id=118429. See also Eric Lipton and Clifford Krauss, "Military to Deliver Fuel to Storm-Ravaged Region," *New York Times*, November 3, 2012.
33. The Pentagon's role in responding to civil disasters is spelled out in U.S. DoD, *Strategy for Homeland Defense and Defense Support of Civil Authorities* (Washington, DC: DoD, 2013).

34. DoD, *National Security Implications of Climate-Related Risks and a Changing Climate*, pp. 4–5.
35. See, for example, Ryan Burke and Sue McNeil, *Toward a Unified Military Response: Hurricane Sandy and the Dual Status Commander* (Carlisle, PA: U.S. Army War College, Strategic Studies Institute, 2015); and U.S. Governmental Accountability Office (GAO), *Civil Support: Actions Are Needed to Improve DoD's Planning for a Complex Catastrophe*, Report to Congressional Requesters, GAO-13-763 (Washington, DC: GAO, 2013).
36. DoD, *Strategy for Homeland Defense and Defense Support of Civil Authorities*, p. 17.
37. Ibid., p. 18.
38. Ibid., pp. 21–23.
39. See, for example, Richard Fausset, Michael D. Shear, Ron Nixon, and Frances Robles, "Slow Pace of Aid Riles Puerto Rico," *New York Times*, September 30, 2017; Luis Ferré-Sadurní, Frances Robles, and Lizette Alvarez, "Frantic Efforts to Offer Care in Puerto Rico," *New York Times*, September 27, 2017; and Robles, Alvarez, and Fandos, "In Battered Puerto Rico, Governor Warns of a Humanitarian Crisis."
40. As quoted in Fausset et al., "Slow Pace of Aid Riles Puerto Rico."
41. As quoted in ibid.
42. Amanda Holpuch, "Hurricane Maria: Puerto Rico Raises Official Death Toll from 64 to 2,975," *Guardian*, August 28, 2018, https://www.theguardian.com/world/2018/aug/28/hurricane-maria-new-death-toll-estimate-is-close-to-3000.
43. As quoted in ibid.
44. USGCRP, *Fourth National Climate Assessment*, vol. 2, p. 47.
45. See ibid., pp. 174–201, 479–511, 638–68.
46. NIC, *National Security Implications of Global Climate Change to 2030*, p. 16.
47. CNA, *National Security and the Threat of Climate Change*, pp. 32, 34.
48. Shuaizhang Feng, Alan B. Krueger, and Michael Oppenheimer, "Linkages Among Climate Change, Crop Yields, and Mexico–U.S. Cross-Border Migration," *Proceedings of the National Academy of Sciences*, vol. 107, no. 32 (August 10, 2010), pp. 14257–63.
49. See the discussion in Steinbruner et al., *Climate and Social Stress*, pp. 112–17.
50. See Oliver Milman, Emily Holden, and David Agren, "The Unseen Driver Behind the Migrant Caravan: Climate Change," *Guardian*, October 30, 2018, https://www.theguardian.com/world/2018/oct/30/migrant-caravan-causes-climate-change-central-america; John D.

Sutter, "One Suspected Driver of the Migrant 'Caravan': Climate Change," CNN, December 11, 2018, https://www.cnn.com/2018/12/11/politics/climate-caravan-honduras-sutter/index.html; and Kirk Semple, "Migrants Flee New Threat: Climate Change," *New York Times*, April 14, 2019.

51. See Jonathan Blitzer, "How Climate Change Is Fuelling the U.S. Border Crisis," *New Yorker*, April 3, 2019, https://www.newyorker.com/news/dispatch/how-climate-change-is-fuelling-the-us-border-crisis; Lauren Markham, "How Climate Change Is Pushing Central American Migrants to the US," *Guardian*, April 6, 2019, https://www.theguardian.com/commentisfree/2019/apr/06/us-mexico-immigration-climate-change-migration; and Jude Webber, "Honduran Farmers Flee the Effects of Climate Change," *Financial Times*, December 13, 2018, https://www.ft.com/content/adc270e2-fd72-11e8-aebf-99e208d3e521.
52. As quoted in Semple, "Migrants Flee New Threat."
53. As cited in Michael D. Shear and Thomas Gibbons-Neff, "Thousands of Troops Will Be Sent to Border," *New York Times*, October 30, 2018.
54. Helene Cooper and Catie Edmondson, "More Troops to the Border as Democrats Raise Doubts," *New York Times*, January 30, 2019; and Matthew S. Schwartz, "Pentagon Deploying 3,750 Troops to Southern Border," NPR, February 4, 2019, https://www.npr.org/2019/02/04/691222383/pentagon-deploying-3-750-troops-to-southern-border.
55. See Robert Burns, "Concern over Using US Military to Help Border Enforcement," Associated Press, June 29, 2018, https://apnews.com/075acbb9ac834fc78080f8305388a793; and Jonah Shepp, "The Military Doesn't Seem to Appreciate Trump's Border Stunt," *Intelligencer*, November 6, 2018, http://nymag.com/intelligencer/2018/11/military-unhappy-trump-border-stunt.html.
56. As quoted in Molly O'Toole, "Marine Corps Commandant Says Deploying Troops to the Border Poses 'Unacceptable Risk,'" *Los Angeles Times*, March 21, 2019, https://www.latimes.com/politics/la-na-pol-marine-corps-border-national-emergency-20190321-story.html. See also Helene Cooper, "Diverted to Border, Troops Forgo Training for Deployments in Europe," *New York Times*, December 25, 2018.
57. Tara Copp, "Pentagon Extends Border Deployment for Active Duty Troops Through September," *Military Times*, January 14, 2019, https://www.militarytimes.com/news/your-military/2019/01/15/dod-extends-border-deployment-to-september/.
58. As quoted in Jamie McIntyre, "Shanahan Ready to Send More Troops

to the Border When Trump Asks: 'Our Support Is Very Elastic,'" *Washington Examiner*, April 12, 2019, https://www.washingtonexaminer.com/policy/defense-national-security/shanahan-ready-to-send-more-troops-to-the-border-when-trump-asks-our-support-is-very-elastic.

59. See Cooper and Edmondson, "More Troops to the Border as Democrats Raise Doubts."
60. Steinbruner et al., *Climate and Social Stress*, pp. 68–70.
61. Interview, Washington, D.C., May 15, 2017.
62. "Defense support [in such situations] is primarily drawn from the existing warfighting capabilities of the Armed Forces," the DoD explains in its *Strategy for Homeland Defense and Defense Support of Civil Authorities*, p. 15.

## 7. NO SAFE HARBORS

1. See Navy Region Southeast Public Affairs, "Florida Navy Bases Prepare for Irma," U.S. Navy News Service, September 6, 2017, http://www.navy.mil/submit/display.asp?story_id=102287; and Barbara Starr, "US Navy to Evacuate 5,000 as Military Preps for Hurricane Irma," CNN, September 7, 2017, http://www.cnn.com/2017/09/05/politics/key-west-navy-evacuation-hurricane-irma/index.html.
2. As quoted in Navy Region Southeast Public Affairs, "Florida Navy Bases Prepare for Irma."
3. Ibid.
4. See Starr, "U.S. Navy to Evacuate 5,000 as Military Preps for Hurricane Irma"; and U.S. Navy, "Naval Station Mayport Sends Ships to Sea Ahead of Hurricane Irma," Navy News Service, September 7, 2017, http://www.navy.mil/submit/display.asp?story_id=102301.
5. As quoted in Charlsy Panzino, "Air Force Evacuates Planes Ahead of Hurricane Irma," *Air Force Times*, September 8, 2017, https://www.airforcetimes.com/news/2017/09/08/air-force-evacuates-planes-ahead-of-hurricane-irma/.
6. Ibid.
7. As quoted in Navy Region Southeast Public Affairs, "NAS Key West Commanding Officer Authorizes All Personnel and Families to Return," U.S. Navy News Service, September 21, 2017, http://www.navy.mil/submit/display.asp?story_id=102563.
8. Dan Lamothe, "U.S. Military Braces for Hurricane Florence, Begins Evacuations," *Washington Post*, September 11, 2018, https://www.washingtonpost.com/world/national-security/us-military-braces-for-hurricane-florence/2018/09/11/8862e446-b5e0-11e8-b79f-f6e31e555258_story.html.

9. Shawn Snow, "$3.6 Billion Price Tag to Rebuild Lejeune Buildings Damaged by Hurricane Florence," *Marine Times*, December 12, 2018, https://www.marinecorpstimes.com/news/your-marine-corps/2018/12/12/36-billion-price-tag-to-rebuild-lejeune-buildings-damaged-by-hurricane-florence/.
10. On Michael's sudden emergence as a powerful storm and possible links to climate change, see John Schwartz, "Storm's Sudden Intensification Surprised Even the Experts," *New York Times*, October 12, 2018. On the storm's devastating punch, see Richard Fausset and Alan Blinder, "'Absolute Monster' Leaves Splintered Path of Havoc," *New York Times*, October 12, 2018.
11. See Dave Phillips, "'Catastrophic Damage' at a Florida Air Force Base," *New York Times*, October 13, 2018; and Joel Achenbach, Kevin Begos, and Dan Lamothe, "Hurricane Michael: Tyndall Air Force Base Was in the Eye of the Storm, and Almost Every Structure Was Damaged," *Washington Post*, October 23, 2018, https://www.washingtonpost.com/national/hurricane-michael-tyndall-air-force-base-was-in-the-eye-of-the-storm-and-almost-every-structure-was-damaged/2018/10/23/26eca0b0-d6cb-11e8-aeb7-ddcad4a0a54e_story.html.
12. See Joe Gould and Valerie Insinna, "Politicos Are Pushing to Rebuild Tyndall, But Should the Air Force Bother?," *Defense News*, October 29, 2018, https://www.defensenews.com/congress/2018/10/29/politicos-are-pushing-to-rebuild-tyndall-but-maybe-it-shouldnt-be-rebuilt/; and Rachel S. Cohen, "USAF Expects to Need Nearly $1B for Tyndall Recovery in FY19," *Air Force*, March 13, 2019, http://www.airforcemag.com/Features/Pages/2019/March%202019/USAF-Expects-to-Need-Nearly-1B-for-Tyndall-Recovery-in-FY19.aspx.
13. See, for example, U.S. House of Representatives, Committee on Foreign Affairs, "How Climate Change Threatens U.S. National Security," Hearings, April 2, 2019, https://foreignaffairs.house.gov/2019/4/how-climate-change-threatens-u-s-national-security.
14. CNA, *National Security and the Threat of Climate Change*, pp. 37, 48.
15. NIC, *National Intelligence Assessment on the National Security Implications of Global Climate Change to 2030*, p. 15.
16. DoD, *Quadrennial Defense Review Report 2010*, pp. 85–86.
17. National Research Council (NRC), Committee on National Security Implications of Climate Change for U.S. Naval Forces, *National Security Implications of Climate Change for U.S. Naval Forces* (Washington, DC: National Academies Press, 2011), pp. 73–75.
18. DoD, Strategic Environmental Research and Development Program (SERDP), *Assessing Impacts of Climate Change on Coastal Military Installations: Policy Implications* (Washington, DC: SERDP, 2013), p. 3.

19. As quoted in Jeff Goodell, "The Pentagon and Climate Change: How Deniers Put National Security at Risk," *Rolling Stone*, February 12, 2015, http://www.rollingstone.com/politics/news/the-pentagon-climate-change-how-climate-deniers-put-national-security-at-risk-20150212.
20. SERDP, *Assessing Impacts of Climate Change on Coastal Military Installations*, pp. 5, 9–11.
21. NRC, *National Security Implications of Climate Change for U.S. Naval Forces*, pp. 63–64, 68, 78.
22. Ibid., pp. 66–67, 73–75.
23. Union of Concerned Scientists (UCS), "The US Military on the Front Lines of Rising Seas: Exposure to Coastal Flooding at Naval Station Norfolk, Virginia," 2016, http://www.ucsusa.org/sites/default/files/attach/2016/07/front-lines-of-rising-seas-naval-station-norfolk.pdf.
24. UCS, "The US Military on the Front Lines of Rising Seas: Exposure to Coastal Flooding at Joint Base Langley-Eustis, Virginia," 2016, http://www.ucsusa.org/sites/default/files/attach/2016/07/front-lines-of-rising-seas-langley-eustis.pdf.
25. As quoted in Nicholas Kusnetz, "Rising Seas Threaten Norfolk Naval Shipyard, Raising Fears of 'Catastrophic Damage,'" NBC News, November 19, 2018, https://www.nbcnews.com/news/us-news/rising-seas-threaten-norfolk-naval-shipyard-raising-fears-catastrophic-damage-n937396.
26. Karen Jowers and Mark D. Faram, "Navy Warships Sail Out of Norfolk While Air Force Planes Fly into the Heart of the Hurricane," *Navy Times*, September 10, 2018, https://www.navytimes.com/news/your-navy/2018/09/10/navy-warships-sail-out-of-norfolk-while-air-force-planes-fly-into-the-heart-of-the-hurricane/.
27. See "Kaine, Warner, and Scott to Introduce Bill to Help Hampton Roads Invest in Sea Level Rise Resiliency Efforts," press release, May 22, 2017, https://www.kaine.senate.gov/press-releases/kaine-warner-and-scott-to-introduce-bill-to-help-hampton-roads-invest-in-sea-level-rise-resiliency-efforts.
28. Megan Eckstein, "Navy Plans to Spend $21B over 20 Years to Optimize, Modernize Public Shipyards," USNI News, April 17, 2018, https://news.usni.org/2018/04/17/navy-plans-spend-21b-20-years-optimize-modernize-public-shipyards.
29. UCS, "The US Military on the Front Lines of Rising Seas: Exposure to Coastal Flooding at Naval Air Station Key West, Florida," 2016, http://www.ucsusa.org/sites/default/files/attach/2016/07/front-lines-of-rising-seas-key-west-naval-station.pdf.
30. Center for Climate and Security (CCS), *Sea Level Rise and the U.S. Military's Mission*, September 2016, https://climateandsecurity.files

.wordpress.com/2016/09/center-for-climate-and-security_military-expert-panel-report2.pdf, pp. 28–29.

31. UCS, "The US Military on the Front Lines of Rising Seas: Exposure to Coastal Flooding at Naval Station Mayport, Florida."
32. CCS, *Sea Level Rise and the U.S. Military's Mission*, p. 29.
33. See Tom Vanden Brook, "Michael Blasted Tyndall Air Force Base in Florida—a Key to Homeland Security," *USA Today*, October 11, 2018, https://www.usatoday.com/story/news/politics/2018/10/11/hurricane-michael-smashed-tyndall-key-air-base-homeland-defense/1601454002/; and Gould, "Politicos Are Pushing to Rebuild Tyndall, But Should the Air Force Bother?"
34. UCS, "The US Military on the Front Lines of Rising Seas: Exposure to Coastal Flooding at Eglin Air Force Base, Florida."
35. Courtney Kube and Mosheh Gains, "Camp Lejeune Is Still a Mess 6 Months After Hurricane Florence. Where's the Money for Repairs?," NBC News, March 30, 2019, https://www.nbcnews.com/news/military/camp-lejeune-still-mess-6-months-after-hurricane-florence-where-n986456.
36. CCS, *Sea Level Rise and the U.S. Military's Mission*, p. 33.
37. UCS, "The US Military on the Front Lines of Rising Seas: Exposure to Coastal Flooding at Marine Corps Recruit Depot Parris Island and Marine Corps Air Station Beaufort, South Carolina," 2016, https://www.ucsusa.org/global-warming/science-and-impacts/impacts/sea-level-rise-flooding-marine-corps-parris-island-air-station-beaufort.
38. CCS, *Sea Level Rise and the U.S. Military's Mission*, pp. 26–27.
39. USGCRP, *Fourth National Climate Assessment*, vol. 2, pp. 98, 149–51, 449, 1008.
40. See Josh Funk and Blake Nicholson, "Late-Winter Storm Moves to Upper Midwest; Flooding Remains," *Denver Post*, March 15, 2019, https://www.denverpost.com/2019/03/15/midwest-bomb-cyclone-flooding/; and Samantha Harrington, "Did Climate Change Cause the Flooding in the Midwest and Plains?," Yale Climate Connections, April 2, 2019, https://www.yaleclimateconnections.org/2019/04/did-climate-change-cause-midwest-flooding/.
41. See Beck et al., "Floods Suggest National Security Threat from Climate Change"; and Steve Liewer, "One-Third of Offutt Underwater; At Least 30 Buildings Damaged in Flood," *Omaha World-Herald*, March 18, 2019, https://www.omaha.com/news/military/one-third-of-offutt-underwater-at-least-buildings-damaged-in/article_631f9b34-5271-50e8-b5eb-19f488daaf32.html.
42. Steve Liewer, "Air Force Seeks $4.9 Billion in Emergency Funds for Storm-Ravaged Offutt, Tyndall," *Omaha World-Herald*, March 28,

2019, https://www.omaha.com/news/military/air-force-seeks-billion-in-emergency-funds-for-storm-ravaged/article_0f70d1ea-1206-5291-9d19-1a981b45608a.html.

43. Rose L. Thayer, "Military Bases in Nebraska Battle Flooding as Offutt AFB, Camp Ashland Remain Under Water," *Stars & Stripes*, March 18, 2019, https://www.stripes.com/news/us/military-bases-in-nebraska-battle-flooding-as-offutt-afb-camp-ashland-remain-under-water-1.573200.
44. Karen Dillon, "Flooding Impairs Drinking Water Treatment for Kansas City, Missouri," KELO News, March 23, 2019, https://kelo.com/news/articles/2019/mar/23/missouri-river-flooding-causes-water-treatment-issues-in-kansas-city/.
45. DoD, *DoD FY 2012 Climate Change Adaptation Roadmap*, p. 3.
46. GAO, *Climate Change Adaptation: DoD Can Improve Infrastructure Planning Processes to Better Account for Potential Impacts*, Report to Congressional Requesters, GAO-14-446 (Washington, DC: GAO, 2014).
47. According to projections compiled by the Intergovernmental Panel on Climate Change, the global extent of permafrost near the surface will diminish by between 37 and 81 percent over the coming decades. IPCC, *Summary for Policymakers*, 2013, p. 25.
48. GAO, *Climate Change Adaptation*, GAO-14-446, p. 14.
49. Ibid., pp. 12–13.
50. Ibid., pp. 15–16.
51. Beth Ford Roth and Claire Trageser, "Tomahawk Fire Jumps Containment Line; Fallbrook Evacuation Orders Lifted," KPBS News, May 15, 2014, http://www.kpbs.org/news/2014/may/14/fire-camp-pendleton-prompts-evacuations/.
52. Justin Ray, "Uncontrolled Wildfire at Vandenberg Air Force Base Continues to Rage," Spaceflight Now, September 20, 2016, https://spaceflightnow.com/2016/09/20/uncontrolled-wildfire-at-vandenberg-air-force-base-continues-to-rage/. See also 30th Space Wing Public Affairs, "Canyon Fire Summary for September 20, 2016," Vandenberg Air Force Base, September 21, 2016, http://www.vandenberg.af.mil/News/Article-Display/Article/950623/canyon-fire-summary-for-september-20-2016/.
53. GAO, *Climate Change Adaptation: DOD Needs to Better Incorporate Adaptation into Planning and Collaboration at Overseas Installation*, GAO-18-206 (Washington, DC: GAO, November 2017), p. 24.
54. CCS, *Sea Level Rise and the U.S. Military's Mission*, p. 27.
55. Carl D. Storlazzi et al., *The Impact of Sea-Level Rise and Climate Change on Department of Defense Installations on Atolls in the Pacific Ocean* (Washington, DC: SERPA, 2017).

56. See, for example, Doyle Rice, "Super Typhoon Vongfong Menaces Japan," *USA Today*, October 8, 2014, https://www.usatoday.com/story/weather/2014/10/08/super-typhoon-vongfong-japan/16912813/.
57. See, for example, Pal and Eltahir, "Future Temperature in Southwest Asia Projected to Exceed a Threshold for Human Adaptability"; and John Schwartz, "Deadly Heat Is Forecast in Persian Gulf by 2100," *New York Times*, October 27, 2015.
58. Anthony J. Parolari, Dan Li, Elie Bou-Zeid, Gabriel G. Katul, and Shmuel Assouline, "Climate, Not Conflict, Explains Extreme Middle East Dust Storm," *Environmental Research Letters*, vol. 11, no. 11 (November 8, 2016), http://iopscience.iop.org/article/10.1088/1748-9326/11/11/114013.
59. Eric Schmitt, "Obstacles Limit Targets and Pace of Strikes on ISIS," *New York Times*, November 10, 2014.
60. Eric Schmitt and Helene Cooper, "ISIS Fighters Seized Advantage in Iraq Attack by Striking During Sandstorm," *New York Times*, May 19, 2015.
61. As quoted in Ben Wolfgang, "Despite Sea Change at White House, Pentagon Steps Up Climate Change Preparations," *Washington Times*, June 3, 2018, https://www.washingtontimes.com/news/2018/jun/3/pentagon-climate-change-plans-avoid-trump-politics/.
62. DoD, *DoD FY 2012 Climate Change Adaptation Roadmap*, pp. 5–6.
63. DoD, *DoD FY 2014 Climate Change Adaptation Roadmap*, pp. 9–10.
64. For discussion of these problems, see GAO, *Climate Change Adaptation*, GAO-14-446, pp. 46–47.
65. DoD, DoD Directive 4715.21, "Climate Change Adaptation and Resilience," January 14, 2016, https://www.defense.gov/Portals/1/Documents/pubs/471521p.pdf.
66. See Wolfgang, "Despite Sea Change at White House, Pentagon Steps Up Climate Change Preparations"; and Danny Vinik, "Why the GOP Is Trying to Stop the Pentagon's Climate Plan," *Politico*, June 12, 2016, https://www.politico.com/agenda/story/2016/06/republicans-trying-to-stop-pentagon-climate-plan-000149.
67. DoD, *Report on Effects of a Changing Climate to the Department of Defense*, pp. 10–13.

## 8. GOING GREEN

1. See "U.S. Navy Starts Alternative Fuel Use," *Maritime Executive*, January 20, 2016, https://www.maritime-executive.com/article/us-navy-starts-alternative-fuel-use; Associated Press (AP), "U.S. Navy Launches First Biofuel-Powered Aircraft Carriers," *Guardian*, January 21, 2016,

https://www.theguardian.com/environment/2016/jan/21/us-navy-launches-first-biofuel-powered-aircraft-carriers; and Katie Fletcher, "U.S. Navy Launches Great Green Fleet with 2016 Kickoff Event," *Biomass Magazine*, January 21, 2016, http://biomassmagazine.com/articles/12820/us-navy-launches-great-green-fleet-with-2016-kickoff-event.

2. As quoted in Michael Casey, "Going Green: Navy Vessels Head to Asia Powered by Cattle Fat," Fox News, January 27, 2016, http://www.foxnews.com/tech/2016/01/20/going-green-navy-vessels-head-to-asia-powered-by-cattle-fat.html.
3. See Brian Dumaine, "Can the Navy Really Go Green?," *Fortune*, September 3, 2012, pp. 107–12. On the congressional fuel-cost requirement, see Noah Shachtman, "Republicans Order Navy to Quit Buying Biofuels," *Wired*, May 14, 2012, https://www.wired.com/2012/05/republican-navy-biofuel/.
4. John C. Stennis Strike Group Public Affairs, "The Great Green Fleet Explained," Navy News Service, June 27, 2016, http://www.navy.mil/submit/display.asp?story_id=95398.
5. Brian J. Davis, "Navy's Great Green Fleet Initiative Powers USS John C. Stennis Carrier Strike Group," Navy News Service, February 2, 2016, http://www.navy.mil/submit/display.asp?story_id=92900.
6. John C. Stennis Strike Group Public Affairs, "The Great Green Fleet Explained."
7. U.S. Navy, "Great Green Fleet," Energy, Environment and Climate Change, n.d., https://navysustainability.dodlive.mil/energy/great-green-fleet/.
8. For background on the Great White Fleet, see Kenneth Wimmel, *Theodore Roosevelt and the Great White Fleet: American Sea Power Comes of Age* (Lincoln, NE: Potomac Books, 1998).
9. Naval History and Heritage Command, "Great Green Fleet Continues Great White Fleet's Legacy of Global Presence," *Navy Live* (blog), June 23, 2016, http://navylive.dodlive.mil/2016/06/23/great-green-fleet-continues-great-white-fleets-legacy-of-global-presence/.
10. Secretary of the Navy (SECNAV), "SECNAV Energy Message to the Fleet," October 30, 2009, https://www.public.navy.mil/bupers-npc/reference/messages/Documents/ALNAVS/ALN2009/ALN09068.txt.
11. Paula Paige, "SECNAV Outlines Five 'Ambitious' Energy Goals," Navy News Service, October 16, 2009, http://www.navy.mil/submit/display.asp?story_id=49044.
12. U.S. Energy Information Administration (EIA), "Europe Brent Spot Price FOB," https://www.eia.gov/dnav/pet/hist/LeafHandler.ashx?n=PET&s=RBRTE&f=M.

13. As cited in Shachtman, "Republicans Order Navy to Quit Buying Biofuels."
14. As quoted in Davis, "Navy's Great Green Fleet Initiative Powers USS John C. Stennis Carrier Strike Group."
15. White House, "Executive Order 13514—Federal Leadership in Environmental, Energy, and Economic Performance," October 5, 2009, http://www.presidency.ucsb.edu/ws/index.php?pid=86728.
16. As quoted in "U.S. Navy Starts Alternative Fuel Use."
17. "U.S. Navy Starts Alternative Fuel Use."
18. DoD, *Quadrennial Defense Review 2010*, p. 87.
19. See August Cole, "For U.S. Troops in Afghanistan, Supplies Are Another Battle," *Wall Street Journal*, December 15, 2009, https://www.wsj.com/articles/SB126075201256889955.
20. Daniel Orchard-Hays and Laura A. King, "Realize the Great Green Fleet," *U.S. Naval Institute Proceedings*, August 2017, https://www.usni.org/magazines/proceedings/2017-08/realize-great-green-fleet.
21. DoD, *Department of Defense Strategic Sustainability Performance Plan, FY [Fiscal Year] 2011* (Washington, DC: DoD, 2011), p. I-2.
22. Michael Breen, interview with the author, Washington, D.C., May 26, 2017.
23. As quoted in Mark Clayton, "In the Iraqi War Zone, U.S. Army Calls for 'Green' Power," *Christian Science Monitor*, September 7, 2006, https://www.csmonitor.com/2006/0907/p01s04-usmi.html.
24. See Summer Barkley, "Operation Dynamo—Power Forward," U.S. Army, March 21, 2013, https://www.army.mil/article/99262/operation_dynamo_power_forward; and David Vergun, "REF: Battlefield Survival Can Depend on Getting Soldiers Critical Gear Posthaste," Army News Service, November 15, 2013, https://www.army.mil/article/115115/ref_battlefield_survival_can_depend_on_getting_soldiers_critical_gear_posthaste.
25. William Price, "India Company, 3/5 Dark Horse Marines Use Solar Power to Brighten Mission Accomplishment," Defense Video Imagery Distribution System, January 6, 2011, https://www.dvidshub.net/news/63126/india-company-3-5-dark-horse-marines-use-solar-power-brighten-mission-accomplishment.
26. DoD, *Energy for the Warfighter: Operational Energy Strategy* (Washington, DC: DoD, 2011), p. 1.
27. As quoted in Orchard-Hays and King, "Realize the Great Green Fleet."
28. Defense Science Board (DSB), *Report of the Defense Science Board Task Force on DoD Energy Strategy: "More Fight—Less Fuel"* (Washington,

DC: DoD, Office of the Under Secretary of Defense for Acquisition, Technology, and Logistics, 2008), pp. 63–71.

29. DoD, *Energy for the Warfighter*, introduction, n.p.
30. Ibid., p. 1.
31. Secretary of the Air Force, "Air Force Energy Program Policy Memorandum," AFPM10-1, December 19, 2008, p. 10.
32. White House, "Fact Sheet: Obama Administration Announces Additional Steps to Increase Energy Security," April 11, 2012, https://obamawhitehouse.archives.gov/the-press-office/2012/04/11/fact-sheet-obama-administration-announces-additional-steps-increase-ener.
33. DoD, *Quadrennial Defense Review 2010*, pp. 84–87.
34. DoD, *Department of Defense Strategic Sustainability Performance Plan, FY 2010* (Washington, DC: DoD, 2010), pp. i–iii.
35. DoD, Office of the Under Secretary of Defense for Acquisition, Technology, and Logistics, *Fiscal Year 2016 Operational Energy Annual Report* (Washington, DC: DoD, 2016), pp. 11–23.
36. Megan Nicholson, "Army's Green Warrior Convoy Emphasizes DoD's Role in Energy Innovation," Innovation Files, May 15, 2012, https://www.innovationfiles.org/armys-green-warrior-convoy-emphasizes-dods-role-in-energy-innovation/.
37. DoD, *Fiscal Year 2016 Operational Energy Annual Report*, Fig. 1, p. 25.
38. DoD, *Department of Defense Strategic Sustainability Performance Plan, FY 2016* (Washington, DC: DoD, 2016), Table 3, p. 19.
39. DoD, *Department of Defense Strategic Sustainability Performance Plan, FY 2011*, p. I-2.
40. Pew Charitable Trusts (Pew), *Power Surge: How the Department of Defense Leverages Private Resources to Enhance Energy Security and Save Money on U.S. Military Bases* (Philadelphia and Washington, DC: Pew, 2014), p. 7.
41. DoD, *Department of Defense Strategic Sustainability Performance Plan, FY 2011*, p. I-2.
42. Ibid., p. I-17.
43. Ibid., p. I-9.
44. DoD, *Department of Defense Strategic Sustainability Performance Plan, FY 2016*, Table 3, p. 19.
45. Ibid., p. 23.
46. Office of the Assistant Secretary of the Navy for Energy, Installations and Environment, "Department of the Navy, Department of Energy, Celebrate the Dedication of 210 Megawatt Solar Facility," Navy News Service, October 14, 2016, http://www.navy.mil/submit/display.asp?story_id=97173.

47. White House, "Fact Sheet: Obama Administration Announces Additional Steps to Increase Energy Security."
48. Heather Ashley, "Solar, Wind Provide Renewable, Secure Energy to Fort Hood," *Fort Hood Sentinel*, June 8, 2017, http://www.forthoodsentinel.com/news/solar-wind-provide-renewable-secure-energy-to-fort-hood/article_5bd61e1a-4b9d-11e7-950e-e75d2e341262.html.
49. DoD, *Department of Defense Strategic Sustainability Performance Plan, FY 2016*, pp. 23–24.
50. Kevin Elliott, "AF's Largest Solar Array Celebrates First Anniversary," Air Force Civil Engineer Center Public Affairs, December 18, 2014, http://www.afcec.af.mil/News/Article-Display/Article/871528/afs-largest-solar-array-celebrates-first-anniversary/; and SunPower, "SunPower Breaks Ground on 28-Megawatt Solar Power System at Vandenberg Air Force Base," press release, May 23, 2017, http://newsroom.sunpower.com/2017-05-23-SunPower-Breaks-Ground-on-28-Megawatt-Solar-Power-System-at-Vandenberg-Air-Force-Base.
51. DSB, *Report of the Defense Science Board Task Force on DoD Energy Strategy*, p. 59.
52. SECNAV, "SECNAV Energy Message to the Fleet," October 30, 2009.
53. U.S. Army, Office of the Assistant Secretary of the Army (Installations, Energy & Environment) (OASAIEE), "Army Vision for Net Zero," October 1, 2011, http://www.asaie.army.mil/Public/ES/netzero/docs/4Oct11_NET_ZERO_White_Paper.pdf.
54. OASAIEE, *Net Zero Progress Report: Net Zero Pilot Installation Initiative 2012* (Washington, DC: OASAIEE, 2013). See also National Renewable Energy Laboratory (NREL), *Army Net Zero: Energy Roadmap and Program Summary, Fiscal Year 2013* (Golden, CO: NREL, 2014).
55. OASAIEE, *2015 Progress Report: Army Net Zero Initiative* (Washington, DC: OASAIEE, 2016).
56. AP, "The Military Is Getting Greener, But That Clashes with Trump's Promises," *Fortune*, January 14, 2017, http://fortune.com/2017/01/14/military-oil-trump-green-power/.
57. DoD, *2014 Climate Change Adaptation Roadmap*, pp. 7–8, 13.
58. U.S. Marine Corps (USMC), *Expeditionary Operations*, Marine Corps Doctrinal Publication (MCDP) 3 (Washington, DC: USMC, 1998), pp. 27–55.
59. USMC, *United States Marine Corps Expeditionary Energy Strategy and Implementation Plan* (Washington, DC: USMC, 2011), p. 5.
60. USMC, *Initial Capabilities Document for United States Marine Corps Expeditionary Energy, Water, and Waste* (Washington, DC: USMC, 2011), pp. iii, 7.
61. Ibid., Appendix F, pp. F4–5.

62. Levi Schultz, "Marine Corps Strives to Be Leaner, Meaner, Greener," Marines.mil, December 9, 2016, http://www.marines.mil/News/News-Display/Article/1025538/marine-corps-strives-to-be-leaner-meaner-gr/.
63. U.S. Department of the Army, *Energy Security and Sustainability (ES2) Strategy* (Washington, DC: Army, 2015), pp. 1–3.
64. As quoted in Jeff Sisto, "Soldiers of the Future Will Generate Their Own Power," Natick Soldier Research, Development and Engineering Center Public Affairs, November 17, 2014, https://www.army.mil/article/138057/soldiers_of_the_future_will_generate_their_own_power.
65. DoD, *Quadrennial Defense Review 2010*, p. 85.
66. DoD, *National Security Implications of Climate-Related Risks and a Changing Climate*, p. 6.
67. John F. Kelly, "Posture Statement of General John F. Kelly, United States Marine Corps Commander, United States Southern Command, Before the Senate Armed Services Committee," March 12, 2015, Washington, D.C., http://www.armed-services.senate.gov/imo/media/doc/Kelly_03-12-15.pdf.
68. See Christopher Klutts, "AFRICOM Supports Disaster Preparedness Initiative," Africom Media Room, July 21, 2015, https://www.africom.mil/media-room/article/25488/africom-supports-disaster-preparedness-initiative; and Samantha Reho, "Cabo Verde Completes Disaster Preparedness Training," Africom Media Room, March 6, 2017, https://www.africom.mil/media-room/photo/28683/cabo-verde-completes-disaster-preparedness-training.
69. DoD, *Report on Effects of a Changing Climate to the Department of Defense*, p. 15.
70. See Tara Copp, "Pentagon Is Still Preparing for Global Warming Even Though Trump Said to Stop," *Military Times*, September 12, 2017, https://www.militarytimes.com/news/your-military/2017/09/12/pentagon-is-still-preparing-for-global-warming-even-though-trump-said-to-stop/; and Renee Cho, "What the U.S. Military Is Doing About Climate Change," *State of the Planet*, Earth Institute of Columbia University, September 20, 2017, https://blogs.ei.columbia.edu/2017/09/20/what-the-u-s-military-is-doing-about-climate-change/.

## CONCLUSION

1. Chuck Hagel, "Secretary of Defense Speech, Conference of Defense Ministers of the Americas," October 13, 2014.
2. DoD, *2014 Climate Change Adaptation Roadmap*, n.p.

3. As cited in Caitlin Werrell and Francesco Femia, "Air Force Chief of Staff: Military Often Has to Respond to the Effects of Climate Change," Center for Climate and Security, April 5, 2019, https://climateandsecurity.org/2019/04/05/air-force-chief-of-staff-military-often-has-to-respond-to-the-effects-of-climate-change/#more-17205.
4. As quoted in "In Niger, Rising Temperatures Mean Barren Fields—But Fertile Ground for Terrorism," *PBS NewsHour,* April 16, 2019, https://www.pbs.org/newshour/show/in-niger-rising-temperatures-mean-barren-fields-but-fertile-ground-for-terrorism.

# ACKNOWLEDGMENTS

The first ideas for this book took shape in the summer and fall of 2013, while I was recovering from a severe illness that kept me bedridden for much of that time. Fortunately, I was blessed by a loving community of family, friends, and neighbors who provided comfort in times of anguish and a responsive sounding board when I could think about future endeavors. I am deeply beholden to all those dear souls and wish to acknowledge their vital role both in smoothing my recovery and helping me envision the contours of this book.

My gratitude begins with my wife, Andrea Ayvazian, who did more than anyone else to help me cope with my illness and then undertake the research and writing that culminated in *All Hell Breaking Loose*. I will be eternally grateful for her support during those difficult times and thereafter. Also critical during the hardest times was the support of our son, Sasha Klare-Ayvazian, and my siblings, Karl and Jane Klare. All three undertook numerous visits and cheered me on. I also wish to acknowledge the careful attention I received from my physicians, Joanne Levin, Timothy Parsons, and Henry Rosenberg. More than provide needed medical care, they offered the caring regard that gave me the confidence to overcome my distress.

As I was recovering, I was fortunate to have a close circle of friends who let me prattle on about my ideas for a new book that would address the issues of climate change, resource scarcity, and national security. Foremost among these are Jim Cason, Tom Engelhardt, Gerald Epstein, Betsy Hartmann, Katrina vanden Heuvel, Laura Reed, Seth Shulman, Adele Simmons, Daniel Volman, Cora Weiss, Barry Werth, and my former student Juecheng Zhao, who tragically passed away in 2018. I cannot recall how many conversations I had with these loyal friends, but I can state with certainty that their patience in listening to and commenting on my ideas represents a significant contribution to this book.

Of equal importance is the role played by my editors at Metropolitan Books, Sara Bershtel and Grigory Tovbis. Both reviewed various early proposals for a book on these issues and helped me narrow the frame to the topic as it stands today. I appreciate not only their critical guidance in this process, but also in their continued support—extended over many years—for my research and writing.

As I proceeded deeper into the research and writing of this book, many people offered vital help and suggestions. I am particularly indebted to several former military officers and officials who afforded me their time early in this process, helping me to better understand the military's stance on climate issues. These include, most notably, Michael Breen, a former Army officer who served two tours of duty in Iraq; Sharon Burke, former assistant secretary of defense for operational energy plans and programs;

John Conger, former principal deputy under secretary of defense (comptroller); Dr. Leo Goff of the CNA Corporation, a former Navy nuclear submarine commander; Sherri Goodman, former deputy undersecretary of defense for environmental security; and Major Danny Sjursen, a former instructor at the U.S. Military Academy at West Point. I also benefited from conversations with members of the staff and advisory board of the Center for Climate and Security, a nonpartisan institute aimed at broadening public and congressional awareness of the links between climate change and U.S. national security. Equally beneficial has been my participation in the Working Group on Climate, Nuclear, and Security Affairs, a project closely associated with the Center for Climate and Security.

Until my retirement from teaching in June 2018, I served as the Five College Professor of Peace and World Security Studies, based at Hampshire College in Amherst, Massachusetts. In addition to teaching at Hampshire, I also taught classes at the other four members of the Five College Consortium: Amherst College, Mount Holyoke College, Smith College, and University of Massachusetts, Amherst. During my thirty-four years of teaching, I benefited enormously from constant interaction with students at the Five Colleges, as well as my many valued colleagues there. I particularly wish to acknowledge the many deep conversations over lunch and coffee with such esteemed colleagues as Aaron Berman, Margaret Cerullo, Javier Corrales, Omar Dahi, Sue Darlington, Vincent Ferraro, Elliot Fratkin, Peter Haas, Kay Johnson, Kavita Khory, Jonathan Lash, Sura Levine, Jon Western, Gregory White, and Andrew Zimbalist.

Many researchers at other institutions have also enriched my understanding of the issues raised in this volume. I particularly wish to acknowledge the contributions of those I've had the opportunity to interact with at scholarly meetings, including

Simon Dalby of Balsillie School of International Affairs in Canada, Corey Johnson of the University of North Carolina at Greensboro, Shannon O'Lear of the University of Kansas, James A. Russell of the Naval Postgraduate School, and Stacy VanDeveer of the University of Massachusetts, Boston.

For the past two years, I've had the privilege of serving as a senior visiting fellow at the Arms Control Association in Washington, DC. I've benefited enormously from my collaboration with ACA's staff and from the opportunity to learn more about the connections between nuclear weapons, international security, and climate change.

Lastly, I wish to acknowledge the generous support provided by the Samuel Rubin Foundation over the years for my research and educational endeavors. While serving as director of the Five College Program in Peace and World Security Studies, I was fortunate to receive a grant from the Rubin Foundation for support of research and teaching on the links between climate change, war, and conflict; among other things, that grant enabled me to attend several scholarly meetings, greatly enhancing my understanding of the topic.

So many other people helped me formulate my approach to this subject just by letting me talk about it that I'm sure I've neglected to mention some, for which I'm truly sorry. I cannot recount all the conversations I had with students and colleagues at the Five Colleges where I gained some new insight, but I will remain eternally grateful for those interactions, and the many others with friends in Western Massachusetts, in Washington, and around the world.

# INDEX

Page numbers in *italics* refer to maps.

Made in United States
North Haven, CT
05 July 2024